WITHDRAWN
UTSA LIBRARIES

D0838492

RENEWALS 458-4574

DATE DUE

GAYLORD			PRINTED IN U.S.A

WITHDRAWN

E. T. A. Hoffmann

Twayne's World Authors Series
German Literature

David O'Connell, Editor
Georgia State University

TWAS 868

E. T. A. HOFFMANN

E. T. A. Hoffmann

James M. McGlathery

University of Illinois–Urbana-Champaign

Twayne Publishers
An Imprint of Simon & Schuster Macmillan
New York

Prentice Hall International
London • Mexico City • New Delhi • Singapore • Sydney • Toronto

Library
University of Texas
at San Antonio

Twayne's World Authors Series No. 868

E. T. A. Hoffmann
James M. McGlathery

Copyright © 1997 by Twayne Publishers

All rights reserved. No part of this book may be reproduced or transmitted in any form or by any means, electronic or mechanical, including photocopying, recording, or by any information storage and retrieval system, without permission in writing from the Publisher.

Twayne Publishers
An Imprint of Simon & Schuster Macmillan
1633 Broadway
New York, NY 10019

Library of Congress Cataloging-in-Publication Data

McGlathery, James M., 1936–
    E.T.A. Hoffmann / James M. McGlathery.
        p.   cm. — (Twayne's world author series ; TWAS 868. German literature)
    Includes bibliographical references and index.
    ISBN 0-8057-4619-6 (alk. paper)
    1. Hoffmann, E. T. A. (Ernst Theodor Amadeus), 1776–1822—Criticism and interpretation.   I. Title.   II. Series: Twayne's world author series ; TWAS 868.   III. Series: Twayne's world author series. German literature.
    PT2361.Z5M34   1997
    833'.6—dc21   97-8269
                                                                          CIP

The paper used in this publication meets the minimum requirements of American National Standard for Information Sciences—Permanence of Paper for Printed Library Materials. ANSI Z39.48-1984. ∞ ™

10 9 8 7 6 5 4 3 2 1

Printed in the United States of America

Contents

Preface

Most of those who think they know nothing of E. T. A. Hoffmann are mistaken. He was after all the author of the tale on which Tchaikovsky's *Nutcracker* ballet ultimately is based. Music lovers will also be aware that Hoffmann and several of his stories are the subject of the still-popular opera by Jacques Offenbach, *Les Contes d'Hoffmann*. Indeed, Hoffmann is well remembered in the music world for other reasons: as the inspiration for Robert Schumann's *Kreisleriana* and a source for the Wagner operas *Tannhäuser* and *Die Meistersinger,* but equally for his essay on Beethoven's *Fifth Symphony* and a much debated interpretation of Mozart's opera *Don Giovanni*. Aside from such acquaintance with Hoffmann by way of music, his literary works continue to be published widely and read throughout the world, not only in the original German and in English translation, but in a number of other languages as well. He clearly occupies an enduring place among classics of world literature.

The present volume is intended as a critical introduction to Hoffmann the author. The first chapter offers a brief account of his life as it relates to his literary career. That information is followed by a history of the critical reception of his literary works and by a brief survey of Hoffmann's own critical writings, beginning with those on music. The focus of this introduction to Hoffmann is on his fiction, however. Chapters 4 and 5 take up, in the order they were completed, the nearly four dozen stories that form the bulk of his literary production. The discussion of these works, many of which are not among his better-known stories, serves as a background against which to view his longer fiction: his seven fairy tales discussed in chapter 6 and the two novels in chapter 7. The conclusion and selected bibliography aim to encourage further reading and study.

All references to Hoffmann's works are to the *Sämtliche Werke in fünf Einzelbänden* edited by Walter Müller-Seidel, Friedrich Schnapp, Wolfgang Kron, and Wulf Segebrecht (5 vols. Munich: Winkler, 1960–1965), the best for scholarly use among the completed editions. Except where otherwise indicated, the translations from foreign languages into English are my own. For reasons of space, references to secondary literature given in the notes are limited to studies that have appeared in the course of the past quarter century, together with examples of commentary by critics contemporary with Hoffmann. For similar notes on secondary sources from the late nineteenth century up to the early 1970s the reader is referred to my earlier study, *Mysticism and Sexuality: E. T. A. Hoffmann* (2 vols. Berne: Lang, 1981–1985).

Acknowledgments

I am grateful to the interlibrary loan service of our university library for locating items not available on campus or through other libraries in Illinois, and to Shannon Murray for helping me secure the secondary sources consulted and for her aid in editing the manuscript, as well as to the Research Board of the Graduate College of the University of Illinois at Urbana-Champaign for the grant to make her service as my research assistant possible. I wish also to thank Professor David O'Connell of Georgia State University, editor for German literature in Twayne's World Authors Series, for the invitation to write this volume and for his advice and help with it.

Chronology

1776   Ernst Theodor Wilhelm Hoffmann born 24 January in Königsberg in East Prussia (now Kaliningrad, Russia). In adoration of Mozart, he later adopts as his pen name "E. T. A. Hoffmann," the *A* standing for Amadeus.

1778   Hoffmann's parents are divorced. Hoffmann and his mother live with her family.

1781   Begins to attend school and also receives instruction in music, drawing, and painting.

1786   Start of his lifelong friendship with Theodor Gottlieb von Hippel, nephew of the prominent author and citizen of Königsberg of the same name.

1792   Enters the study of law at the University of Königsberg.

1794   Meets Dora Hatt ("Cora"), to whom he gives music lessons and with whom he falls in love.

1795   Completes his studies and begins work in the Prussian judiciary.

1796   Goes to Glogau in Silesia (now Glogów, Poland) to live with his mother's brother, Johann Ludwig Doerffer, and his family.

1798   Becomes engaged to one of the uncle's daughters, Minna Doerffer. Passes the examination to become a referendar and is posted to Berlin. Takes music lessons from the noted composer Johann Friedrich Reichardt.

1800   Passes the third law examination in March, advances to assessor, and is posted to the superior court at Posen in Polish Prussia (now Poznan, Poland).

1802   Breaks his engagement to Minna Doerffer. His caricatures of prominent members of the German elite in Posen result in his disciplinary posting to the Polish town Plock, though with advancement to full status in the Prussian judiciary as councilor (*rat*). On 26 July he

marries a young Polish woman, Marianna Thekla
Michaelina Rorer, in Posen.

1803   His first publication, about the use of a chorus in
       Schiller's play *Die Braut von Messina,* appears in the
       journal *Der Freimüthige.*

1804   Transferred to Warsaw, then the capital of the province
       of South Prussia. There, through Zacharias Werner and
       Julius Eduard Hitzig, judiciary colleagues, he becomes
       acquainted with the writings of German Romantic
       authors.

1805   Helps found the Musical Society in Warsaw. Perfor-
       mances are given of his musical compositions: the
       operetta *Die lustigen Musikanten* to the text by the
       romantic author Clemens Brentano; his *Mass in D-
       Minor;* his *Symphony in E-flat Major.* Birth of his daugh-
       ter Caecilia.

1806   Loses his position in the judiciary after the French,
       under Napoleon, enter Warsaw.

1807   His wife and infant daughter go to stay with her par-
       ents while he moves to Berlin in search of means to
       support himself and his family. The daughter dies in
       Posen.

1808   Takes the position of kapellmeister at the theater in
       Bamberg but soon relinquishes the duties of conductor,
       retaining only that of composer.

1809   Resigns his remaining position with the theater and
       earns money instead by giving music lessons. He
       begins to write for the *Allgemeine Musikalische Zeitung,*
       where his first tale, "Ritter Gluck," appears.

1810   His friend Franz von Holbein takes over direction of
       the Bamberg theater. Hoffmann helps with the direc-
       tion and as composer, stage painter, and set designer.
       His review of Beethoven's *Fifth Symphony* appears in the
       AMZ.

1811   Becomes deeply devoted to and infatuated with his
       adolescent voice pupil Julia Marc.

1812   Holbein gives up the direction of the Bamberg theater, and Hoffmann loses his position with it. Julia Marc marries and moves to Hamburg.

1813   Accepts the offer of theater director Joseph Seconda to become kapellmeister in Dresden and signs a contract for the *Fantasiestücke* with the Bamberg wine merchant, lending librarian, and publisher, Carl Friedrich Kunz.

1813   Kapellmeister with Seconda's troupe alternatingly in Dresden and Leipzig. Composition of the romantic opera *Undine* (libretto by Fouqué). Begins to write his fairy-tale masterpiece *Der goldne Topf.*

1814   Completion of *Der goldne Topf.* Following a quarrel with Seconda he leaves his position with the troupe. Completion of the first volume of his novel *Die Elixiere des Teufels.* Return to service in the Prussian judiciary with the Kammergericht in Berlin. Meets leading literary figures including especially Tieck, Chamisso, and Fouqué. The first two of the four volumes of *Fantasiestücke,* published by Kunz in Bamberg, appear at Easter, followed by *Der goldne Topf* as volume 3 in the fall.

1815   The fourth and final volume of *Fantasiestücke* is published by Kunz, and the first volume of the two-volume *Elixiere des Teufels* by Duncker and Humblot in Berlin.

1816   Appointed as councilor at the Kammergericht. The second, concluding volume of *Die Elixiere* appears. Premiere of Hoffmann's opera *Undine* on the birthday of the Prussian king Friedrich Wilhelm III. The first volume of the *Nachtstücke* with "Der Sandmann" is published by Reimer in Berlin.

1817   Publication of the second, concluding volume of *Nachtstücke.*

1818   Hoffmann's essay in dialogue form, *Seltsame Leiden eines Theater-Direktors,* published by Maurer in Berlin, with the date 1819. Renewal of Hoffmann's circle of literary friends on St. Serapion's Day, 14 November.

1819   Kunz publishes the second, revised edition of the *Fan-tasiestücke,* now in two volumes instead of four. Reimer in Berlin brings out the first volume of Hoffmann's *Die Serapionsbrüder* containing chiefly stories he published in literary annuals known as "Taschenbücher." The second of Hoffmann's fairy tales to appear as a separate volume, *Klein Zaches,* is published by Dümmler in Berlin. Hoffmann takes a course of treatment at the baths in Warmbrunn in Lower Silesia (now in Poland). Hoffmann is named to the king's commission to investigate so-called demagogic activities. The second volume of *Die Serapionsbrüder* appears in the fall, published by Reimer, and the first volume of Hoffmann's novel *Kater Murr* in December, published by Dümmler.

1820   The third volume of *Die Serapionsbrüder* is published by Reimer. The third of Hoffmann's four fairy tales to appear as separate volumes, *Prinzessin Brambilla,* is brought out by the publisher Max in Breslau (now Wroclaw, Poland).

1821   Named to the superior appeals court of the Kammergericht. Reimer publishes the fourth and last volume of *Die Serapionsbrüder*. The second volume of *Kater Murr* is published (the planned concluding third volume remained unwritten at the time of Hoffmann's death the following June).

1822   Falls mortally ill. The manuscript of his fairy tale *Meister Floh* is confiscated by the Prussian government, which initiates an investigation and disciplinary action against Hoffmann for having satirized the activities of a police official in an episode contained in the work. The fairy tale, minus the offending episode, is brought out by the publisher Wilmans in Frankfurt am Main. Hoffmann dies on 25 June at age 46 as a result of paralytic illness.

Chapter One

Hoffmann's Life

E. T. A. Hoffmann first attracted wide interest among critics and readers alike in 1814, with the publication of three volumes of his *Fantasiestücke in Callots Manier* (*Fantasy-Pieces in the Manner of Jacques Callot,* the fourth and final volume appeared the following year). Over the short period of eight years that followed before his death from a paralytic illness on 25 June 1822 at age 46, Hoffmann's literary production came to total some four dozen tales and two novels as his success with the reading public grew continuously. Following his death, interest in him declined in his native Germany but grew markedly beyond its borders, notably in England and then in France and Russia, helped along as it happened by a rather negative but widely noticed critical review by Walter Scott (1772–1831) in 1827. Hoffmann since has come to be considered a classic of world literature and a perhaps unsurpassed master of the fantastic tale. Before turning our attention to the history of critical interest in Hoffmann and then to discussion of the literary works that gave rise to it, we need to consider the life out of which this contribution to world literature arose.

At the time Hoffmann began writing what became the *Fantasiestücke* he was an essentially unemployed former official of the Prussian judiciary. He had lost his post in Warsaw as a result of Napoleon's defeat of Prussia and his ensuing invasion of territory that had been annexed by that country in the partitions of Poland during the last decades of the eighteenth century. In his 30s and married, Hoffmann had relocated in September 1808 to Bamberg in southern Germany (in Upper Franconia, now a part of the German state of Bavaria), where he had hoped to realize his lifelong ambition to make a career in music as a composer, conductor, and music director. His appointment in that capacity with the theater in Bamberg, which had drawn him there, was short-lived, so that he soon was reduced to relying largely on giving private music lessons to make a living.

The dream of success as a musician gave rise, meanwhile, to the literary activity that led to Hoffmann's fame as a writer. To make a name for himself in the music world, as well as to help his finances, he began to contribute reviews and satirical essays to the leading music journal, *Allgemeine Musikalische Zeitung*, published by Breitkopf and Härtel in Leipzig and edited by Friedrich Rochlitz (1769–1842). Hoffmann's first piece for the *AMZ*, with which he introduced himself to the editor and asked to become a contributor, was a novelistic sketch about an encounter with an eccentric music enthusiast who claims to be Christoph Willibald Gluck (1714–1787), even though at the time of the narrator's meeting with the enthusiast the composer had been dead for more than 20 years. Hoffmann was perhaps speculating that since Rochlitz had published a piece of his own about an insane musician in the *AMZ*, his "Ritter Gluck" ("Chevalier Gluck," 1809) would stand that much better chance of being accepted. With this story Hoffmann had in any case found his gift for mingling fantasy and reality in strikingly convincing fashion. Not surprisingly, he subsequently used "Ritter Gluck" to introduce himself to the readers of his volumes of *Fantasiestücke*, making it the first of these "Leaves from the Diary of a Traveling Enthusiast," as the subtitle of the—anonymously published—work identifies them.

There are other ways in which Hoffmann's situation in Bamberg gave rise to his stunning success as an author. Precisely his failure to find the measure of acceptance as a musician he had hoped for there helped suggest to him a poetic alter ego in the figure of the still-young composer Johannes Kreisler. Kreisler became a vehicle for satirizing the pretentiousness of artistic taste and lack of genuine understanding of the arts among the upper classes in provincial towns like Bamberg. Through his sketches about Kreisler, Hoffmann was able to promote his musical career by becoming identified with this sublime, poetically minded composer while at the same time gaining revenge for the hurt that he suffered both in his musical aspirations and in his personal dignity.

One way the years in Bamberg (1808–1813) helped launch and shape Hoffmann's career as a writer was his contact with leading figures in the emerging medical specialty that became known as psychiatry. Through these contacts he became familiar with the relevant literature. The mingling of fantasy and reality that characterizes his poetic works can be said to involve depiction of thoughts and emotions that lie below the level of consciousness. Fantasy in Hoffmann's works is, as he is wont to announce or otherwise indicate to his readers, a representation of an inner world, but an inner world that is intimately connected with the world outside. Of special interest to Hoffmann was psychiatric literature, as represented especially by the books of Johann Christian Reil (1759–1813) and Gotthilf Heinrich Schubert (1780–1860), that offered descriptions and interpretations of psychic phenomena, including those connected with mesmerism and somnambulism. Such books find mention now and again in Hoffmann's tales and other writings.

Foremost among psychiatric experts in Bamberg was the physician Adalbert Friedrich Marcus (1753–1816). That physician's young niece Julia Marc (Juliane Mark, originally Marcus, 1796–1865) who, by becoming the object of Hoffmann's adoration, provided a further, and perhaps ultimately decisive, impetus to his writing career. This adoration of "Julchen," who was 12 when Hoffmann became her voice teacher shortly after his arrival in Bamberg in the fall of 1808 and was 16 when she left at the end of 1812 to marry the son of a Hamburg banker, is best described as a guilty, or at least embarrassed and despairing, adulterous infatuation. That love from afar, of which Julchen was unaware— at least consciously so—until she and Hoffmann bid one another farewell in December 1812, provided him with yet another object for satire, or in this case, good-natured humor: the older man foolishly in love with a young girl, like the figure of Pantalone in the commedia dell'arte, the form of older comedy to which Hoffmann later paid special tribute with his novella "Signor Formica" ("Sir Ant," 1819; first published in *Taschenbuch zum geselligen Vergnügen,* 1820) and his fairy tale *Prinzessin Brambilla* (*Princess Brambilla,* 1820).

Shortly after Julchen's marriage Hoffmann's disappointed love for her found bitterly satirical form bordering on the unseemly in the fanciful dialogue entitled "Neueste Schicksale des Hundes Berganza" ("The Latest from the Life of the Dog Berganza"; written 1813, published 1814 in the second volume of *Fantasiestücke*), and then mellower, self-humorous form in the subsequent fantasy piece "Die Abenteuer der Silvester-Nacht" ("Adventures of a New Year's Eve," 1815, in volume 4). Thereafter, with the exception of the autobiographical novel *Lebensansichten des Katers Murr* (2 volumes, 1819 and 1821; a third volume was planned, but Hoffmann's death intervened), depictions of Hoffmann's passion for Julchen became less direct, being confined to portrayals of an older man's usually veiled feelings for a young girl. The importance of Hoffmann's unfulfilled passion for Julia Marc as an impetus for his writing career, on which he embarked in earnest soon after her engagement, can be seen in his choice of her 17th birthday, 18 March 1813, as the date for signing the contract for publication of the *Fantasiestücke*.

Hoffmann was 37 when he signed the contract. His artistic development began of course much earlier, in his childhood and adolescence in Königsberg, then the capital of East Prussia (now Kaliningrad, capital of a Russian province of that same name), where he was born on 24 January 1776, the son of Christoph Ludwig (1736–1797) and Lovisa Albertine (née Doerffer, 1748–1796) Hoffmann. The circumstances of Hoffmann's early years inclined him to turn inward. His parents' marriage was unhappy, and they separated when he was still an infant. He remained with his mother, while an older brother lived with his father. His mother withdrew to herself, so that he was raised more by her sisters and brother than by her and grew up in effect much as an orphan cared for by relatives. What is known about his childhood is largely from autobiographical passages in his late novel *Kater Murr*. There the composer Johannes Kreisler, a romanticized self-portrait, tells how he was specially devoted to one of his mother's sisters, Charlotte Wilhelmina Doerffer (1755–1779). However, she died when he was three years old. Responsibility for his upbringing in later childhood and adolescence passed to his mother's brother, Otto Wilhelm Doerffer (1741–1811), who was unsuited to the role and whom the youth repaid for that ineptitude with pranks and practical jokes.

The lack of parental guidance, authority, and affection left Hoffmann, in childhood, rather more to his own devices and encouraged him to dwell in the realm of his own especially fecund imagination. His mother's brother, Uncle Otto, was a man of some education, having been trained as a jurist, and was a sufficiently accomplished musician to host gatherings for purposes of performing music. In the Doerffer household Hoffmann was introduced to music, art, and literature as a child. From the beginning, the development of his imagination occurred in relation to his familiarity with and enthusiasm for the arts, which in view of his lonely childhood meant much more to him than might otherwise have been the case.

The loneliness Hoffmann experienced as a child was alleviated in adolescence through his friendship with a schoolmate, Theodor Gottlieb Hippel (1775–1843), whose uncle and namesake (1741–1796) was a noted author and among the most prominent and celebrated citizens of the city. More important for Hoffmann's later career as an author was that young Hippel became the trial audience for his artistic endeavors. Appropriate to the ages of the two schoolboys, the theme of these early attempts at poetic expression was love and friendship. The subject of one of Hoffmann's earliest known efforts at graphic depiction was a young girl of whom he was enamored from afar; and to help cement his friendship with Hippel, he did for him a portrait miniature of Hippel's mother.

Once their school days were at an end and they had entered the study of law at Königsberg's university, Hippel became Hoffmann's confidant regarding his romantic involvement with a married woman, Dorothea Hatt (née Schlunck, 1766–1803), who lived with her husband and children in the same building with Hoffmann's family and to whom he had been engaged to give music lessons. This romantic attachment to an older woman coincided with Hoffmann's first serious efforts at writing fiction and likely provided inspiration for the two novels he wrote at this time, one titled "Cornaro," which he submitted unsuccessfully for publication, and the other "Der Geheimnisvolle" ("The Mysterious Man"), which he presumably did not complete (nothing of "Cornaro" has survived, and of the other novel, only a brief passage quoted by Hoffmann in a letter to Hippel[1]).

Hoffmann's chief literary model at the time of these early attempts at fiction was the most fashionable serious German novelist of that day, Jean Paul Friedrich Richter (1763–1825), whose literary star was rising precisely in those middle years of the 1790s. Jean Paul, as he came to be known, in turn had been much influenced by the English novelist Laurence Sterne (1713–1768), particularly Sterne's mingling of authorial caprice, learned wit, and wistful sentimentality. Especially the latter quality in Jean Paul's novels attracted Hoffmann, together with that author's penchant for the scurrilous and grotesque, to judge from numerous passages in Hoffmann's letters to Hippel of those years.

In Hoffmann's student days, the new romantic direction in German literature was only on the threshold of its arrival. It was instead the literature of the late Enlightenment, to which Jean Paul still belonged, that shaped Hoffmann's early poetic world: Johann Wolfgang Goethe's (1749–1832) novel *Die Leiden des Jungen Werthers* (*The Sorrows of Young Werther,* 1774) and Schiller's (1759–1805) plays *Die Räuber* (*The Robbers,* 1781) and *Don Karlos* (1787), and the occult story "Der Geisterseher" ("The Visionary"), together with gothic romances by authors now largely forgotten. In music, Hoffmann's passion was for the operas of Wolfgang Amadeus Mozart (1756–1791). Among foreign authors, Jean-Jacques Rousseau (1712–1778) and especially William Shakespeare (1564–1616) were the greatest influences.

There is no indication that Hoffmann found inspiration in his courses at the university. He appears to have done what was necessary to complete his law study and nothing further. There is no record that he attended the lectures of the philosopher Immanuel Kant (1724–1804), by then long since renowned, whom Hoffmann never so much as mentions. Hoffmann's dedication was, from the start, to art as distinguished from ideas as such. Philosophy and theology appear to have interested him only in connection with the manifestation of human emotions.

Hoffmann's passion for Dora Hatt came to be a public embarrassment for his family about the time that he finished his law studies and began a practical apprenticeship in the law. Both for that reason and for his professional advancement, the family arranged for him to remove to Glogau in Silesia, where one of his mother's brothers, Johann Ludwig Doerffer (1743–1803), was well established in the provincial Prussian judiciary and where Hoffmann could continue his apprenticeship and prepare for his examination while living with his uncle and family.[2]

The uncle had two daughters. Hoffmann seems to have found himself attracted to the younger one, Wilhelmina (1775–1853), to whom he became engaged. The move to Glogau proved to have been a good idea for advancement of Hoffmann's career as a jurist, especially when the uncle was promoted and transferred to the Prussian capital Berlin a short time later, in 1798, only some two years after Hoffmann had joined the household. In the meantime, Hoffmann had passed his second law examination with a performance rated exceptionally good in every respect. Hoffmann being by then his cousin's fiancé, a place for him was found in Berlin, too, as an intern (*referendar*) at the same high court (the Kammergericht) where he later served as judge up to the time of his death. The move to Glogau had also widened young Hoffmann's experience of the life of artists, through his friendship with the Italian painter Aloys Molinary (1772–1831), who had been commissioned to do the interior of a Jesuit church there. In Glogau, too, Hoffmann became acquainted with a composer, Johannes Hampe (1770–1823).[3]

The two years (1798–1800) Hoffmann spent as *referendar* in Berlin enabled him to experience artistic life in the Prussian capital firsthand and to make the personal acquaintance of leading figures in the world of German literature, music, and painting, as well as critics and publishers. In Berlin in 1799 he wrote the text and composed the music for an operetta (*singspiel*), *Die Maske* (*The Mask*), which he submitted unsuccessfully to the director of the Royal Playhouse (Königliches Schauspielhaus) in Berlin, the acclaimed actor August Wilhelm Iffland (1759–1814). Hoffmann's career in the judiciary advanced with his successful completion of the third examination and his being named to probationary rank (assessor) and posted to Posen (today Poznan), in the province of South Prussia. That jurisdiction had been created in the course of the partitioning of Poland in the closing decades of the eighteenth century. Hoffmann arrived there in the summer of 1800.

Most prominent of the authors Hoffmann encountered in these years was Jean Paul himself, who was engaged to a close friend of Hoffmann's fiancée Minna Doerffer and whom Hoffmann met at Christmas 1800 in Berlin, during a visit to Minna. This connection to Jean Paul proved an embarrassment to Hoffmann and a source of ill feeling toward him on the famous writer's part, however, when Hoffmann subsequently broke off the engagement to Wilhelmina.

In Posen Hoffmann, then in his mid-20s, was somewhat removed from artistic life. While in his new post, however, he composed and achieved the performance of the operetta *Scherz, List und Rache* (*Jest, Cunning, and Revenge*) after the text of that title (1784) by Goethe, to whom Jean Paul sent Hoffmann's score for the operetta. Hoffmann was here for the first time also off on his own, out from under the wing of the Doerffer family. Posen offered him an opportunity for carousing, an activity encouraged by the young Prussian men's service in newly acquired, foreign territory and accommodated by more fun-loving Polish cultural traditions. Hoffmann became enamored of an appealing young Polish woman, Marianna Thekla Michaelina Rorer-Trzcinska (1778–1859), with whom, reportedly, he wished to make love rather than marry.[4]

Hoffmann's involvement in the production and distribution of caricatures of top military officers and civil officials of the Prussian provincial government during the German community's Mardi Gras (*Fasching*) celebrations resulted in a disciplinary posting to Plock in the province New East Prussia, farther into formerly Polish land on the Vistula River downstream from Warsaw. He probably could not have brought Cousin Minna to Plock as his bride in any case. Michaelina followed him there as Frau Hoffmann (they were married on 26 July 1802). At the time of his ill-fated use of talent for graphic art, Hoffmann was about to be promoted to the status of a regular official of government, as councilor (*regierungsrat*), an advancement that enabled him to consider marriage. That prospect forced him to decide whether to honor his promise to Minna, whom he seems not to have been attracted to with the sort of passionate desire he reportedly felt for "Mischa." His marriage to Mischa coincided with his advancement in rank and disciplinary posting to the unfavorable location.

During the almost two years in Plock (summer 1802 to spring 1804) Hoffmann's efforts to make a name for himself in the arts increased.

There the isolation was much greater, the inhabitants being almost wholly Polish and Jewish, the city being smaller and out of the way, and Hoffmann no longer being young and free for the first time from family supervision but instead a married man. His diary for 1803, which survived, shows that he took refuge from boredom and isolation in musical and literary efforts, as well as in domestic life with Mischa, together with whom he became something of an instant parent when her eight-year-old niece, Michalina Gottwald (1795 to after 1859), came to live with them following the arrest of her father for embezzlement.

In Plock Hoffmann had his first success in getting something published, a short essay concerning the controversy over Schiller's introduction of the chorus from ancient Greek tragedy into contemporary drama in his *Die Braut von Messina* (*The Bride of Messina*), which premiered that year (1803). Hoffmann was unsuccessful, though, in attempts to get his compositions—music for the piano and church music—published. He failed, too, to win a contest, advertised by the leading popular playwright of the day, August von Kotzebue (1761–1819), for the best comedy (*lustspiel*). Hoffmann's submission was the farce "Der Preis" ("The Prize"), the text of which has not survived.

Hoffmann's exile to Plock ended after two years with his transfer to Warsaw in the spring of 1804, where he was able to find again both the stimulus of cultural life that he had lost with his departure from Berlin four years before and the buoyant Polish ambiance that he had first experienced in Posen. The three years in Warsaw were happy and important for Hoffmann as an artist. For the first time, he was able to assume the role of music director, conductor, and composer, as a leading figure in the German community's Musikalische Gesellschaft (Musical Society), founded in 1805. Among the pieces he conducted at the Society's concerts was a Beethoven symphony and his own E-flat major (es-dur) symphony, on the score of which he used *A.* (for Amadeus) as his third name for the first time, out of enthusiasm for Mozart's music.[5]

On the literary side, he now became acquainted, through his judiciary colleague Julius Eduard Hitzig (1780–1849), with the writings of the authors of the new romantic movement in German literature: Ludwig Tieck (1773–1853), Friedrich Schlegel (1772–1829), Novalis (pseud. for Friedrich von Hardenberg, 1772–1801), and Clemens Brentano (1778–1842), for whose newly published comedy, *Die lustigen Musikanten* (*The Merry Musicians,* 1804), Hoffmann wrote music that was performed in the Warsaw production of that play. In Warsaw, too, Hoffmann became more closely acquainted with the playwright Zacharias Werner (1768–1823), who had been a neighbor's child in the same building where Hoffmann lived with his mother and her family, and for whose play *Das Kreuz an der Ostsee* (*The Cross on the Baltic Sea,* 1806) Hoffmann wrote stage music.[6]

With Napoleon's entry into Warsaw in the fall of 1806, following his decisive defeat of the Prussian forces at Jena and Auerstedt in Germany, Hoffmann and the other Prussian officials in that city lost their positions. Hoffmann now had to think in terms of making a career in the arts—instead of in law—a prospect not entirely unwelcome to him. Though he fell seriously ill during that winter of 1806 to 1807, he had the freedom to devote himself fully to the arts during the months between the French entry into Warsaw and the expulsion of the Prussian officials the following year before the signing of the Treaty of Tilsit on 7 July 1807. Moreover, Hoffmann led the life of a grass widower during his last months in Warsaw. Since he had to survive on his share of the provincial judiciary's moneys that the displaced officials had divided among themselves as a kind of severance pay, Mischa and their infant daughter went to Posen to her family until Hoffmann might again be able to support them. Fulfillment of his dream of a career in music now took on added urgency if he was to be reunited with his wife and child.

Forced to leave Warsaw, rather than swear allegiance to the new government, Hoffmann went to Berlin. He had some faint hope of receiving reinstatement in the judiciary or at least some modest support from the government. Failing that, perhaps he could secure a position as music director, composer, and conductor at a theater, on the strength of his experience in those capacities with the Musical Society in Warsaw. The year spent in Berlin, from June 1807 to the following June, was the most desperate of his life. He reportedly found solace in an affair with a grass widow who was also lonely and despondent. Berlin was crowded with Prussian officials from the lost Polish provinces who like Hoffmann were seeking reinstatement or a pension from the government. Economic life in the capital of the defeated land was depressed. From Berlin Hoffmann applied for positions elsewhere and ultimately received the appointment in Bamberg, at a theater supported by private means and in shaky financial condition.

The call to the theater in Bamberg, which Hoffmann received in April 1808, enabled him to be reunited with Mischa, whom he picked up in Posen on the way to the new position. Their infant daughter, though, had died the previous August, during the parents' separation. Hoffmann's debut as conductor with the theater's orchestra on 21 Octo-

ber 1808 did not find favor with the audience, at least partly owing to
his conducting from the piano rather than with the violin, as the the-
atergoers had come to expect. Hoffmann gave up conducting at the theater, where he remained music director, and as a result had to supple-
ment his income by giving music lessons.

That necessity brought him into contact with Julia Marc, then a 12-
year-old, toward whom he conceived an at first surely paternal devotion
that developed over the next four years into romantic passion. When his
niece Michalina Gottwald had ceased living with Hoffmann and his
wife, she was at the time around 12, Julchen's age when Hoffmann met
her. Since it had been, moreover, just over a year since the death of Hoffmann's infant daughter, there is reason to believe that at the time he
became Julchen's voice teacher he had an emotional need for a substitute object of paternal adoration. A music enthusiast, he had named the
baby daughter Caecilia for the patron saint of music; and music was the
medium of his emotional involvement with Julchen, who was 20 years
his junior, he being at the time of their first acquaintance 32.

Julia's mother, Franziska Marc (née Marcus, 1770–1849), was the
widow of an important local figure, Philipp Marc (originally Marcus,
1739–1801), American Consul for Franconia in Bamberg, and sister of
Bamberg's most prominent physician, Adalbert Friedrich Marcus.
Through her and other music-lesson patrons, Hoffmann gained entrance
to the town's leading social circles. His professional background as a Prussian judiciary official assured him a measure of respect, and his new career in
music and the theater added an intriguing dimension. He chafed, though,
at being cast in the role of servant to people of wealth and power and gave
vent to his resentment through the creation of his fictional alter ego
Johannes Kreisler, whose musical sufferings ("Des Kapellmeisters Johannes
Kreislers musikalische Leiden," 1810) appeared in the *Allgemeine Musikalische Zeitung* less than two years after Hoffmann's arrival in Bamberg.

To the extent it was possible in a provincial city like Bamberg, Hoffmann escaped into the bohemian world of the local theater, across from
which he and Mischa had their apartment. Most to his liking was the
Rose Tavern (Wirtshaus zur Rose), attached to the theater, where he
could hold forth in conviviality with others, including actors, who liked
to drink wine and indulge in flights of humorous poetic fantasy. His
happiest times appear to have been divided between the voice lessons
with Julchen and his work in the theater, especially after his actor friend
from his first years in Berlin, Franz von Holbein (1779–1855), took
over the direction of the Bamberg theater in 1810.

Hoffmann cultivated a friendship, too, with the wine merchant Carl Friedrich Kunz (1785–1849), almost 10 years his junior, who could provide him not only with good things to drink but books from his extensive private library, as well as an appealing young wife with whom Hoffmann was at times likely to flirt. During Hoffmann's years in Bamberg, Kunz decided to turn his collection into a lending library and engaged Hoffmann to help him catalog the books. With Kunz's help, Hoffmann was able to inform himself concerning the latest developments in literature. It was through Kunz, for example, that Hoffmann became acquainted with one of his chief sources for depicting mesmerist and other spiritualistic beliefs and practices, the writings of the natural philosopher *(naturphilosoph)* Gotthilf Heinrich Schubert, whose subsequent influential book *Symbolik des Traumes* (*The Symbolism of Dreams,* 1814) Kunz himself was later to publish.[7]

Among members of Bamberg society, Hoffmann's most important intellectual associates appear to have been Julia Marc's uncle, Adalbert Friedrich Marcus, and the latter's nephew Friedrich Speyer (1782–1839), her cousin. They were both physicians with a strong interest in philosophy and literature and especially in the emerging field of psychiatric medicine. Through them Hoffmann not only became familiar with the pioneering classics on psychiatry by Reil and Philippe Pinel (1745–1826) but was afforded the opportunity to visit insane asylums and to discuss the treatment of mentally ill patients with the physicians. Already in "Ritter Gluck," published in the *AMZ* within a few months of Hoffmann's arrival in Bamberg, he had depicted a character possessed of bizarre beliefs about himself. In his work as a jurist, mental and emotional aberrations in defendants and plaintiffs must have intrigued him long before. It was in Bamberg, though, that his interest in the subject deepened in such a way as to shape the fiction that he was just then beginning to write and that would make him famous.[8]

By odd coincidence, it was Dr. Marcus's niece and Dr. Speyer's cousin, namely Julchen Marc, who became the object of Hoffmann's fears that he himself might be losing his mind or be driven to suicide. The romantic passion that he conceived for her, about which his diaries inform us, dates from the time after she turned 14, on 18 March 1810, probably late in that year (for which Hoffmann did not keep a dairy). Certainly the crisis of passion began in connection with his visions of her as Katie of Heilbronn in Heinrich von Kleist's new play of that name (*Das Käthchen von Heilbronn,* first published 1810), which Hoffmann was helping Holbein to produce at the Bamberg theater. Hoffmann used the code abbreviation "Ktch" in his diary when referring to Julchen during this emotional crisis. Kleist's heroine—a girl of 14 like Julchen when she had a dream about her ideal beloved—is so completely wrapped up in that dream of love that nothing else matters to her, not her family, reputation, or even life and limb.

Hoffmann yearned to believe that through some such visionary experience his Julchen would discover in him her dream beloved. It may have been precisely that slightly embarrassed association of Julchen with Kleist's heroine that caused Hoffmann to resume his diary when he did on New Year's Day 1811. Perhaps he hoped that Julchen might that New Year's Eve have had a dream experience like Käthchen's. In the play, on New Year's Eve when Käthchen is 14, she engages in fortune-telling with her maid to find out if she, a commoner, will marry a handsome knight. After the fortune-telling she retires to bed and dreams about being visited in her bedroom by just such a—to that point unknown—knight.

Once the dream beloved has actually entered the life of Kleist's young heroine, she becomes an object of romantic and also strongly erotic attraction for him. Hoffmann's fantasies about Julchen as Käthchen likewise were not confined to the spiritualistic. An early crisis in his relationship with Julchen's mother was occasioned by the erotically tinged verses he wrote for the daughter on her 15th birthday (18 March 1811) likening her to a blossoming rose, a comparison the Frau Consulin found inappropriate for a voice teacher to use in reference to his pupil.

Hoffmann's emotional crisis over Julchen took on the character of jealous passion with her engagement the next year, following her 16th birthday, to Johann Gerhard Graepel (1780–1821), son of a Hamburg banker of the same name. At the time of the engagement Graepel, some four years younger than Hoffmann, was in his early 30s. Hoffmann's new role as the disapproving avuncular mentor and friend of the family perhaps contributed to his excitement about a poetic work by another contemporary, Friedrich de la Motte Fouqué (1777–1843). In Fouqué's mermaid tale *Undine* (1811), a water nymph from the realm of elemental spirits yearns to marry a mortal. To oblige her, her devoted uncle, a water sprite, maneuvers a handsome knight into position to fall in love with the blossomingly appealing, innocently alluring niece, Undine. When the knight, after learning that he has married a magical being, turns away from his bride to marry a mortal woman, Uncle Kühleborn is angered and acts to return the niece to their submarine realm. Hoffmann's offer to Fouqué to compose the music if the latter would recast the story as an opera libretto was perhaps not unrelated to Hoffmann's seeing himself as the mermaid's uncle in the tale. Hoffmann's sketch for Fouqué of the final scene for the opera has Uncle Kühleborn hovering over the niece and her dead beloved, as though for the uncle this is the desired happy ending—an ending such as Hoffmann in his jealousy might fancifully have conceived for himself with regard to Julchen and her bridegroom.

Hoffmann's jealous love of Julchen culminated in an outburst during an outing that September (1812) that resulted in termination of his role as her teacher and in his banishment from her mother's house. When Julchen's bridegroom, who had become inebriated, lost his equilibrium and fell to the ground, Hoffmann denounced him as unfit for marriage to her. Thus deprived of his accustomed access to Julchen's presence, Hoffmann turned still more seriously to his artistic pursuits, and to writing in particular. In the wake of his banishment from Julchen Hoffmann began serious discussion with Kunz about contributing to a planned theater journal that the latter wished to publish. For that venture Hoffmann wrote the fanciful sketch "Don Juan," a music enthusiast's account of his uncanny experiences surrounding a performance of Mozart's opera *Don Giovanni*. A connection between this first-person narrative, which was later included in the first volume of *Fantasiestücke,* and Hoffmann's jealous love of Julchen can be seen in the revisionist interpretation of the opera offered by the enthusiast, who prefers to believe that Donna Anna will not marry her fiancé Octavio but will pine away instead for the dead rake Giovanni, whose seduction of women the enthusiast interprets as motivated by despair over unfulfilled transcendent yearning. In his passion for Julchen, Hoffmann hoped that his sense of the sublime would win him her love, just as his enthusiast in "Don Juan" fantasizes about Mozart's Don Giovanni awakening Donna Anna's passion because of the unfulfilled spiritual yearning that lay behind his compulsion to seduce women.

That same fall of 1812 Hoffmann also conceived the plan to write a fanciful memoir based on his experiences in Bamberg, in particular those related to Julchen's engagement to the unwelcome suitor. This satirical narrative, in dialogue form, became the "Nachricht von den neuesten Schicksalen des Hundes Berganza" ("Report of the Newest Fortunes of the Dog Berganza") in the second volume of *Fantasiestücke*. In the dialogue, the dog, taken from a work by Miguel de Cervantes Saavedra (1547–1616), is clearly Hoffmann's mouthpiece, and—as was obvious to those who knew about Hoffmann's feelings toward Julchen, though not to other readers—the scene in the bridal chamber when the dog attacks the bridegroom as he is about to consummate his marriage with Caecilia is an only thinly disguised depiction of what Hoffmann wished he had been in a position to do to Julchen's Graepel.

By the time Hoffmann signed the contract with Kunz for the *Fantasie-stücke* on Julchen's birthday the following spring (1813), she had left with Graepel for Hamburg. Hoffmann knew then that he, too, would be leaving soon to accept a position as conductor and composer with Joseph Seconda's opera company that alternated engagements between Leipzig and Dresden, the major cities in the kingdom of Saxony. The first two volumes of *Fantasiestücke,* which Kunz published at Easter the next year (1814), consist by and large of material Hoffmann had written in Bamberg. Most of what was included in the first of the two volumes had appeared in the *AMZ* in the years since 1809. The second volume was largely devoted to the Bamberg memoir, "Berganza," which Hoffmann surely would not have published while still residing in that city.

The nearly a year and a half (April 1813 to September 1814) that Hoffmann spent in Leipzig and Dresden marked the beginning of his career as author of tales in the narrower sense. In these months he wrote his first actual story, "Der Magnetiseur," about how a young maiden's attraction to a mesmerist physician subverts her marriage to her bridegroom—a subject obviously related to Hoffmann's jealous love for Julchen. Together with the "Berganza" satire, that story filled the second volume of *Fantasiestücke.* These months also saw the creation of his first—and as he himself thought, perhaps in some ways best—fairy tale, *Der goldne Topf* (*The Golden Pot*), in which like Huldbrand in Fouqué's *Undine*—of which Hoffmann at that time was making an opera—a young man embraces, in the end, union with a magical beloved over marriage to a mortal woman. Moreover, in the spring of 1814 Hoffmann completed the first half of his first novel, *Die Elixiere des Teufels* (*The Devil's Elixirs*), a monk's account of how he triumphed over the madness engendered in him by fleshly lust and jealous passion.

As had Hoffmann's engagement with Count Julius Soden's theater in Bamberg, his appointment with Seconda's troupe ended badly, so that by spring he was again unemployed. In the meantime, however, Napoleon had been defeated (Hoffmann had personally witnessed the battle at Dresden in August 1813 and the allies' siege of the city that October and November). As a result of an unexpected visit by Hoffmann's friend from his youth, Hippel, whom he had chanced to meet in

Dresden the previous spring when Hippel was in the entourage of the Prussian Chancellor Carl von Hardenberg (1750–1822, a relative of the poet Novalis), Hoffmann had the prospect of reinstatement in the judiciary. Despite the failure in Bamberg and the more recent one with Seconda, a career as composer, conductor, and music director continued to be his dream. The move to Berlin, for updating his familiarity with the judiciary through unsalaried work at the Kammergericht, offered as well the prospect of becoming involved in the world of music and theater in the Prussian capital.

When Hoffmann arrived in Berlin toward the end of September 1814, the first two volumes of his *Fantasiestücke* had already made him a celebrity in the literary world. He was feted at a gathering organized by his former judiciary colleague in Warsaw, Hitzig, who had gone into publishing. The reception was attended by prominent authors of the romantic literary movement, including Tieck, Adelbert von Chamisso (1781–1838), and Fouqué. The success of his *Fantasiestücke* encouraged Hoffmann to keep writing after his arrival in Berlin, as did his financial need as an unsalaried collaborator at the Kammergericht. A means to earn money and spread his literary acclaim presented itself immediately in the form of requests for contributions from *Taschenbücher,* annuals of collected short poetic works published in pocket-size format (hence the name "pocket books") and nicely bound to serve as gifts, especially for the Christmas market. The first summer in Berlin (1815), Hoffmann presumably completed the second half of his novel *Die Elixiere des Teufels,* and that fall he began the collection of stories entitled *Nachtstücke* (*Night-Pieces*) that he published in two volumes (1816, 1817), the first story of which is one of his best known, "Der Sandmann" ("The Sandman").

Hoffmann's greatest and indeed only notable success as a musician came in these first years back in Berlin, during which his literary celebrity grew so rapidly. His opera *Undine,* to Fouqué's text, premiered on the Prussian king Friedrich Wilhelm III's (1770–1840) birthday, 3 August 1816. The opera was favorably received and continued to be performed until a fire the following summer destroyed the theater, together with the costumes and the expensive, highly praised set designed by the famous architect and painter Karl Friedrich Schinkel (1781–1841). Hoffmann's *Undine* is considered to have pioneered the genre of German Romantic operas, the best-known example of which remains *Der Freischütz* by Carl Maria von Weber (1786–1826), which premiered at the new Royal Theater in Berlin shortly after it opened in the spring of 1821, replacing the structure that had burned. The success of that premiere contributed to an invitation to Hoffmann to revise his *Undine* for reintroduction on the Berlin stage, but his illness and death intervened.

By the time of his opera's premiere, Hoffmann had been reinstated as a salaried official of the judiciary with full seniority and rank as councilor (*rat*). Nevertheless, he had wanted to avoid such return to full official duties to leave himself more time for his artistic pursuits. Aside from the financial security it provided, the reinstatement of his rank lent him a degree of social prominence and contributed to the respect he enjoyed as the composer of *Undine*. His literary celebrity had already resulted in invitations to so-called aesthetic teas and brought him in contact with upper levels of Berlin society. His collaboration with Fouqué on the opera contributed to his celebrity among the socially prominent, for the latter was very well connected in those circles, including even that of the Prussian royalty.

Another result of the collaboration with Fouqué on *Undine* were two contributions to a literary annual edited by him, the *Frauentaschenbuch* (*Ladies' Pocket Book*), for the years 1816 and 1817. Both stories have music enthusiasm as their theme. The first of the two tales, "Die Fermate" ("The Pause"), was inspired by a painting at an exhibition in Berlin and does not belong among Hoffmann's masterpieces. The second story, however, which appeared in the *Frauentaschenbuch* as "Ein Brief an Fouqué" ("A Letter to Fouqué"), has become one of Hoffmann's most famous as "Rat Krespel" ("Councilor Krespel"), a title referring to the central figure that was given to the tale by editors after Hoffmann's death (some English translations are entitled "The Cremona Violin").

Hoffmann's collaboration with Fouqué in these years also resulted in another of his most celebrated stories, "Nußknacker und Mausekönig" ("The Nutcracker and the Mouse-King"), which served as the inspiration for the ballet set to music by Peter Ilyich Tchaikovsky (1840–1893). Hoffmann created the nutcracker story for a volume of *Kinder-Mährchen* (*Children's Fairy Tales*) for the Christmas market in 1816 with contributions by Hoffmann, Fouqué, and another literary friend, Carl Wilhelm Salice Contessa (1777–1825). That enterprise followed by only a year the publication of the second volume of the Grimm brothers'—Jacob (1785–1863) and Wilhelm (1786–1859)—*Kinder- und Hausmärchen* (*Children's and Household Tales*) in Berlin, the first volume of which had appeared in 1812. While the Grimms were criticized for publishing stories that were deemed not entirely appropriate for children, it was claimed that Hoffmann's "Nutcracker" showed he was completely incapable of writing children's literature. A second volume of *Kinder-Mährchen* to which he contributed the following year (1817) enabled Hoffmann to prove the critics wrong. He arranged to have his wholly innocent, vaguely pious story, "Das fremde Kind" ("The Strange Child"), placed in that volume in such a way as to give the impression that it had been written by one of the other two contributors.

While the impetus to the demand for children's fairy tales given by the Grimms' collection, and the rising vogue of such stories generally, helped result in Hoffmann's "Nutcracker" story that later inspired Tchaikovsky, the vogue of historical novels like those of Fouqué and Walter Scott's Waverly novels of the post-Napoleonic years was a major factor in Hoffmann's turn in 1817 and 1818 to producing tales with historical settings. Two of these proved especially influential. His poetization of the life and times of master craftsmen in sixteenth-century Nuremberg in the tale "Meister Martin der Küfner und seine Gesellen," ("Meister Martin the Cooper and His Journeymen," 1818) was a major source of inspiration for Richard Wagner's later depiction of that milieu in his opera *Die Meistersinger von Nürnberg* (*The Mastersingers of Nuremberg,* 1862). Hoffmann's "Das Fräulein von Scuderi" ("Mademoiselle de Scudéry," 1819), which ranks among the best known of his tales, is considered to be an important example of the emerging popular genre of crime stories and a forerunner of the later detective stories.

The year 1819 brought a turn in Hoffmann's storytelling toward the satirical vein that had characterized his essays and sketches from the Bamberg period for the *Fantasiestücke,* such as those gathered together in the "Kreisleriana," and his Bamberg memoir, "Die neuesten Schicksale des Hundes Berganza." Hoffmann's return to satire was related to the restoration of absolutist governmental forms in the wake of Napoleon's defeat and the resistance that development met among those citizens eager for change. The change sought was either constitutional monarchy or other forms of representative government that in some German lands had been promised in order to defeat French domination. For some the goal was simply unification of the separate German states as one land.

Hoffmann was certainly no political activist and there is no evidence he favored representative government or unification of Germany as a single national state. As a jurist, though, he was committed to the rule of law; and as a member of the professional burgher class and jealous guardian of his personal dignity he could not abide condescension, much

less arrogance, on the part of the ruling nobility or anyone else in a position of power and authority. Already in his fairy tale *Klein Zaches* (*Little
Zachary,* 1819), which he completed toward the end of 1818, he satirized contemporary attempts to impose autocratic rule and the sub-
servience, obsequiousness, and corruptness engendered by despotism.
The first volume of his autobiographical novel *Lebensansichten des Katers
Murr* (*World Views of the Tomcat Murr,* 1819, 1821) depicted the political
restoration in even more scurrilous fashion through the groundless pretense, arrogance, and condescension of a prince who continues to behave
as an autocratic ruler even after his land has been mediatized, or taken
from him, pursuant to territorial rearrangements effected at the Congress of Vienna of 1815.

As a result of Hoffmann's position at the Kammergericht, the Prussian king appointed him that fall (1819) to a commission to investigate
"demagogic activities." The commission was formed in the wake of the
political assassination of the playwright Kotzebue by a student, Karl
Ludwig Sand (1795–1820), that spring and the resulting Carlsbad
Decrees issued that summer by the federated German governments and
aimed at suppressing unauthorized political activity. Hoffmann proved
to be a strong voice on the commission rejecting punishment for the
holding of opinions as distinguished from the committing of acts against
the government. He was especially instrumental in securing the release
from custody of one of the leading figures among the "demagogic"
activists, Friedrich Ludwig Jahn (1778–1852), better known as Turn-
vater Jahn for having been the father of gymnastic training as a means
to build patriotic spirit, to rid Germany of political domination by
France, and to preserve German independence. Jahn had been one of the
leaders of the resistance to Napoleon and therefore retained somewhat
the status of a popular national hero. In the course of the nineteenth
century he became a hero for German nationalists, and in the twentieth
century his popular fame was exploited by the National Socialists in
support of their aggressive war aims. At the time of the Carlsbad
Decrees, however, Jahn was viewed by German rulers with suspicion
and as a threat to lead populist uprisings against the restoration of the
older order that had been effected only a few years earlier by the Congress of Vienna.[9]

Hoffmann's experiences on the commission gave further impetus to
satirical tendencies in his writing during these years, 1819 to 1822. The
second volume of his autobiographical novel, *Kater Murr,* which
appeared at the end of 1821, contained still more unflattering depic-

tions of the established order—whether rulers, aristocrats, or academics—than had the first volume. In his contributions for the *Berlinischer Taschenkalendar*—"Die Brautwahl" ("The Choice of a Bride") and the two-part story "Irrungen" ("Mistakes") and "Die Geheimnisse" ("The Secrets")—Prussian government officials and Prussian aristocrats cut ridiculous if not wholly unsympathetic figures, as do the aristocrats in the fairy tale "Die Königsbraut" ("The King's Bride"). By far the most direct reflection of Hoffmann's experiences on the investigatory commission, however, was his satire on police methods in his last fairy tale, *Meister Floh* (*Master Flea*), completed only several months before his death. This time Hoffmann used material to which he was privy only as a member of the commission, so that not only was the object of the satire identifiable to those familiar with the commission's documents, but Hoffmann was clearly guilty of at least an indiscretion toward his government. Even so, the target of the satire might not have been recognized if Hoffmann had not boasted about the blow he was going to strike in the tale, much of which, including the relevant passages, was already in press that January of 1822. The police official who was satirized there as "Knarrpanti" got wind of the matter and through his influence succeeded in having the offending episode removed before the tale was printed.

Even in these last years, Hoffmann's writing tended less to biting satire than to the good-natured, jovial, humorous sort, though the satirical element was stronger in this period. Already in 1817 he had withdrawn from attending so-called aesthetic teas frequented by celebrities and members of polite society. He preferred the more boisterous conviviality of the wine houses, in particular Lutter and Wegner's, where he became a fixture with his actor friend Ludwig Devrient, attracting business to the establishment with his jests, storytelling, and impromptu caricatures drawn on napkins. In his writings, he managed to make fun of vanity and pretense in a wide assortment of positions and professions. Beyond the tales referred to earlier, there are such examples as the biologists in the stories "Haimatochare" (first published in *Der Freimüthige oder Unterhaltungsblatt für gebildete, unbefangene Leser,* 1819) and "Datura fastuosa" (first published in *Taschenbuch der Liebe und Freundschaft gewidmet,* 1823), the Italian actor in the fairy tale *Prinzessin Brambilla* (*Princess Brambilla*), and the two claimants to the throne in a tiny principality in "Die Doppeltgänger" ("The Doubles"; first published in *Die Feierstunden,* 1822).

These late tales, like Hoffmann's earlier fiction, nonetheless continue to revolve around erotic desire and its sublimations. Unsurprisingly, considering that Hoffmann's writing career began in earnest only in the wake of his emotional crisis over his passion for his voice pupil Julia Marc, the jealous paternal or avuncular love of an older man for a young maiden is an oft-portrayed subject in these stories, and increasingly so in Hoffmann's last years when his health was failing. Such focus on the relationship of a father or uncle to a daughter or niece is particularly strong in stories such as "Signor Formica" and "Die Marquise de la Pivardiere" ("The Marchioness de la Pivardière"; first published in *Taschenbuch zum geselligen Vergnügen,* 1821) and in the two stories Hoffmann completed on his deathbed, "Meister Johannes Wacht" ("Master Johannes Wacht"; first published in *Geschichten, Märchen und Sagen,* 1823) and "Die Genesung" ("The Recovery"; first published in *Der Zuschauer,* 1822), the latter surely depicting secretly, on the eve of his death, the tender avuncular feelings he had felt for his Julchen.

Another of Hoffmann's very last works, "Des Vetters Eckfenster" ("The Cousin's Corner Window"; first published in *Der Zuschauer,* 1822), amounts to a last statement about his nature as a writer. This testament has the form of a report by a writer's cousin about a visit to the dying relative. The writer, confined to a wheelchair, is reduced to viewing the world from his window but makes a virtue of this necessity by close observation of certain figures he spies in the marketplace and by envisioning things about them from their appearances and actions as seen from his vantage point. Hoffmann's often repeated principle that a writer can only portray convincingly what he or she has actually seen is stated here one last time. Seeing, though, means in this case far more than just observing. Hoffmann, the writer, was able to envision a whole life, in the sense of poetic characterization, from a few externals. As "Des Vetters Eckfenster" suggests, he was busy at this creative activity almost to the exact moment when the rising paralysis reached his lungs and he died of suffocation on 25 June 1822. Ever since, the question for readers of Hoffmann's fantastic, always enigmatic tales has remained: Just how does he characterize these figures he has made come to life because he has actually "seen" them, and how are they, as characters, to be understood?

Chapter Two
Critical Reception

Excitement is evident in reviews of Hoffmann's *Fantasiestücke* that appeared in 1815. That year saw the fourth and final volume follow the three that were published the year before. Two critics in particular were enthused over the fairy tale *Der goldne Topf,* which they understood to have philosophical import. An anonymous commentator, writing in the influential journal *Morgenblatt für gebildete Stände* (*Morning Paper for the Educated Classes*), judged that the work's subject is the question: "*What is the ultimate purpose of human existence? How is it achievable?*"[1] Similarly, but from a specifically romantic viewpoint, Hoffmann's literary contemporary and acquaintance Friedrich Gottlieb Wetzel (1779–1819), in the *Heidelbergische Jahrbücher* (*Heidelberg Yearbooks*), concluded that Hoffmann was writing about "the mystery of all mysteries, the great mystical secret of all temporal creation, of the falling away and the return of the Transitory into Original Being."[2]

Two other critical voices, however, were not so sure that the ostensible philosophical meaning was to be taken seriously. The critic in the *Leipziger Literatur-Zeitung* (*Leipzig Literary Newspaper*) wrote of the tale's spirit of "jesting irony."[3] In the *Jenaische Allgemeine Literatur-Zeitung* (*Jena General Literary Newspaper*), another critic, though singling out *Der goldne Topf* as the most thoroughly successful of the *Fantasiestücke,* did not find the central figure convincing as an ideal: "Nothing about the student Anselmus, except at most his awkwardness, testifies to his poetic sensitivity, which indeed he does not possess."[4]

What distinguished Hoffmann in the eyes of readers, though, was surely his genius in mingling the familiar and the fantastic. As another critic noted, referring to the first of the *Fantasiestücke,* "Ritter Gluck": "Vision and reality here are blended very boldly into one."[5] In a review of Hoffmann's *Prinzessin Brambilla* (1820), another critic celebrated Hoffmann as the master of the artistic fairy tale as pioneered by the German Romantics: "Ever since *Tieck* and *Hardenberg* [i.e., Novalis] opened up, like a hidden door in one's everyday living room, the new miraculous fairy tale realm, in which everything can be explained, dissolved, and formed anew, and yet still remain mysterious and independent, a number of authors have followed this path; none yet seems to have found his way so happily through this romantic wilderness as Hoffmann."[6]

Less well received than this mingling of everyday life and the fantastic was Hoffmann's related depiction of symptoms of insanity or seeming madness. A critic in the *Morgenblatt für gebildete Stände* complained about the deranged amateur musician in Hoffmann's since widely acclaimed story "Rat Krespel": "If the narrative part of this essay stood in a medical journal, we would account it a grippingly and vividly portrayed story of a very curious partial confusion of the mind, but when the author invents the story of such a terrible affliction and elaborates it in the most horrifying detail over forty pages, then we look with melancholy at his mood and questioningly up at Art."[7] A similar complaint was voiced two years later about another of Hoffmann's tales that, like "Rat Krespel," later came to be considered among his best. Writing about "Das Fräulein von Scuderi" (first published in *Taschenbuch, der Liebe und Freundschaft gewidmet,* 1820), this critic was bothered by the depiction of compulsive murder-lust in the figure of the goldsmith René Cardillac.[8] That complaint was echoed by another critic two years later, who found that Hoffmann had "misused his talent through the invention of a despicable moral monster."[9] In her diary of those years, Rahel Varnhagen von Ense (née Levin, 1771–1833), too, found the story of Cardillac's compulsion "hideous, sick, useless." She wondered at Hoffmann's great popularity with the reading public: "*Such is the grand pleasure*—of Hoffmann. And *long live the author* cries the German reading public. Utterly beyond comprehension."[10]

"Das Fräulein von Scuderi" was indeed an immediate popular success. Hoffmann's literary contemporary, Therese Huber (1764–1829), in a review for the *Morgenblatt für gebildete Stände* very shortly after the story's appearance, praised it as "suspenseful and well costumed." She was referring to the narrative's qualities as both a detective story—an important early example of the genre as noted by some—and a historical novella, set in Paris during the reign of Louis XIV. It was indeed especially as a portrayer of earlier times that Hoffmann succeeded with the critics. His "Meister Martin der Küfner und seine Gesellen" ("Master Martin the Cooper and His Journeymen," 1818; first published in *Taschenbuch zum geselligen Vergnügen,* 1819) was praised immediately in the *Zeitung für die elegante Welt* (*Newspaper for Elegant People*) as "a most congenial and appealing family portrait from those genuine, warm, and powerful times to which our generation, not entirely without justification, looks back longingly."[11] That opinion was seconded by Therese Huber in the *Morgenblatt,* who wrote that "[t]he costume of this story, both the *mores* and the way of thinking, seem to us to be most authentic!"[12]

Konrad Schwenk, however, raised a dissenting voice several years later in commenting on Hoffmann's tale "Der Kampf der Sänger" ("The Minnesinger's Contest," 1818; first published in *Die Serapionsbrüder,* vol. 2, 1819) that portrayed the medieval troubadours Wolfram von Eschenbach and Heinrich von Ofterdingen. Schwenk compared Hoffmann's depiction unfavorably with Walter Scott's historical novels that were taking the literary world by storm in those years: "Stories of this sort cannot possibly transport the reader to the Middle Ages, since for that many more peculiarities of the age have to be portrayed, as Walter Scott does in giving us a clear and vivid picture of bygone times."[13]

Positive responses to Hoffmann concerned not only presumed philosophical import of his tales, their mingling of fantasy and reality, or their depiction of bygone times. Critics also wrote about his ability to grip his readers. A reviewer of the third volume of the collected tales published as *Die Serapionsbrüder* (*The Serapion Brethren,* 4 vols., 1819–1821) commented that "an irresistible power is exercised by the spirit that holds sway in these poetic writings."[14] Another contemporary reviewer wrote about the tale "Spielerglück" ("Gambler's Luck"): "The abyss into which the gambling compulsion can plunge even a rather noble person cannot be portrayed more grippingly, truly, and movingly."[15] The unexplained ending of that story found favor with Konrad Schwenk: "[T]he horrifying uncertainty of how Angela actually died [is] magnificent in a way that is seldom encountered."[16] That judgment was echoed by another critic, who found that the story "leaves a wounding thorn in the reader's soul, since the only noble creature to appear here dies finally in a way that remains unclear."[17]

There were, at the same time, complaints about confusion and lack of clarity in Hoffmann's stories. Referring to the role of spiritualistic fantasy in "Der Elementargeist" ("The Elemental Spirit"; first published in *Taschenbuch zum geselligen Vergnügen,* 1822), the poet Wilhelm Müller (1794–1827) asked, "will this man of many talents never tire of entertaining the public with confused, feverish dreams?"[18] Another critic raised a similar objection about the fairy tale *Prinzessin Brambilla:* "[T]he author's forcing [us] to follow him through a labyrinth of dream and insanity without a saving thread is as inartistic as it is unnatural."[19] The praise Hoffmann was accorded for his stories in which magic and the supernatural play little or no role also shows that this element was not universally applauded. A case in point was his late story "Die Räuber" ("The Robbers," 1821; first published in *Rheinisches Tachenbuch,* 1822), in which the only uncanny aspect is that the central figures become involved with a family that in its composition and the names of its members seems to have stepped from the pages of Friedrich Schiller's play of that title. One critic sighed, "If the gifted author would only give us more such poetic works full of nature and truth, instead of his numerous grotesqueries."[20] Another wrote, "the Robbers, by Hoffmann, grips the reader all the more certainly since the author's vivid imagination has known here how to keep itself within the bounds of physical possibility and psychological probability."[21] A third critic, though, found that precisely Hoffmann's transformation of Schiller's play "into the realm of the natural" had deprived it "of its grandeur."[22]

Another element in Hoffmann's works that attracted contemporary critics was humor. His fairy tale *Klein Zaches* (*Little Zachary,* 1819) moved a critic to write that "after reading through this Märchen one gains an insight into what it means to elevate oneself humoristically above life, and how refreshing such a successful attempt can be for the mind and soul."[23] Commentary on the splenetic humor in Hoffmann's autobiographical novel *Kater Murr* was rather negative, however. One critic complained that Hoffmann "too often omits the *mediating* point of view and robs himself and his readers of the most sublime enjoyment of *that* irony which throws the rainbow bridge of *bold* courage across the terrifying chasm of Existence and Being, and mocks even mockery itself."[24] The author and critic Ludwig Börne (1786–1837) found the novel's romantic hero, the composer Johannes Kreisler, to be a "degenerate human being [who] tears down the bridge which a good sense of humor builds across all rifts and divisions in life."[25] Another reviewer measured Hoffmann against a—platonic—ideal of humor the critic found fulfilled in the novels of Jean Paul Friedrich Richter: "Humor, in the higher sense of the term, we define as the universal view of the world which, by encompassing the limits of human knowledge and by relating the most sublime in spiritual contemplation to the lowest of ordinary phenomena, dissolves the conflicting opposites into an essential unity and puts the observer at a vantage point from which, beyond the dissension and conflict of earthly relationships, the view of a higher, conciliatory world of ideas is opened to him. . . . [H]is [Hoffmann's] portrayals are by no means imbued with genuine humor in the above sense."[26] Börne's rejection of Hoffmann's humor, meanwhile, was absolute: "The humor in the writings of the author of the *Fantasiestücke* is sick."[27]

The young Heinrich Heine (1797–1856), at the beginning of his illustrious writing career in 1822, and only a few weeks before Hoffmann's demise, referred to the dying author's gift for fathoming of the psyche. That judgment shows itself in Heine's complaint about Hoffmann's last fairy tale, *Meister Floh:* "The psychic realm which Hoffmann knows how to depict so magnificently is treated most prosaically in this novel [sic]. . . . The grand allegory into which everything dissolves at the end did not satisfy me. . . . I believe that a novel should not be an allegory."[28] Hoffmann's plumbing of psychic depths hardly met with universal understanding or approval, though. One critic, for example, was understandably revolted by the ghoulish tale "Vampirismus" ("Vampirism"; first published in *Die Serapions-Brüder,* vol. 4, 1821): "although we are not at all averse to [portrayals of] the horrifying, still we believe that this must find its limit when a higher moral power in man is no longer able to control it, and therefore we have to call this whole story a repulsive, diabolical invention."[29]

Hoffmann's critical reception in England dates from shortly after his premature death in 1822 at age 46. He was welcomed as an author of horror literature, as a practitioner of a genre pioneered by English authors, the so-called gothic novel. An anonymous critic, reviewing a translation of Hoffmann's venture into that genre, *Die Elixiere des Teufels,* singled out for praise "the skill with which its author has contrived to mix up the horrible notion of the double-goer with ordinary human feelings of all kinds."[30] Even for English readers accustomed to such fare as Matthew Gregory Lewis's (1775–1818) gothic novel, *The Monk* (1795), though, Hoffmann's depictions apparently exceeded the bounds of acceptability. The reviewer, at any rate, applauded the translator's decision to "prune off all the indelicacy of the German original."[31] A similar attitude among the British toward German writers generally was reflected, shortly after the review of Hoffmann's novel, in the preface to a translation of works by German Romantic authors that included Hoffmann's "Fräulein von Scuderi." The translator ventured the opinion that "German authors, if anglicized . . . [by] a remaniement or refacimento, will prove infinitely more acceptable than they have ever yet been to the British public."[32]

The most influential of all British reactions to Hoffmann's works was that by the then immensely popular author Walter Scott, who had taken literary Europe by storm with his Waverly novels. In his review of Hoffmann, which appeared some five years after Hoffmann's death, Scott, whose historical novels were praised for their realism, complained that with all of "the Fantastic mode of writing" popular in Germany, the reader cannot expect "to discover either meaning or end further than the surprize of the moment."[33] Scott considered Hoffmann a prime example. Influenced surely by Julius Eduard Hitzig's biography of Hoffmann that had appeared the year after Hoffmann's death, where Hoffmann's gift of fantasy was attributed to excessive consumption of alcohol, Scott in his review compared him to an opium eater and asserted, "we cannot help considering his case as one requiring the assistance of medicine, rather than of criticism."[34] Scott's judgment was not shared universally in England, though, as the assessment by the author Thomas Carlyle from the same year (1827) shows. Carlyle reasoned that "if Rabelais continues, after centuries, to be read . . . the products of a mind so brilliant, wild and singular as that of Hoffmann may long hover in the remembrance of the world: as objects of curiosity, of censure, and, on the whole, compared with absolute Nonentity, of entertainment and partial approval."[35]

Scott's rejection of Hoffmann found resonance in Hoffmann's native Germany.[36] The grand old man of German letters, Johann Wolfgang Goethe (1749–1832), asked, in commending Scott's review of Hoffmann to his readers, "what loyal participant in the concern for national culture has not been grieved by seeing that the pathological works of this ailing man were so influential in Germany for a number of years."[37] The following year the German critic Wolfgang Menzel, in his book about German literature, echoed the view of Scott and Goethe—as well as some others before them—that Hoffmann's writings were those of a mentally ill man: "His whole poetic work is infected with this sickness [mental illness], and its subject even is sickness."[38] The German philosopher Georg Friedrich Wilhelm Hegel (1770–1831), too, in his lectures on aesthetics at the University of Berlin, censured Hoffmann as exemplifying "this inner, unstable discord which travels the whole range of the most repulsive dissonances" and spoke disapprovingly of his humor as one of "repulsiveness and an ironic burlesqueness."[39]

The rise of a Hoffmann vogue in France beginning around 1830, which led to a similar one in Russia in the ensuing decade, owed much to the attention called to him by Scott's disapproving review.[40] Hoffmann came to be championed by French writers and critics who wanted to free creativity from fetters of moralism and good taste, such as insisted upon in England. These writers and critics were identified with what came to be called the movement of *l'art pour l'art* (art for art's sake). Closely allied with and hailed by that movement, was the renowned German-Jewish author Heine, a literary sensation in his native land in the 1820s who had removed to Paris in the wake of the July Revolution of 1830 there. In his ironically humorous fashion, Heine, in his history of the romantic movement in Germany, asked with reference to views of Hoffmann like those expressed by Scott, Goethe, and Menzel "is poetry perhaps a sickness of man, just as the pearl is only the infectious matter from which the poor oyster is suffering?"[41] What does it matter, Heine asks, if poetry originates in pathology, as long as the product, like the pearl, is beautiful? This since famous statement from Heine surely contributed to Hoffmann's becoming acknowledged as a forerunner by the advocates of *l'art pour l'art*. That standing was disapprovingly acknowledged by Hoffmann's German Romantic contemporary, Joseph von Eichendorff (1788–1857), in his history of German literature published in his late years: "[I]t is in no way accidental that the whole immoral so-called Romanticism in France acknowledges him as their avant garde."[42]

Heine's and the *l'art pour l'art* adherents' romanticization of Hoffmann's works as the product of sickness was echoed subsequently by the French author Champfleury (pseud. Jules Fleury-Husson, 1821–1889), in the introduction to his translation of Hoffmann's posthumously published stories. Champfleury addressed that introduction to his fellow champion of realism, the painter Gustave Courbet (1819–1877). Champfleury wrote that Courbet would see from "the torments, anguishes, and sufferings" of Hoffmann's "nervous existence that the envious, the impotents and philistines are not the artist's only tormentors. . . . [B]ehind the artist there is always a tormentor who makes him suffer a thousand tortures, a thousand anguishes keener than those invented by the jealous. Isn't that tormentor Art itself?"[43] For the French poet Charles Baudelaire (1821–1867), forerunner of the movement that came to be called symbolism, Hoffmann's art did not have its origins in sickness but was instead a study of mental illness. Baudelaire likened Hoffmann to "a physiologist or a physician of the more profoundly insane and who amuses himself by clothing that deep science in poetic forms, like a wise man who speaks in fables and parables."[44]

The image of Hoffmann as an artist whose creativity was owing to drunkenness, sickness, or spiritual torment was especially dominant in the second half of the nineteenth century, a view characteristic, not surprisingly, of representatives of the emerging profession of psychiatric medicine. In his influential, widely read book on genius and insanity, the Italian physician Cesare Lombroso (1836–1909) declared Hoffmann to

be "a mad drinker" whose "drawings became caricatures, his tales horror-inspiring, his music a chaos of notes, and thus he became the actual
founder of fantastic poetry. . . . For many years he suffered paranoia with
hallucinations, during which he saw the fantastic figures of his tales
transform themselves into real persons and things."[45] That explanation
of Hoffmann's creative genius, which echoed the depiction in Hitzig's
biography of him, was repeated by subsequent psychiatric writers,
including an American who claimed that "[i]n all probability, had Hoffmann not been spurred by disease into morbid introspection, he would
not have produced anything, but would have settled into a humdrum
lawyer."[46] A French psychiatrist devoted a book-length study to Hoffmann (1908), in which he argued that Hoffmann's tales were written
"in a state of mental disequilibrium in which the images succeed one
another without connection, without logic, at the mercy of external
things; and, above all, these dreams are born of illness."[47]

Generally speaking, though, the turn to the twentieth century saw a
shift toward decidedly positive assessments of Hoffmann's poetic inspiration. The change accompanied a developing neoromanticism that
emphasized a yearning for transcendence of earthly bounds. The German writer Ricarda Huch (1864–1947), in her history of German
romanticism, depicted Hoffmann as longing "for a spirit realm where
there would be no such tormenting corporeality as that which had fallen
his lot."[48] The theme of Hoffmann's need for liberation was struck also
in the introduction to a standard edition of his works by the scholar
Georg Ellinger, whose biography of him in the 1890s had helped direct
attention to Hoffmann in a distinctly positive way. Even Ellinger,
though, echoed the references to Hoffmann as subject to hallucination,
explaining the Satanic themes in his works as "the poet's striving, in the
treatment of his subject matter, to free himself through artistic creativity from the uncanny power of the hallucinations that were oppressing
him."[49] As in this example, the neoromantic direction in criticism saw
Hoffmann, one way or another, to be involved with a transcendent,
supernatural, or otherworldly realm.

Thus, for Hermann Hesse (1877–1962) Hoffmann's "pure works"
were those that were "without earthly residue."[50] A British literary
scholar in a study of the German novella found that in Hoffmann's
works "[a]rt, and more particularly music, is the channel through which
the daemonic, incalculable forces of the universe burst in upon the ordinary, calculable life of man, with an elemental force, and set up tremendous upheavals of the personality."[51] A French scholar, likewise writing

in the 1930s, wrote that Hoffmann's message was that "[i]nvisible reality, imperceivable through ordinary means, chooses all sorts of devious paths to alert us to its presence and to make us sense that we belong to it at least as much as to the world of our occupations, our morality, our petty everyday lives."[52]

Neoromantic or neoidealistic interpretations of Hoffmann, with their neoplatonic origins or affinities, continued in the post–World War II period. Another French literary scholar argued that the mission of the central figure in Hoffmann's tales is "to play his part in that harmonious symphony which constitutes the universe."[53] A Swiss scholarly critic similarly wrote that for Hoffmann salvation is "everything that enables the soul to begin its flight to heaven—above all, Love and Art."[54] Meanwhile a German scholar, in his history of German literature, claimed that for Hoffmann "another, higher existence protrudes into ours."[55] A leader in the establishment of comparative literature as an academic discipline, the Czech-born and Czech-educated scholar René Wellek, in his preface to a new English translation of selected writings by Hoffmann, similarly wrote that "Hoffmann shared his German contemporaries' view of music as not only an emotional release and exaltation but a secret language of the beyond, a door to the supernatural and divine."[56]

In the 1970s one still found views expressed such as that "Hoffmann . . . had a definite concept of a transcendental sphere, which relates itself to the physical by the medium of music"[57] or that "Hoffmann ultimately demonstrates that the bourgeois conception of madness is identical with celestial inspiration."[58] A variation of the platonic view was offered by another critic who saw Hoffmann's use of myth and miracle as a vehicle to "portray the transcendence of the usual."[59] Another critic similarly found Hoffmann's use of dreams to show "the only . . . possibility of salvation from the 'fetters' of an oppressive 'reality.' "[60]

The neoromantic understanding of Hoffmann has been quite persistent—justifiably so, since he not only left himself open to but encouraged that perception by various means in writings for his romantic contemporaries. Not all critical comment on him in the twentieth century has been of that type, however. Some Hoffmann criticism shows the influence of existentialism, the dominant direction in Western intellectual discourse since World War II. Existentialism has many themes, among them the individual's search for authenticity or justification. This theme is found in a German literary scholar's study of Hoffmann, published the year Hitler invaded Poland, where it is said that in Hoffmann's "most beautiful works he perceived essentiality, the miracle of the self in its identity with itself, or rather the way to this identity despite all manner of temptations and devilments."[61]

In the aftermath of World War II, existentialism came to emphasize especially the theme of lostness and alienation in an incomprehensible world and chaotic universe. In a German doctoral dissertation from 1961, Hoffmann's concern was understood by the question "What is at stake is the answer to the Existential question: How can the image of man be saved?"[62] A dozen years later, a professor of German literature in the United States argued that "Hoffmann portrayed the disintegration of the individual in a world of uncontrolled forces."[63] Another scholar found in Hoffmann a depiction that "the world familiar to man . . . has on its fringes . . . a realm accessible to the imagination and even more dreaded and deadly because of its inchoate form."[64]

What about the view of Hoffmann under fascism and communism? For a German scholar of nationalistic leanings writing in the post–World War I decade, Hoffmann's acclaim in that period had been a symptom of disintegration. Wilhelm Kosch's opinion was that "[i]n the period of collapse, of feverish chaos, of the traditionless [Weimar] Republic, Hoffmann necessarily became the classic of classics." Hoffmann was associated in Kosch's mind with a moral, ethical, and aesthetic permissiveness and cultural rootlessness he found characteristic of Germany in the 1920s: "When everything goes into dissolution, when the religious, moral, national, economic, and literary lawlessness celebrates real triumphs, the author least indigenous, least burdened with 'prejudices,' the least self-controlled becomes the nation's cultural hero."[65] Unsurprisingly, Hoffmann was not particularly in favor under the ensuing National Socialist regime.

As viewed from Kosch's perspective, Hoffmann would not find favor with any totalitarian regime, nationalist or otherwise. At the time of the worker's revolt of 1953 in the communist German Democratic Republic, a revolt in reaction to the imposing of totalitarian rule under Soviet auspices, the author of a Leipzig doctoral dissertation declared that "Hoffmann was not able to go the way of affirming the law. He did not see beauty in moderation, in lawfulness."[66] In other ways, too, the acclaim Hoffmann's works found in the capitalist West posed a challenge for critics in the communist East. Should they embrace or reject him as a classic, and on what basis? An East German scholar remarked that "[t]he adherents of the most varying decadent movements looked for support to the mystical, reactionary, and otherworldly elements in his work. These traits connect Hoffmann's works with Existentialism and similar pessimistic currents in the literature of the twentieth century."[67] As this remark indicates, East German critics looked to other aspects of Hoffmann's work, notably the element of social criticism and class resentment embodied in his satirical humor. The leading critic of the communist East, Georg Lukács, had shown the way by writing in the immediate post–World War II years that "the Philistinism against which [Hoffmann] tirelessly and unrelentingly fights is the manifest form of the deprivation of rights and degradation of man through the German *misère* under the conditions of emerging capitalism."[68]

Even the "otherworldly elements" could be fitted into the Marxist interpretation of history and society. In his preface to a prominent edition of Hoffmann's works, the leading East German literary scholar Hans Mayer, who later defected to the West, showed how Hoffmann could be seen by Marxists as a poet of social realism. Mayer argued that "[a]lmost all of Hoffmann's great tales . . . agree in their portrayal of reality in so far as the coexistence of both worlds, the real and the mythical, is necessary, since the artist as artist necessarily would perish in the German reality [of Hoffmann's day]."[69] Mayer's assessment from the late 1950s was echoed then in the early 1960s in the standard East German scholarly monograph on Hoffmann, by Hans-Georg Werner, who explained that the "suprasensory world" symbolically depicted in the romantic author's works is a reflection of "his deep discontent with the given concrete environment, which he experienced as a constant threat and as endangering his creativity."[70]

In addition to Marxist interpretations of the supernatural in Hoffmann's works as reflecting his reaction to life under feudalism and capitalism, existentialist views of the supernatural as representing uncontrollable cosmic forces, and neoromantic claims of Hoffmann's belief in or yearning for transcendence, there have been psychoanalytical interpretations of his works with regard to the element of the fantastic. The founder of psychoanalysis himself, Sigmund Freud (1856–1939), made Hoffmann's tale "Der Sandmann" the focus of an influential essay on "The Uncanny" published just after the end of World War I. Freud interpreted the supernatural adventures as projections of sexual fantasies of an oedipal nature told from the perspective of the emotionally disturbed central character.[71]

Freud's attention may have been drawn to Hoffmann by a psychoanalytical study of another of his tales that had been published in Freud's journal *Imago* five years earlier. In that essay, the central figure's involvement with a supernatural Queen of the Mine is seen as occurring in reaction to the death of his mother: "Elis's libido is constantly fixed on his mother. He returns to her from his sea voyages as others to their beloveds. When, on one homecoming, he finds her no longer among the living, he succumbs to the illness, whose cause we may perceive as nothing but the resulting failure of an erotic need which remained on an infantile level."[72] The focus on depiction of sexuality in Hoffmann's tales initiated by the Freudians is found also in a study from the 1980s by an American scholar.[73] In addition to interpretations based on Freudian theory, there has been commentary on Hoffmann stories from divergent psychoanalytical viewpoints. The emphasis on a battle of the sexes and inferiority complexes, as associated with the theory of Freud's pupil, Alfred Adler (1870–1937), appears reflected in a 1918 doctoral dissertation's view of Hoffmann's "Elementargeist" as portraying "anxiety regarding the female partner . . . [and] fear of woman, who is here made into a destructive demon."[74]

In recent decades, the influence of the theories of the most famous of Freud's fallen-away disciples, Carl Gustav Jung (1875–1961), has been especially evident in interpretations of Hoffmann from a psychoanalytical perspective. The way was shown by one of Jung's collaborators, Aniela Jaffé, in her 1950 study of Hoffmann's fairy tale *Der goldne Topf.*[75] Characteristic of Jungian interpretations is reference to a quest for the inner self, exemplified in an American literary scholar's view of the central figure's dream vision near the end of Hoffmann's *Meister Floh* as a "descent into the lower regions of consciousness which allows the hero to become aware of the totality of his personality."[76] A prominent British scholarly critic, Siegbert S. Prawer, likewise saw Hoffmann as anticipating Jung, in this case with his "Sandmann": "For Hoffmann the personal unconscious is a means of gaining contact with something larger and deeper . . . which we may equate with Jung's 'Collective Unconscious.' "[77] A Jungian approach was taken subsequently by another British critic who wrote that it was to Hoffmann's "credit as a psychologist of the artist that [he] stressed, rather, the bridge between the two equally necessary and equally valid worlds," between everyday reality and the " 'Other Realm.' "[78] Also in the early 1970s, a major study emphasizing poetic creativity, as the Jungian critics mostly do, argued that Hoffmann was depicting the "absolute autonomy of the productive power of imagination."[79]

Beginning in the 1960s and at first influenced by Marxist criticism literary studies sought to emphasize the connection of texts with the society, culture, and intellectual climate in which they arose. This was precisely the aspect that neoromantic, existential, and psychoanalytical criticism had ignored or neglected. A greater emphasis on seeing Hoffmann in the context of his times is evident in the series of editions of his writings and of material about him issued over the course of the 1960s and 1970s by the Winkler publishing house in Munich.[80] Not only do the volumes containing his poetic works and essays, his correspondence, and his diaries have notes and commentary to help in that regard; there is also a likewise annotated edition of his legal opinions as a jurist and one collecting what was written about him by his friends and acquaintances.

This historical orientation as it applied to Hoffmann criticism is reflected in a study published in the late 1970s about mesmerism in relation to its depiction in literature.[81] There are many good examples of Hoffmann's use of the imagery and language of mesmerism are offered. Then, in the 1980s, a monograph was devoted to the broader question of medical science in Hoffmann's time and its depiction in his works.[82] In particular, this study provides a great deal of information about psychiatric medicine in its beginnings around 1800.

Related to this emphasis on historicity (*geschichtlichkeit*)—an emphasis that had its origins to a great extent in social issues—was the rise of a feminist approach to literature, which related poetic portrayals to the history of women's role and situation in society. This direction in literary study, closely associated with the women's liberation movement dating from the late 1960s and the 1970s, was the basis for a study in the 1980s on the function of women in early German romanticism and in Hoffmann's narratives.[83]

The 1970s saw a particular interest in how texts are understood by different readers, in connection with debate among scholarly critics about reception theory (*rezeptionstheorie*). The history of literary criticism and scholarship thereby came to be seen as crucially important to discussion of the meaning of poetic works. An aid to that sort of investigation was provided toward the end of the 1980s by the appearance, finally, of a volume on Hoffmann in the series of handbooks (*handbücher*) on authors and other literary subjects by the Metzler publishing house in Stuttgart.[84]

In addition to the question of how texts are understood by readers, there was the related interest in how authors use language to achieve their effects and the far larger question of how language conveys meaning. Hoffmann's strategies for involving his readers was the subject of a book by an American Germanist in the early 1970s.[85] Later in that decade a British literary scholar published a monograph on Hoffmann that aimed "to investigate what kind of rhetoric an author employs in order to make a reader's flesh creep."[86] In the 1980s there followed a German critic's investigation of the use of the metaphor of the puppet or marionette as a rhetorical device in German literature of the early nineteenth century, including its employment by Hoffmann.[87]

Directions in twentieth-century literary scholarship such as formalism, new criticism, and structuralism posited a principle of unity in poetic texts as one of the marks of creative genius. The century's last two decades have seen the emergence of a contrary critical movement, deconstructionism, that has sought to investigate the various provenance of significations and meanings contained in the language of a given literary work. In criticism on Hoffmann, an early example of this direction was an essay by an American scholar using a "structural-semiotic approach."[88]

A German doctoral dissertation of the late 1980s on Hoffmann's tale "Der Sandmann," while not avowedly written from a deconstructionist perspective, does seem influenced by that direction in criticism. A great deal of information about society in Hoffmann's time is introduced, and reference is made to a wide spectrum of interpretive and theoretical perspectives. The intended result is not to uncover the poetic or aesthetic unity of the work but to show the diversity of elements contributing to its production and the multiplicity of meanings to be found in it. One of the avowed interdisciplinary aims of the study was to shed light on Hoffmann's tale by referring to the social history of his time, an aim reflecting the currently dominant trend among Germanists and historians generally. Another goal was inclusion of a broad spectrum of theoretical viewpoints, including that of feminism. Reference thus is made to many theorists, especially those such as Jacques Derrida, Michel Foucault, Jacques Lacan, Jean Piaget, and Tzvetan Todorov, much discussed among academic critics over recent decades, as well as ones often cited still earlier, including Freud, Hegel, Martin Heidegger, Søren Kierkegaard, Käte Hamburger, Gustav René Hocke, and Karl Kerényi.[89] More recently, there appeared a monograph taking a semiotic approach to Hoffmann's tales with special attention to the question of intertextuality.[90] Among most recent studies is one that applies to two of Hoffmann's works the ideas of the Russian aesthetician and cultural philosopher Mikhail Bakhtin about the subversive function of carnivalesque elements, as exemplified in the writings of François Rabelais (1494–1553).[91]

A survey of criticism on Hoffmann such as offered here can help prepare us for making up our own minds about him as a creative artist. Hoffmann, though, was not only an author but a critic as well. Turning our attention now to Hoffmann the critic and essayist may aid in establishing a framework for better understanding him as a poetic author.

Chapter Three

Essays and Criticism

As we remember from our account of Hoffmann's life, he made his writing debut as a music and theater critic, first with his short essay (1803) on Schiller's reintroduction of the chorus from Greek antiquity in his play of that same year *Die Braut von Messina* (*The Bride of Messina*) and then a half-dozen years later (1809) with his initial contribution to the *Allgemeine Musikalische Zeitung* about a music enthusiast who believed himself to be the long since dead composer Christoph Willibald Gluck. Hoffmann's published thoughts on art and life thus have their beginnings in his ideas about music.[1] An understanding of those ideas is best arrived at by considering first his discussions of instrumental music.

Hoffmann accorded music for instruments as opposed to music for voice or vocal accompaniment a special place. In a review (1809) of two symphonies by Friedrich Witt (1770–1836), he argued that instrumental pieces intended for the concert hall should provide purely musical pleasure devoid of poetic reference. He criticized the use of exotic instruments like the tambourine, triangle, and kettle drum in Witt's "Turkish" symphony not only as too loud for the size of contemporary orchestras and concert halls and as simply "bad sounding," but also for aiming to make the listeners think they have been transported to Turkey. Such illusion, Hoffmann argues, is appropriate for theater music, but not for the concert hall.[2]

The same ideal of pure symphonic music devoid of poetic reference is evident in Hoffmann's since famous review of Beethoven's *Fifth Symphony* (1810). There he claims that music is "the most romantic of all the arts." In doing so he defines the function of romantic art by saying—with reference to the story of Orpheus's opening of the gates of the underworld with his lyre—that music reveals to us "an unknown realm." That realm is a world "that has nothing in common with the external world accessible to our senses." In the world opened to us by music, "all emotions that can be determined through concepts" are left behind as we surrender ourselves "to the ineffable." Instrumental music, Hoffmann thereby implies, is potentially the most romantic of all music because, more fully than vocal music, music for vocal accompaniment, or music for the theater, it is capable of evoking a sense of surrender to inexpressible feeling (*SzM*, 34).

Because music opens for us an unknown realm, so Hoffmann goes on to say, in song or the opera, "where the accompanying poetry indicates particular emotional states," music's "magical power" envelops every passion with "the purple glow of romanticism." As such even what we have experienced emotionally in life "leads us out from life into the realm of the infinite" (*SzM*, 34–35). Not every composer achieves this effect, however; nor is its appreciation by listeners universal. Only a very few composers are capable of playing Orpheus's lyre in such a way as to "unlock the miraculous realm of the infinite."

Among those who can do so best are Joseph Haydn (1732–1809), Wolfgang Amadeus Mozart, and Beethoven. For Hoffmann, Haydn in his music "conceives of human things in human life romantically," while Mozart's music addresses itself to "the superhuman, the miraculous" elements that dwell in the inner spirit. Beethoven's music, though, using the "levers of awe, fear, horror, and pain," awakens "that boundless longing which is the essence of romanticism." Beethoven, therefore, is the most romantic of all composers. As a purely romantic composer his genius lies in instrumental music, since vocal music does not permit expression of indeterminate longing, "only emotional states, as indicated by the words," albeit emotional states experienced "as in the realm of the infinite" (*SzM*, 36).[3]

In subsequent reviews, Hoffmann continued to champion the romantic or transporting and transcendent capability of music. In commenting (1811) on Louis Spohr's (1784–1859) first symphony, he grants that the piece is characterized by a "quiet dignity" but observes that it lacks "the wild fire" of the Mozart and Beethoven symphonies that "penetrates deep into the soul of the listener" (*SzM*, 76). Hoffmann found further demonstration that Beethoven "carries the romantic spirit deep in his soul" in two of the composer's piano trios he reviewed (1812, 1813; *SzM*, 119). Reviewing (1813) Carl Anton Braun's (1788–1835) fourth symphony, he pointed again to Haydn, Mozart, and Beethoven as having been the first to bring that musical genre into its own, rendering it the highest form of instrumental music so that it became "the opera of instruments" (*SzM*, 145). And commenting (1814) on a piano sonata by Johann Friedrich Reichardt (1752–1814), Hoffmann declared music's "peculiarly own, most marvelous area" to be that in which "words perish in the intimation of the divine"—an intimation that "fills one's breast with unutterable longing" (*SzM*, 204).

The idea that romantic music's mission is the expression of ineffable transcendent yearning is evident, too, in Hoffmann's reviews of church music, which he believed should express a simple piety oriented heavenward.[4] Commenting (1809) on the "Pater noster" of Andreas Romberg (1767–1821), he praised it for "a piety such as dwells in a childlike, happy soul that, unbent by any earthly burden, intimates the joys of heaven" (*SzM*, 31). He found the ideal of church music realized in a service he attended in the Pietistic community of Herrnhut, an experience he described in reviewing (1812) Anton Heinrich Pustkuchen's (1761–1830) book of choral music. In contrast to Lutheran and Reformed church services, Hoffmann remarks, in which the congregation is expected to join in the singing as a devotional exercise, so that the louder one sings the greater the witness to one's piety, in the Pietistic service "no one wants to stand out, no one wants to disavow the quiet devotion with which one has approached the supreme being." As a result, the singing not only remains "pure," but the three-part harmony of the chorale can also be heard properly (*SzM,* 91–92).

Expression of simple faith in church music is likewise urged in Hoffmann's review (1813) of Beethoven's C-major mass. He observes that only a composer with "a rare depth of spirit and a high degree of genius" such as possessed by Haydn, Mozart, and Beethoven can remain "serious and dignified, in short, church-like" when employing highly figured vocal music and the "whole wealth of instrumental music." Mozart achieved the ideal in his *Requiem* (1791), which is "truly romantically holy music emanating from his innermost soul." Haydn, too, in some of his masses, succeeded excellently in this regard. Hoffmann proceeds to express his surprise that Beethoven, whose "genius otherwise so gladly sets in motion the levers of awe and horror," conveys in his mass the impression of a "childlike, happy soul that, relying on its purity, devoutly trusts God's grace and prays to him as to a father who wants the best for his children and grants their requests" (*SzM*, 156–57).

Hoffmann's interest in church music as expressive of the romantic yearning for transcendence is evident, too, in his review (1813) of an oratorio by August Bergt (1772–1813). The text of oratorios should be taken solely and wholly from the Bible because they "speak directly about the supreme mystery of our religion." An oratorio's music, meanwhile, must come from the innermost depths of the composer's soul "inflamed by faith and love": "[E]very note has to have been conceived in religious inspiration, in such a way, however, that the whole, as though divinely consecrated, glorifies what is exalted and holy and fills the listener with true reverence, so that, torn away from earthly things, his spirit turns completely toward heaven, which fills his soul with faith, love, hope, and comfort" (*SzM*, 180–81).

That Hoffmann's ideal of church music was born not of Christian faith but of his romanticism is indicated in his essay (1814) contrasting older and modern church music. His heroes Haydn, Mozart, and Beethoven even in their church music were inspired not by Christian piety, but in Hoffmann's judgment by its counterpart in an emerging nature mysticism, as represented most obviously and prominently by his German Romantic contemporaries, the philosopher Friedrich Wilhelm Joseph Schelling (1775–1854) and the poet Novalis. This inspiration is described by Hoffmann as arising from a "wondrous striving to discern the governing force of the enlivening spirit of nature, indeed our existence in that spirit, our superterrestrial spiritual homeland, that reveals itself in science." This transcendent striving was alluded to in music by "the intimating tones that spoke ever more variously and completely about the marvels of the faraway realm." In this way, Hoffmann explains the heights music had reached in the age of Haydn, Mozart, and Beethoven as resulting from the advance of natural science and, in particular, the nature mysticism to which it contributed (*SzM*, 230). At the same time, Hoffmann expresses a wish for renewed appreciation of the "old, exalted masters" of church music, from Palestrina to Johann Sebastian Bach (1685–1750), who in their way were inspired by the dream of transcendence. Now, after the defeat of Napoleon, Hoffmann yearns in this essay for a return to peaceful and joyous times in which music "may stir its seraphic pinions in order once again to begin its flight to the Beyond, which is its homeland and from which comfort and redemption shine down into man's unhappy breast" (*SzM*, 235).

The inherently transcendent expressiveness of music remains a theme in Hoffmann's comments on its place in the theater. As we remember, his first publication was a brief essay on Schiller's attempt, in his *Braut von Messina,* at revival of the chorus from ancient Greek tragedy. There, to be sure, Hoffmann's concept of transcendent musical transport is not yet evident. He had at that point not yet been introduced to the writings of German Romantic contemporaries and the nature mysticism of a Schelling or Novalis. What is already apparent in that essay, however, is Hoffmann's consistent focus as a critic on the emotional impact of music on the listeners, here in the negative sense of a comic effect produced by the introduction of theater conventions from antiquity into an otherwise wholly contemporary drama.

He has his "monastic clergyman" inquire of the "friend in the capital" whether, as in the Roman author Lucius Anneas Seneca's (ca. 1 A.D. to 65 A.D.) description of the choruses in Greek tragedy, in the performance of Schiller's drama, there are flute players accompanying "the declamation throughout the whole piece" or only when the chorus speaks, and whether the actors wear masks and cothurns. Above all, he wants to know about the effect of the chorus on the audience, "whether they were deeply moved" or did the actors meet the fate of "the late Professor Meibom, who was laughed off the stage by the whole of Queen Christina's [the Swedish ruler's] court when he began to sing a Greek aria" (*SzM*, 15).

Hoffmann's rejection of spoken choruses on stage, such as used in Schiller's play, is made clear in a letter he wrote five years later (1808) to his future employer, Julius Soden (1754–1831), director of the Bamberg theater. Hoffmann considers having several persons declaim the same verses "a great blunder." At least people with an ear for music "cannot endure any such declaiming in chorus." Referring to Seneca as he had done in the essay, he observes that this blunder is indeed something new, because the Greek choruses did not declaim, but sang and were accompanied by musical instruments (*SzM*, 19).

Here we see a reflection of Hoffmann's strong championship of recitative in opera. In a review of Gluck's *Iphigénie en Aulide* (1810), he deplores the effect of the popularity of operettas (*singspiele*) on opera singers, who having thereby become accustomed to singing that is interrupted by dialogue are rendered incapable of recitative. Hoffmann blames that development for the rarity with which Gluck's operas are performed. Worse still, contemporary composers are neglecting opera seria entirely, with the result that "soon, the highest achievement of which poetry allied with music is capable will disappear entirely from the stage" (*SzM*, 61–62).

The connection between Hoffmann's championship of operatic recitative, or "through-composed" opera, and his romantic view of music as the language of transcendence is quite clear in his critique (1816) of Étienne Nicolas Méhul's (1763–1817) *Ariodant*. Opera interrupted by dialogue is "surely an absurdity that we tolerate only out of habit." Opera is supposed to transport us to a "higher poetic realm, in which language is music," but in the operetta we are "every minute hurled down and come into contact with the earth." Not only is the poetic spell broken, but the songs in operettas, unlike the aria in opera, do not carry the action forward by depicting "an inner spiritual condition" as the dramatic monologue does. Instead the songs bring the action to a halt for "elaboration of a maxim" or, on the model of the composer Pietro Metastasio (1698–1782), even to elaborate an allegory (*SzM*, 311–12).

Plot and character were important for producing the romantic transport that Hoffmann cherished in opera. In a review (1810–1811) of Ferdinando Paer's (1771–1839) *Sofonisbe,* he complained that Paer's opera, like more recent Italian opera music, aims at giving singers opportunity to show off their artistry to best advantage and thereby neglects "that which is actually dramatic, the expression of the action and situation" (*SzM*, 68). German opera composers, on the contrary, are wont to pay attention to this element. Those like Hoffmann "who strictly demand from opera all the requirements of musical drama and who therefore deeply revere the classical works of Gluck and Mozart will hardly want to hear operas like this *Sofonisbe* through to the end" (*SzM*, 74–75).

The arias should express the characters' emotional situations chiefly through the music, Hoffmann comments in a review (1814) of songs by the composer Wilhelm Friedrich Riem (1779–1857). Arias require only a few words, "in which the poet gives exact expression to the dominant emotional mood." The composer employs "the whole musical scale of passion" so that everything "that has appeared inwardly" unfolds for us "brightly, colorfully, and powerfully." As a result, in the aria the words are only a "symbolic indication of the feelings, which in the untiring succession of their slight nuances can only make themselves known through the music." In songs, by contrast, the poet makes the inner emotional experiences known fully in words, often requiring a number of stanzas (*SzM*, 237–38).

Hoffmann's concern with the musical depiction of emotion seen in these remarks about arias also is evident in his comments about dance. Reviewing polonaise music for piano (1814), he reports that during his years in Warsaw he often found in that dance as performed by "a handsome, powerfully built young man with a charming young woman" the whole of a chivalric novel from the time of King Arthur. In particular such dancing revealed to him, in the peculiar twists and turns the couple executed, "all the trials and tribulations of the pair of lovers out of which they finally emerge brightly and magnificently in the full majesty of their beauty" (*SzM*, 252–53). Ballet on the other hand, as Hoffmann confesses in a theater review two years later (1816), does not convey to him what he looks for in dance, namely "the emotional state streaming forth from the soul," which, so he humorously remarks, he cannot accustom himself "to look for in feet" (*SzM*, 308).

In his opera reviews, Hoffmann's championship of the romantic element is paramount. In his first such piece of commentary (1810), on
Joseph Weigl's (1766–1846) *Das Waisenhaus* (*The Orphanage*), he argues
that when Mozart and other great composers wrote masterpieces to bad
texts, it was because, "as opera indispensably requires," there was "a
romantic idea" underlying the text as a whole, as is most obviously the
case with Mozart's *Die Zauberflöte* (*The Magic Flute*, 1791; *SzM*, 52). The
composer must be filled with the "fantastic idea of the whole." The text
of Weigl's opera lacks the requisite romantic element, the quality of
transcendent fantasy. The scenes of ordinary burgher existence depicted
there, "which show human beings in the most oppressive requirements
of their journey through earthly life," are unsuitable for depiction in the
theater. Such scenes are still less suited for the operatic stage, where
"human nature is raised to a higher power, where speech is song, . . .
and which altogether exists only in the marvelous realm of the romantic." The author of Weigl's text meant to tug at the audience's heart-
strings, to produce a "touching" effect, an aim running directly counter
to Hoffmann's poetic goal of romantic transport (*SzM*, 52–53).

The lack of an underlying romantic idea is Hoffmann's criticism
(1812) of the drama for which Beethoven's since famous *Coriolan Overture* was written. The text in question was not Shakespeare's *Coriolanus*
but a version by a contemporary of Hoffmann's. Beethoven, Hoffmann
writes, is better suited to writing music to plays by Shakespeare or
Calderón.

A review that same year (1812) of an opera *Der Augenarzt* (*The Eye
Doctor*) by Adalbert Gyrowetz (1763–1850) provided Hoffmann opportunity to renew his complaints about dramas designed to appeal to philanthropic sentimentality. He comments that such touching depictions of
family relationships, which "had taken over our stage until they
drowned in their own oceans of tears," now appear to "want to be resus-
citated by music in order to return to the stage as operas" (*SzM*, 104).
Following the example of his German Romantic contemporary Ludwig
Tieck, who some dozen years earlier had mocked the vogue of these
tear-jerking domestic dramas for the stage with his *Gestiefelter Kater* (*Puss
in Boots*, 1797) and other fairy tale plays, Hoffmann makes the text of
the Gyrowetz opera the target of his satiric wit.

As summarized by Hoffmann, the story in the Gyrowetz opera is as
follows: "[T]wo blind persons—lost children, a little young gentleman
and a little young lady who, having been taken in and raised by a good-
hearted pastor, then are reduced now to going around with his daughter

to beg for food—have fallen in love with one another and so lead an anxious, tormented life. It is they on whom a skillful surgeon operates, and as a reward receives the pastor's daughter as his bride" (*SzM*, 105). Hoffmann then claims to have hit upon a subject for an opera that in the sense of misery it evokes "would almost outdo" the piece under review. It would be about "an older, extremely virtuous, very poor man" who has a hard time feeding his family, among whom there is "a very pretty, sixteen-year-old daughter."

During a fire the man rescues a child from the flames but in doing so seriously injures his leg. Because he cannot pay for a skilled surgeon and "despite the most attentive care by his daughter," the injury develops in such a way as to become life threatening. The poverty of the family, which has been joined by the child he had saved (its parents died in the fire), has increased to the point where they have not eaten for three days. Then "a young, most noble surgeon sees the beautiful girl; he falls very much in love, learns the reason for her distress, hurries over with wine, hearty soups, and his surgical instruments, and through a skillful amputation of the bad leg saves the father's life, for which he receives the latter's daughter as his wife. Some prince or count can then easily become involved in the matter and shower the family with gifts" (*SzM*, 105).

By exaggerating the "touching" aspects in this spoof on such *Familiengemälde* (domestic comedies), Hoffmann holds them up to ridicule. At the same time, though, he lends romantic elements to the genre, both by offering the story as imaginary, as poetic fantasy, and by making erotic attraction the decisive factor in the denouement in place of philanthropic sentiment. In particular, Hoffmann's focus on the beauty and blossoming maidenhood of the 16-year-old daughter—the age of his beloved Julchen Marc at the time of his just-passed emotional crisis—serves to shift this supposed touching family piece to the realm of fantasy and poetic transport.

In concluding his review of the Gyrowetz opera, Hoffmann expresses sympathy for the impossibility of the task confronting the composer in writing music for "the main moment of the piece, as the operation has succeeded and the blindfolds have been removed from the patients." The emotional situation, Hoffmann comments, is such as "can only cripple fantasy," because "[a]ll the truly touching utterances of those who have been successfully operated on in the bosom of any family whatsoever or in a hospital have to degenerate into meaningless sentimentality as soon as one brings them onto the stage, where such scenes do not admit of any poetic exaltation whatsoever" (*SzM*, 113).

Precisely the depiction of romantic love that Hoffmann considers the main theme in Goethe's drama *Egmont* (1788) explains Beethoven's success in his—now-famous—music for that play, so Hoffmann claimed in his review of that music (1813). In his overture, Beethoven hewed to the "deeper, truly romantic intention" of the play, the love between Egmont and Klärchen. For Hoffmann it is particularly Klärchen's rapturous love for Egmont that provides the element of fantasy, transport, and transcendence he considers requisite for romanticism in the arts: "[E]levated far above her immediate environment, the magnificent maiden can only—with an ardor that is truly superterrestrial, that disdaining life's petty circumstances strides forth beyond everything of this world—attach herself to the hero of her fatherland, to live only in him. And without his clearly sensing it, she is for him herself the higher being that nurtures the divine fire that burns in his breast for freedom and his country" (*SzM*, 171–72). In other words, Egmont's and Klärchen's ardent patriotism is intimately bound up, however unconsciously, with their romantic attraction to one another.

In another review written that same year (1813), Hoffmann refers to an example of passionate patriotism in another context and on the part of a theater audience as opposed to the characters on stage. In Warsaw in 1807 the Poles, having been promised restoration of their empire by Napoleon, celebrated with a production of the opera *Andromeda* by Joseph Elsner (1769–1854). Hoffmann recalls that "the opera was meant entirely as an allegory, so that fettered Andromeda was supposed to represent solely the fatherland, and Perseus, rushing to her aid, to represent Poland's victorious heroes." Hoffmann comments humorously that allegories of this sort were long since popular in Poland, especially everything that contained any mention at all of the fatherland, "even the mere word itself, even when it occurred without any further reference, for example, the line 'I am going to the fatherland,' was met with strong applause" (*SzM*, 191).

The challenge to artistic inspiration and poetic transport arising from patriotic concerns and political upheaval provides the framework for a dialogue between two romantic enthusiasts, "Der Dichter und der Komponist," that Hoffmann published in the *Allgemeine Musikalische Zeitung* (1813) and reprinted in the first volume of *Die Serapionsbrüder* (1819). The dialogue is set at the time of the battles in and around Dresden that August between the allies Prussia, Austria, and Russia and the Napoleonic forces, humbled the winter before in their ill-fated Russian campaign of 1812. Hoffmann, who had been in Dresden at the time (late

August 1813), introduces the dialogue with a depiction of the composer Ludwig "in his little back room, completely engrossed and submerged in the magnificent, colorful, fantastic world that had opened up to him at the piano" and oblivious to the battle that was raging. Ludwig had just finished a symphony that was supposed, "like Beethoven's compositions of that type, to speak in divine language about the magnificent marvels of a faraway romantic land in which we live submerged in ineffable longing." The music was meant "to enter, like one of those marvels, into our confined, impoverished life and to lure out of it, with lovely siren-like voices, those who willingly surrender themselves." That is to say, Ludwig—the name Hoffmann gave him surely points to Hoffmann's esteem for Beethoven—is the epitome of the romantic enthusiast.[5]

The dialogue about literature and music is occasioned by Ludwig's chance meeting with a friend from his youth, Ferdinand, a poet serving at the time as an officer with the allied forces. The composer complains of a lack of suitable opera texts. When his poet friend suggests that he write his own libretti, Ludwig objects that the composer of an opera would run out of poetic inspiration if he had to produce the text before he could proceed to set it to music. Ludwig undertakes instead to describe what is required for writing the sort of libretto he would want. The poet should prepare himself for "bold flight into the faraway realm of romanticism" where he will find "the marvels that he is to carry back into life, alive and in brightly shining color, so that people shall willingly believe in those marvels, indeed so that as in a beatific dream, themselves removed from paltry everyday life, they wander in the flower gardens of a romantic land and understand only its language, words that sound forth in music." What Ludwig in his enthusiasm describes is of course Hoffmann's ideal of romantic transport. As Ludwig confesses to Ferdinand, he considers romantic opera to be the only true one "for only in the realm of the romantic is music [truly] at home" (*SB,* 83–84).[6]

In the end, the two friends' discussion ultimately turns from romantic to comic opera. As Ferdinand, believing that he has understood his composer friend correctly, says, if the "indispensable requirement of opera" is the romantic element, then in opera buffa it would be replaced or represented by the element of the fantastic. By that quality Ferdinand means that for opera buffa the poet's art consists not only in having the characters appear "fully rounded out and poetically true" but also just as though they had been "taken right from life as we know it" and are so individualized that "one immediately says to oneself, 'Look there! That's my neighbor with whom I spoke every day! That's the student who goes on his way to class every morning and sighs terribly in front of his girl cousin's windows, etc.' " (*SB,* 90–91).

Comic opera, as described here, transports the audience to a poetic realm by clothing creatures of fantasy in ordinary garb and by making what is strange, extravagant, or superterrestrial seem familiar.[7] While romantic opera lends a strange, marvelous, transcendent quality to what is familiar, comic opera accomplishes the reverse of that romanticization: It lends a familiar quality to what is strange, extravagant, or marvelous.[8] As we shall see, Hoffmann's fairy-tale masterpiece, *Der goldne Topf,* which he wrote just after this dialogue between the poet and composer, is the narrative equivalent of comic opera as defined here. Indeed, the suggestions for comic depiction in this vein that Ferdinand gives here (the neighbor, the lovesick student) echo what is found in that "fairy tale from modern times" (the subtitle of *Der goldne Topf*), especially as Hoffmann reported his original concept of it to his publisher Kunz.[9]

The example Ludwig had just offered shows that it is particularly the theme of languishing desire that he—and Hoffmann with him—associates with opera buffa: " 'Imagine an honorable gathering of male and female relatives with a languishing little daughter, and in addition a few students who praise the eyes of the girl cousin in song and play their guitars in front of the windows.' " The special, romantic fun begins when, as Ludwig says, " '[t]he spirit of droll humor rushes in among them with teasing apparitions, and then everything is thrown into confusion with mad imaginings, all sorts of strange leaps and odd grimaces' " (*SB,* 90). In *Der goldne Topf* Hoffmann proceeded to fill that prescription for romantic opera buffa, most particularly with the wild punchbowl scene (ninth vigil).

An "almanac" of opera texts by the contemporary, highly popular playwright August von Kotzebue gave Hoffmann opportunity to repeat his views on what opera should and should not be. In the review (1814), he refers to and summarizes what he had said in the dialogue "Der Dichter und der Komponist" about the subject: "[T]hat true opera can be produced only from truly poetic material, that . . . romanticism is the most proper area for opera"; that in romantic opera everything depends on introducing "the marvelous phenomena of the spirit-realm into life with such poetic truth that we willingly believe in them"; that "as the actions of higher beings visibly occur, a romantic existence opens before our very eyes in which even language is raised to a higher power, or rather is appropriated from that faraway realm, that is, it is music and song"; that we are transported to where "even the action and situation, floating in powerful sounds and tones, seize us and transport us the more powerfully." All of this has to start with the opera text. The "indispensable requirement for true opera" is that the music "arises directly and necessarily from the poetic work itself." In comic opera, "odd and fantastic things enter into ordinary life, and out of this contradiction true jest is engendered" (*SzM*, 262–63). Kotzebue's often crude or coarse farces are unsuited to true comic opera, Hoffmann finds, because they do not meet this requirement of entry of the fantastic into life.

Kotzebue's model was French farce, which Hoffmann in a review (1814) of an opera by Adrien Boieldieu (1775–1834) declared generally contrary to the spirit of comic opera. According to Hoffmann, jest in the true sense of the word is foreign to the French and is replaced by the joke, as evidenced by the text to the Boieldieu opera. Equally foreign to the French is the element of the "romantically fantastic," which Hoffmann finds to rule the opera buffa of the Italians, arising there "in part from the animation of the individual characters, in part from the ghostly play of happenstance." The French therefore have no actual comic operas, only comedies "in which the singing enters in as a coincidental admixture, and which then are unjustly called comic operas" (*SzM*, 268).

Even in drama as opposed to opera Hoffmann looked to the element of romanticization and romantic transport. In his report (1812) about the production of Pedro Calderón de la Barca's (1600–1681) plays at the Bamberg theater, he singled out for special comment the closing scene in *Die Andacht zum Kreuze* (*The Worship of the Cross*), which depicted Eusebio's apotheosis and his beloved Julia's ascension heavenward to join him. As described by Hoffmann and portrayed on the Bamberg stage, the miracle seems to occur in response to Julia's embracing of the cross and in answer to the prayer that gesture denotes: "As Julia in the end embraced the cross, which was set up at the back of the stage, her masculine disguise disappeared and one saw her in nun's habit kneeling at the cross, which lifted itself into the air with her. The clouds separated, and as though transfigured Eusebio appeared with his arms longingly outstretched toward Julia."

Hoffmann finds that this arrangement, which was not indicated in the text of the play, was better than the ending given there because in the Bamberg production "Eusebio's and Julia's transfiguration was depicted for the senses as a miracle; and it is entirely in keeping with the spirit of Catholicism to appeal to the senses in portraying that which is supersensual" (*SzM*, 598). We note here that Hoffmann does not say that the Bamberg stage's depiction of the young lovers' transfiguration

meant to interpret their union as a miracle, beyond merely lending it
the romantic quality of the marvelous or miraculous. The lovers' erotic
devotion and desire rather than the Christian faith is glorified through
this poetization, which does not, however, violate principles of Catholic
art.[10]

For the actor as well as the poet fantasy is the indispensable ingredi-
ent, so Hoffmann has one of his two dialogue partners ("the one in
gray") assert in his *Seltsame Leiden eines Theater-Direktors* (*Curious Sufferings of a Theater Director,* 1818). The role as conceived by the author or
the actor is created by "the inspired individual, . . . by the hidden poet."
At the same time, the author or actor's conscious power of understanding was responsible for enticing the hidden poet out from within "and
endowing it with the power to enter life rounded out with flesh and
bone." Thus, while inspiration is the key, it must be "ruled and reined in
by the power of understanding" to create a classic work of art. A kind of
double activity (*duplizität*) is required, of which only a few people are
capable. Actors possessed of this ability often, as a result, "shape a character in a way the author did not envision at all."[11]

True comedy, the other partner ("the one dressed in brown") argues
later in the dialogue, involves a further kind of doubleness. Deep in
human nature lies an irony, "which, indeed, determines that nature in its
innermost being and out of which jest, wit, roguishness beam forth with
the most profound seriousness." Convulsions of pain and despairing
lament "empty into a river of laughter expressing marvelous delight,"
delight that, "indeed was just only engendered by pain and despair."
(One may think here about how often joy and laughter are accompanied
by tears.) "The full recognition of this peculiar organization of human
nature" might be what we mean by humor, the humoristic, and the
truly comic. That recognition, too, dwells "in the breast of those actors
who draw their representations from the depths of human nature." Such
actors, as a result, are able to play both comic and tragic roles "with
equal power and truth" (*FuN,* 654).

The meaning of irony here is indicated in the remarks made by the
other dialogue partner (the one dressed in brown). Referring to "those
wonderful roles of Shakespeare's" that are based on humor in the narrower and truer sense, Hoffmann's theater director speaks of the "feeling of the incongruity that exists between the inner spirit and all the
external earthly doings around it" and that this feeling engenders "the
abnormal state of excitation that breaks out in bitterly mocking irony."
The feeling is "an unhealthy tickle" experienced by a "painfully affected,

wounded soul" whose laughter is only "the suffering cry of longing for the spiritual home that makes itself felt within." The irony in question is therefore a romantic one that concerns the incongruity between the spirit's yearning for transcendence and the confines of its terrestrial existence. The Shakespearean character in whom Hoffmann's theater director finds this romantic irony best exemplified is—unsurprisingly—Hamlet (*FuN*, 658–59). Drama's function, from this romantic perspective, is to help respond to the yearning for transcendence. As Hoffmann's fellow in brown asks rhetorically: "In what else does the divine power of drama, which like no other work of art so irresistibly takes hold of us, actually consist than that, transported with the swiftness of a magic spell, we see the marvelous happenings of a fantastic existence right before our eyes" (*FuN*, 663).

As much as Hoffmann was a devotee of theater and an opera enthusiast, he was not himself a dramatist. Nevertheless, in his narrative fiction he aimed to achieve what he saw as the stage's special charm.[12] He proclaimed as much in introducing the first two of the four volumes of his *Fantasiestücke in Callots Manier*. There he explains the reference to the French graphic artist Jacques Callot (1592–1635) in his title as being appropriate for a poet or writer to whom, as to himself, "the figures from everyday life have appeared in his inner romantic spirit realm" and who now portrays them "in the luster in which they are bathed there and as though in a strange, peculiar dress" (*FuN*, 13).[13]

Moreover, Hamlet, as the epitome of the romantic hero, is the model for Hoffmann's poeticized alter ego, the composer Johannes Kreisler, in the essayistic pieces collected in the *Fantasiestücke* as "Kreisleriana."[14] In the third item of the first set of these pieces, "Gedanken über den hohen Wert der Musik" (*AMZ*, 1812), Kreisler gives ironic expression to the view held of romantic music by enthusiasts like himself. Such enthusiasts believe that "art lets man sense the higher principle of his existence and leads him forth from the foolish doings and bustle of ordinary life into the temple of the goddess Isis, where nature speaks to him in sounds never before heard yet comprehensible" (*FuN*, 39). In a similarly ironic piece—number five in the second set of "Kreisleriana" for the fourth and last volume of *Fantasiestücke*—about an enthusiast whom others considered an enemy of music ("Der Musikfeind," *AMZ*, 1814), Kreisler's friend reports to him that when it often seems as though the characters in an opera would be unable to speak otherwise than "in music's powerful accents" and when it is as though "the realm of the marvelous opens up like a flaming star," he has great difficulty "holding on in the gale that seizes him and threatens to cast him into infinity" (*FuN*, 312).

For Kreisler—as expressed in the earlier piece about music's great worth and in the last of the "Kreisleriana," his letter of completed apprenticeship written to himself—music is the language of nature, of the natural universe, not of a spiritual realm above or beyond it. Indeed, Kreisler's artistic quest is one of seeking to understand nature. He asks himself in the letter of completed apprenticeship: "May not the musician relate to nature which surrounds him as the hypnotist does to his medium, in that the musician's spirited volition is the question that nature never leaves unanswered?" Music is "the general language of nature" and speaks to us in "marvelous, mysterious accords." The musician, however, can only struggle in vain "to capture those accords in musical notation" (*FuN*, 326).

The aim of the *Fantasiestücke* to demonstrate the power of poetic imagination to lend a romantic cast to the experience of life manifests itself further in the "Nachricht von den neuesten Schicksalen des Hundes Berganza." With the *Fantasiestücke*'s subtitle, "Leaves from the Diary of a Traveling Enthusiast," the reader is put on notice that these pieces, even as poetic fiction, are from the pen of a narrator with an overactive imagination. Among the fantasy pieces, "Berganza" is one introduced in such a way as to remind us that our narrator is ever eager to find realized in life the products of his romantic yearnings and poetic imaginings.

One evening as he was leaving a party in a foul mood, the enthusiast tells us, he heard sighs and went to see who it was, sensing that he might encounter something very special, "which in this everyday, prosaic life is always my wish and prayer" (*FuN*, 79). When it turns out that the sighs were coming from a talking dog out of the pages of a novella by Cervantes, a work published in the 1600s, we know that our narrator is imagining things.[15] We suspect, moreover, that the imaginary dialogue partner is one "right after the heart" of the narrator or that the narrator is speaking with an imaginary self. The reality is indicated later in the encounter when the dog comments to the enthusiast: "In a certain sense every mind that is even a little eccentric is insane, and appears to be so all the more, the more fervently it endeavors to set our external, dull, lifeless existence ablaze through its glowing inner visions" (*FuN*, 98). The talking dog himself, in other words, is just such an inner glowing vision from the mind of the enthusiast.[16]

We know as Hoffmann's readers during his lifetime did not that beyond being a mouthpiece for his views on art and life the talking dog is an autobiographical self, and a most personal one at that. Berganza's account of the devoted relationship between himself as house pet and a widow's beautiful young daughter "Cecilia" (for the patron saint of music) is a fanciful, "glowing inner vision" of Hoffmann's relationship to his voice pupil Julchen Marc. With that fanciful image, Hoffmann expressed both his resentment at the subservient position he had held in the household of Julchen's widowed mother and his yearning to believe that he had been the daughter's most loyal friend. In the end, following the outing during which he denounced Julchen's fiancé for being inebriated, her mother had in his mind "treated him like a dog," whereas he felt in denouncing the bridegroom he had shown loyalty such as in poetic tradition was represented emblematically with the image of a dog.

The fanciful vision of himself as Julchen's loyal house pet enabled Hoffmann to portray graphically his feelings, in his self-appointed role as devoted guardian, about her marriage. Berganza, seeing himself as Cecilia's guard dog, slips unnoticed into the bridal chamber on her wedding night, and when the drunken bridegroom begins to assert his marital rights in crude and coarse fashion Berganza reports, " 'in rage I leapt onto the bed, seized him by the thigh with a powerful bite [Berganza is a bulldog], and dragged him across the room to the door . . . [and] out into the hallway. As I tore him to shreds, so that he lay covered with blood, he raged in pain, and the horribly high-pitched tones that he let out roused the whole house' " (*FuN*, 123). The enormity of this depiction, which was preceded by Berganza's account of how he sniffed Cecilia's wedding-night attire in the bridal chamber just before she entered the room, suggests that Hoffmann's conception of this fantasy was not devoid of humor concerning the intensity of his passion for Julchen.

As indicated earlier, the talking bulldog is himself an enthusiast. This is unsurprising, since he is the imaginary dialogue partner of choice for the enthusiast narrator, who in turn is a poetic, ironic guise for Hoffmann. Occasion for the bulldog to expound on the arts is provided by his relating that when Cecilia's mother chased him away he joined up with a theater troupe (a self-humorous depiction of what happened in Hoffmann's life not long after his banishment by Julchen's mother). Hoffmann has Berganza, as his mouthpiece, declare that art's highest purpose is "to awaken in man that sort of delight that liberates his whole being from all earthly torment, from all oppressiveness of everyday life, as from unclean slag, and lifts him up in such a way that, raising his head proudly and joyfully, he beholds that which is divine, indeed comes into contact with it."

Likewise, the true purpose of theater is to engender such delight and to elevate us to a poetic vantage point from which we "willingly believe in the marvels of that which is purely ideal, indeed become intimately familiar with them" and we see "ordinary life, too, with its manifold, variegated phenomena transfigured and glorified through the luster of poetry." What lends that luster to life's phenomena is "the gift of being able to see them as arising from the whole [of nature] and again reaching down deeply into its mechanism." Without that gift one cannot be a playwright in the truest sense, Hoffmann's bulldog concludes (*FuN*, 132–33).

The ability to fathom nature is the key to poetic depiction of life. That appears to be Berganza's creed. As a canine halfway transformed into a human being he can speak with a certain authority on that point. This explains why he seconds the praise of the German Romantic poet Novalis that he quotes from another of Hoffmann's poetic alter egos, Johannes Kreisler. Berganza says of Kreisler, with whom the bulldog reports he lived for a time, "In his childlike soul shone the purest rays of poetry, and his pious life was a song of praise that he sang in magnificent tones to the supreme being and to the sacred marvels of nature" (*FuN*, 136).

Just which "marvels of nature" particularly interested Hoffmann is indicated by the framing dialogue in the first volume of his tales collected in *Die Serapionsbrüder*. In that framing dialogue the circle of literary friends who function as the tellers of stories Hoffmann published earlier in journals, almanacs, and annuals (or, in a few cases, wrote especially for the collected tales) are discussing the case of an insane man who believes he is the martyred saint Serapion who was put to death many centuries earlier. The friends come to call themselves the Serapion brethren in tribute to the man's reputed gift for vivid storytelling.[17] Despite, or rather perhaps because of, his madness, he is able to believe uninhibitedly in the products of his poetic imagination. As Cyprian tells the other literary friends about this "Serapion," the man defended himself against Cyprian's challenge to him about his madness by saying, "[m]any people have . . . expressed the opinion that I am only imagining that I am seeing things actually taking place in life outside that have simply taken shape as products of my mind, of my [power of] fantasy. . . . [Yet] if it is the mind alone that perceives the event [happening] in front of us, then what the mind acknowledges as having happened has indeed really taken place" (*SB*, 26).

It is not just Serapion's capacity to believe in the reality of his poetic perceptions and hence the effectiveness of his storytelling that interests the literary friends. They are also attracted by the potential of insanity like his for offering revelation about nature and about humans as creatures of nature. Cyprian, at least, explains his interest in the mad hermit—a certain Count P . . . who left a high successful career in diplomatic service to live alone in the forest—and his interest in insane people generally by saying he has always believed that especially in such cases of abnormality "nature grants us glimpses into its terrible depths" and that indeed "in the horror itself that often seizes [him] in that odd social intercourse," intimations and images have come to him that "invigorated and animated [his] mind for odd flights of fancy" (*SB,* 29).

The discussion about the hermit culminates in a judgment concerning his insanity given by another of the literary friends in this framing dialogue. Lothar speaks of fate having robbed the man of "the knowledge of the doubleness (*duplizität*) by which alone our terrestrial existence is conditioned." This doubleness concerns the fact that while there is "an inner world, and the mental power to view it in complete clarity" and most vividly, as Serapion does, it is our earthly fate that "precisely the external world into which we are inserted works as the lever that sets that mental power in motion." In other words, the workings of fantasy, of the spirit, of the poetic imagination are triggered by our physical existence. The spirit is imprisoned in the body, and the body in the world around it. Indeed, what we perceive inwardly does not actually soar beyond the external world; the mind and spirit are only able to transcend that world "in dark, mysterious intimations that never form a clear image."

When Lothar goes on to speak as though addressing his remarks to the hermit, he makes it still more apparent that with the idea of doubleness he is talking about a process of cause and effect. We may think that the mind asserts its freedom by seeing, hearing, feeling, and perceiving, yet "the world outside compels the spirit imprisoned in the body to carry out those functions as it [the world outside] pleases." Here Lothar evidently means by "the outside world" the forces of nature; the workings of the mind are subject to the dictates of nature (*SB,* 54–55).

With reference to nature's dictates it must be observed that the Serapion brethren's club is one devoid of women, as Hoffmann has the brethren note in the opening pages of the framing narrative. Being literary friends, the brethren note this absence of women as a departure from poetic tradition. In Hoffmann's immediate model, Tieck's collection *Phantasus* (1812–1817)—and in Giovanni Boccaccio's (1313–1375) *Decameron* (1348–1353), Goethe's *Unterhaltungen deutscher Ausgewan-*

derten (1795), and even the *Arabian Nights*—the storytelling takes place in mixed company. The brethren's male exclusivity is the object of some humor on their part, notably in their jesting comparison of themselves to an all-male club that had as its symbol a rooster straining to lay eggs (*SB*, 14, 17). One may guess that that symbol was intended in the spirit of such formerly traditional, jestingly misogynistic expressions as "you can't live with them and you can't live without them"—an expression that women were as likely to use referring to men. At least partly in jest, the brethren speak of women as something of "a race apart," and in doing so tell us a good deal about Hoffmann's poetic view of relations between the genders. That subject in turn, as we shall see, is a major object of depiction in his tales.

The issue of women comes up again toward the end of the first volume of *Die Serapionsbrüder*. The proposition put forth is that women, as a rule, lack a sense for or appreciation of ironic humor. Hoffmann's aim here, among others, is surely to tease his many female readers into accepting the challenge to fathom the mystifications in such stories as the one just told, "Der Artushof," and the equally ironic one to come, "Die Bergwerke zu Falun." Hoffmann further mocks his female readers —while perhaps expressing his actual view—when he has the Serapion brother Theodor, the one most closely identifiable with himself, remark that it is fine with him when women lack ironic humor, "which is completely opposed to the nature of women."

The support he offers for that assertion has to do with what he finds appealing in a woman. " 'Tell me,' " he says, 'would you, even for a short time, enjoy conversing with a humorous woman, would you want to have her as your beloved or your wife?' " (*SB*, 169–70). He goes on to make clear that social intercourse with women interests him only when a degree of erotic attraction is involved, or is at least not excluded. As he humorously puts it, " 'I am of the opinion that any closer contact whatsoever with a female being can only be interesting when at the thought that that female being might become one's beloved or one's wife, one is at least not terrified, and that the more this thought finds comfortable space in one's mind, the higher that interest climbs' " (*SB*, 170). In short, Theodor's every involvement with a woman involves something like a mating instinct.

Depiction of the mating instinct at work in women, of their wanting to make themselves interesting and appealing to men, is made by the Serapion brethren in the course of their participation in the then-current debate about mesmerism. Hoffmann's interest in mesmerism centered on the degree of romantic transport and states of poetic exaltation involved. He has his Serapion brethren express varying opinions as to the truth of claims for mesmerism's power to heal physical ailments or to render persons called mediums clairvoyant. Since the mesmerists were invariably men and their patients and mediums mostly women, these relationships lent themselves to interpretation as involving a desire to render oneself interesting to the opposite sex.[18]

The examples Hoffmann's Serapion brethren offer are of this latter sort. In one, the supposedly clairvoyant medium is an older woman whom Theodor judged to be a fake. Two young women, envious of the attention the woman was getting from the young men in attendance, were also present. Theodor relates that " 'Disregarding the two silly girls who were eager to emerge from the uninteresting position of inactive spectators, I could not ward off the thought that the somnambulistic lady on the sofa [in reclining position] was playing a prepared, well thought through, thoroughly rehearsed role with much artistry' " (*SB,* 268). Theodor goes on to cite the opinion of an old physician friend about the allure of mesmerism for the romantically inclined: " 'The attraction of existing in an elevated spirit realm is, he said, too enticing for poetic souls or those in a permanently exalted mood for them, with their ardent longing for that state [of existing in an elevated spirit realm] not to indulge in all sorts of imaginings' " (*SB,* 271).

The other example Theodor gives concerns a 16-year-old village girl who was withering away until she was brought to a hospital and cured by a young doctor treating her under an older physician's supervision. After a few weeks under the young physician's care the girl becomes clairvoyant. Being a village girl, she had no knowledge of mesmerism whatsoever. That fact helped convince Theodor that she really had achieved the state described in a contemporary mesmerist treatise. In that state "the connection with the mesmerist is so intimate that the clairvoyant patient not only knows instantaneously when the mesmerist's thoughts are distracted and not directed toward the patient's condition, but also that the patient is able to perceive the mesmerist's mental images [dwelling] in his soul most clearly."

The ironic point made by Theodor here is the humorous one that a girl with a "crush" on her young physician can perhaps do all of this without the aid of mesmerism. The same holds true for what Theodor, also surely tongue in cheek, goes on to report: "The patient, on the other hand, now comes entirely under the will of the mesmerist, through whose psyche alone the patient is able to think, speak, act. That was exactly the case with the somnambulistic peasant girl." Theodor offers as the best proof of working mesmeristic powers that in her clairvoyant state the girl "spoke the pure educated idiom of her mesmerist physician. She expressed herself in her answers—which she gave to him mostly with a charming smile—discriminatingly, educatedly, in short entirely the way the physician was wont to speak. And while she did this her cheeks and her lips blossomed with a purple glow and her facial features appeared ennobled!" As Theodor's concluding exclamation indicates, the ironic point of his account is that the power of romantic attraction, not mesmerism, is at work here (*SB*, 271–73).

Hoffmann's focus on the romantic appeal that mesmerism and similar spiritualistic enthusiasms held for women is evident, too, in a letter supposedly from his poetic alter ego, the composer Johannes Kreisler, that Hoffmann published the same year (1819) that volume 2 of *Die Serapionsbrüder* appeared. The subject was the renewed enthusiasm for the so-called musical glasses (*glasharmonika*) that Benjamin Franklin had invented (1763). As Kreisler mentions in his letter, Anton Mesmer (1734–1815) had used musical glasses to treat patients—in ways better left unsaid, Kreisler indicates. Mozart and Beethoven were among the musicians who composed music for this odd instrument, with which tones may be produced by touching inverted spinning bell jars with moist fingers. Kreisler writes in the fictive letter that enthusiasm for the instrument at the time among "sentimental souls" arose from the claim that the musical glasses "exerted a magical effect on the nerves." Kreisler, with satirical humor, claims that "[f]or every girl of some education it would have been highly inappropriate, just as soon as the musical glasses were touched, not to faint in acceptable fashion." Otherwise she would have run the risk of becoming immediately uninteresting "to every tender youth who had been looking languishingly and sweetly at her." At such performances with the musical glasses "even women grown older were transported back ten to fifteen years by the pain of blessed rapture and received a heart and a romantic love affair in addition" (*Nachlese,* 330).

Later, in volume 3 (1820) of *Die Serapionsbrüder,* the literary friends touch once more on the enticements of spiritualistic fantasy, again as regards women. In this case the discussion concerns reports in a late-sixteenth-century chronicle about trials for witchcraft. Theodor comments to Lothar that he finds it curious that "many supposed witches" confessed—quite freely and without being compelled—to having been allied with the devil. Indeed, he goes on, the accused women had particularly confessed "quite freely and shamelessly their lewd relationship with the filthy hellish lover, sometimes even without being summoned to do so." Lothar's cryptic reply to Theodor's questioning that possibility is that "with their belief in the devilish alliance came the alliance itself" (*SB,* 527). What Lothar apparently means is that such alliances were appealing fantasies for these women, who therefore were quite eager to believe in the reality of their fantasy.

The chronicle's reports of the devil's doings in sixteenth-century Berlin provide Hoffmann opportunity to explain the spirit of ironic humor he aims to engender through the mingling of familiar reality and the fantastic in his tales. As one of the Serapion brethren, Lothar, comments, regardless of what may have occasioned the chronicler Peter Hafftitz's (ca. 1525–after 1601) account of "how the devil led a middle-class life" in the Berlin of his time, the matter remains for people of his—Lothar's—time "purely fantastic." Therefore, Lothar continues, even the uneasiness and ghostliness that for us otherwise attaches to the devil as "the terrifyingly negative principle of creation" can, because of the comic contrast in which it makes its appearance, produce in us "only that curious feeling that, being a peculiar mixture of horror and irony, creates a tension in us that is not at all unpleasant" (*SB,* 526).

Mingling the fantastic with depiction of familiar life serves Hoffmann's poetic purpose of shedding humorously ironic light on that reality. The subject is revisited in reference to the *Arabian Nights* later in the framing narrative of the third volume of *Die Serapionsbrüder.* Theodor asserts that poetic depiction of the fantastic sort has to start with life as we know it before transporting us to the realm of the marvelous. Theodor's metaphorical explanation is that "the bottom of the ladder to the heavens, on which we want to ascend into higher regions, has to be anchored in life so that everyone is able to climb up after us."[19] Moreover, this way the connection between the fantasies depicted and life as we know it will be established. The reader will therefore recognize fantasy's magical realm as belonging to life and as being "actually the marvelously most magnificent part of it" (*SB,* 599).

Life as depicted in the *Arabian Nights* appears familiar, Ottmar asserts, because of the convincing portrayal of human nature. What gives the stories "life and truth" is that "[a]ll the shoemakers, tailors, porters, dervishes, merchants, etc. in those tales are figures such as one saw them daily on the streets; and since life in the actual sense does not after all depend on the times and customs, but remains, and must remain, in its deeper condition eternally the same, it therefore happens

that we believe that those people, to whom in the midst of their everyday lives the most marvelous magic revealed itself, are still walking
around among us" (*SB,* 599 – 600). As we shall see, what Ottmar claims
here about the *Arabian Nights* can equally well be said about the tales of
Hoffmann, which we shall now proceed to discuss. In doing so, we will
start in each case not with the bottom of the "ladder to the heavens," its
anchor in life, but instead with its top, the "higher regions" into which
Hoffmann leads us. That is to say, we will look first at the element of the
miraculous or fantastic in the given story, then descend the ladder to
investigate the situation in everyday life out of which the supernatural
adventures arise.

Chapter Four
Earlier Tales (1809–1817)

Hoffmann's first tale is as much a piece of music criticism in dialogue form as it is a story.[1] The dialogue partners are two music enthusiasts who themselves compose music; but unlike the poet and composer in "Dichter und Komponist" and the two theater directors in *Seltsame Leiden eines Theaterdirektors,* the enthusiast whom the narrator encounters in "Ritter Gluck" (1809, in the *Allgemeine Musikalische Zeitung;* then 1814 in the first volume of *Fantasiestücke*) is mentally deranged. Like the mad hermit in *Die Serapionsbrüder,* the deranged dialogue partner here has the ironic function of mouthpiece for Hoffmann's viewpoint on the nature and role of art. More than in Cyprian's report of his encounter with Serapion, however, the enthusiast's account of his meeting up with the man who thinks he is the deceased composer Gluck forms a story, too, for we learn a good deal about the nature of the man's fantasies.[2]

The narrator, finding that the man has joined him uninvited at a table in a pavilion at the Berlin Tiergarten, becomes intrigued by the stranger's request to the restaurant's orchestra to play the overture to Gluck's opera *Iphigenia in Aulis* (1774) and then by the man's acting as though he were conducting the piece from his seat at their table. The stranger, who appeared to the narrator to be in his 50s, recounts how he arrived at his musical inspiration, of which the narrator has experienced a sample in the stranger's humming of variations on the chorus of priestesses from Gluck's *Iphigenia in Tauris* (1779). Many seek to be composers, the stranger says, but only a few manage to enter the realm of dreams, and still fewer find their way through that realm to discover truth. However, the stranger's description of his discovery of truth suggests that his sojourn in the land of dreams was in reality a succumbing to benign madness.

Truth, in the stranger's account, was revealed to him in the form of a large, bright eye that causes beautiful music to sound from an organ. The eye smiled at him and promised that the man would see the eye again and that its melodies would become his. When he encountered the eye once more, it appeared to him in the calyx of a sunflower. Upon seeing the eye, melodies poured forth from him as they had done from

the organ in the earlier vision; and in response, he reports, " 'the sunflower's petals became larger and larger—flames flowed out from
them—they surrounded me—the eye had vanished and I disappeared in
the calyx' " (*FuN,* 19). The man's abrupt departure after uttering these
last words suggests that he does not want to be challenged concerning
the reality of his claim to have disappeared into the sunflower.[3]

When the narrator chances to meet up with the man on the street on
his way home, a further indication of the stranger's mental derangement
appears in his excusing his abrupt departure by saying that "[i]t got too
hot, and the 'Euphon' began to sound." The same problem with the
sounding of this mysterious "Euphon" occurs when he goes to see
Mozart's *Don Giovanni* (1787), even when he has, as he says, " 'prepared
[himself] with fasting and prayer' " (*FuN,* 20). This second conversation
ends almost as abruptly as the first, with the man rushing away just
after the narrator has observed that currently everything is being done
to promote the Gluck operas.

Once we have discovered, at the end of the narrator's account, that
the stranger has surrendered to the delusion that he is the composer
Gluck returned from the dead, we can surmise retrospectively that the
man's rushing away this second time concerns his struggle with the
temptation to reveal himself right then and there as "Ritter Gluck."
Actually, in each of his first two conversations with the narrator he had
given a hint of his imagined identity. In the initial encounter when they
have gone into a room in the restaurant to enjoy a glass of wine, the
stranger, as he is sitting down, throws open his frock coat to reveal an
attire of the sort that had been worn by noblemen in the previous century. He then carefully rebuttons the coat. Such behavior, one can imagine, is in keeping with that of an insane person who wants to reveal
something of his supposed true self. A further hint is dropped in the second conversation when the man refers to *Don Giovanni* as "my young
friend's opera" (*FuN,* 20), Mozart having been Gluck's much younger
contemporary. Interestingly, the narrator does not report having registered any surprise at either of the man's revelations.

When "smiling oddly" the stranger in the end declares to the narrator " 'I am the Chevalier Gluck' " (*FuN,* 24), the man's earlier hints
about that imaginary identity become important for showing that he is
not jesting but rather, on the contrary—like the hermit Serapion in the
later narrative—believes in the identity he has assumed. It is perhaps
enough to understand that the man here reveals himself to be insane
and that this insanity takes the form of his believing himself to be the

famous composer as the object of his enthusiastic veneration and his aspiration. Yet when we examine the particular objects of the man's imaginings and enthusiasms, his insanity may involve a negative motivation, a sublimation of desire. We note for example the erotic character of his imaginary disappearance into the calyx of the sunflower, and that vision along with seeing Mozart's opera about sexual seduction makes his "Euphon" sound and arouses him too much. Judging from the implied reference in the Greek roots represented in "Euphon," the man fears hearing too much of some "good sound"—perhaps as from a "good-sounding instrument" as the musician Chladni called the version of the *Glasharmonika* he invented and promoted.[4] The danger consists in experiencing an unbearable excess of aural pleasure, analogous perhaps to sexual climax for a music enthusiast.

We see first the man's enthusiasm for the two Gluck operas about the pure virgin Iphigenia, beginning with his request to the pavilion orchestra to play the overture to *Iphigenia in Aulis* and then with his humming of the chorus of priestesses from *Iphigenia in Tauris,* in which the heroine is sung about as a "chaste maiden." In the end, moreover, we see that the man's enthusiasm extends also to the Gluck opera about seduction, his *Armide* (1777), and in particular to the heroine's concluding aria where she laments the failure of her charms to captivate Rinaldo. One may imagine that the fiftyish stranger, presumably a confirmed bachelor, envisions himself in some way as the handsome knight who has caused the beautiful seductress such grief over his resistance to her charms. Understood this way, by singing the role of Armide to the narrator the stranger is in reality singing the aria to himself, out of enthusiastic transport at the thought of being the object of the beautiful seductress's unrequited passion.

In what may be properly considered the second of the four dozen stories that Hoffmann subsequently wrote, "Don Juan" (1812, published 1814 in the first volume of *Fantasiestücke*), we have a far clearer depiction of a music enthusiast's fantasy of himself as the object of an operatic heroine's passion. Indeed, as the title indicates, this tale is about the opera, Mozart's *Don Giovanni,* that in the previous story caused the stranger's "Euphon" to sound. While in "Ritter Gluck" the man's belief that he is the dead composer suggests that he is insane, in "Don Juan" we have simply, as the subtitle tells us, the account of "A Marvelous Event that Happened with a Traveling Enthusiast." This fabulous occurrence is related by the enthusiast himself, whom we are expected to trust; but one quickly judges that the so-called event is a product of romantic fantasy. Still more clearly than in "Ritter Gluck," Hoffmann's ironic humor is at work here.

The enthusiast's fantasy about having attended a performance of Mozart's opera in a box just down the hallway from his room in an inn culminates in a romantic reinterpretation of the Mozart opera that the enthusiast makes in a letter to his friend Theodor—an interpretation that was destined to become a bone of contention in music circles ever after.[5] Don Giovanni's seducing of women is explained as a romantic version of Hamletian spleen. The young Spanish nobleman had sought to still his boundless yearning for spiritual union with superterrestrial powers through "love, through pleasure with women," and then, disappointed in that hope, set about to be revenged on "nature and the creator" by going on to seduce still more women. Donna Anna, being a "divine woman over whose pure soul the devil had no power," becomes the special object of Don Giovanni's satanic lust (*FuN*, 76).

In the enthusiast's interpretation, when the opera begins Don Giovanni has not only killed Donna Anna's father but also succeeded in seducing her. Her father had come upon them too late: "She was not rescued! When [Don Giovanni] fled, the deed had been done. The fire of a superhuman sensuality, flames from hell, ran through her innermost being and made any resistance impossible. Only he, only Don Giovanni, could ignite the voluptuous insanity in her with which she embraced him" (*FuN*, 77). Donna Anna, so the enthusiast proposes in making this interpretation in a letter to his friend Theodor, is then torn between guilt over her seduction by her father's murderer and ardent passion for her seducer. As a result, she acts to bring about Don Giovanni's downfall and consignment to the powers of hell even though it will cause her own earthly demise because she will lose her love. Accordingly, the enthusiast chooses to believe that Donna Anna will die before her marriage to her fiancé Don Ottavio can take place: "Don Ottavio will never embrace her whose pious soul saved her from becoming Satan's consecrated bride" (*FuN*, 77).[6]

The enthusiast's interpretation of *Don Giovanni* for Theodor follows upon the performance of the opera the enthusiast claims to have witnessed shortly before. During the performance he received a visit from the Italian actress portraying Donna Anna while she was simultaneously playing that role on stage. The actress is transported to him in body as well as in spirit, a transport resulting from her recognition in him of a composer akin to Mozart, whose music she is singing on stage. The enthusiast reports that she declared to him, " 'for I know that to you, too, has been revealed the marvelous romantic realm where dwells the heavenly magic of musical sounds,' " whereupon he responded: " 'Can it be, magnificent, wondrous woman, that you know me?' " Her answer amounts to fulfillment of his wildest dream as composer and music enthusiast: " 'Did not the magical insanity of eternally yearning love depicted in the role of *** in your most recent opera issue forth from within you?—I have understood you: your soul has opened itself to me in song!—Yes, (here she called me by my first name), I have sung you, just as your melodies are me' " (*FuN,* 71–72).

The enthusiast's adventure culminated in his discovery the day after the performance that the singer of the role of Donna Anna had died that night. Her death confirmed that the actress had understood the role exactly as the enthusiast interpreted it. The conversation at table in the inn during the noon meal, as related by the enthusiast, concerns the intensity with which the actress always played that particular role and how the day before she seemed to be especially engulfed by it. The actress's death parallels the prediction for Donna Anna made by the enthusiast in his interpretation; she died at the very moment—two o'clock in the morning—the enthusiast finished conveying that interpretation in the letter to Theodor. Indeed, if the enthusiast is to be believed, at that very moment he had felt "a warm electrical breath" glide over him and had caught scent of "the gentle fragrance of fine Italian perfume" he smelled when the actress visited him in his box during the performance (*FuN,* 78). In other words, her departing spirit had paid him a last visit, as a token of their spiritual union through shared musical understanding and enthusiasm.

Hoffmann's third story, "Der Magnetiseur" ("The Hypnotist," 1813; published 1814 in the second volume of *Fantasiestücke*), no longer concerned musical inspiration but a different romantic enthusiasm, belief in spiritualistic phenomena associated with mesmerism. Whereas in "Ritter Gluck" the stranger's musical enthusiasm is connected with his insanity and in "Don Juan" the enthusiast's musical transport is supposedly a contributing factor in an actress's death, in "Der Magnetiseur" a young bride's mortal faint at the altar is attributed to her having come under the spell of a young mesmerist physician.

Marie's spiritualistic fantasies about the physician, Alban, are revealed in a letter she writes to Adelgunde, the sister of her fiancé Hypolit (*FuN,* 163–68). During a period of nervous illness she had dreamed of a "beautiful serious man" who despite his youth had instilled "genuine awe" in her. He was always dressed "in long robes, with a diamond crown on his head" and appeared to her "like the romantic king in the fairytale-like spirit world and removed every evil spell." In particular, he reminded her of Sarastro in Mozart's *Zauberflöte,* which she had seen at the court theater. She then recognized in Alban at first glance "that romantic king from my dreams."

As Marie writes to Adelgunde, she had met Alban before when her brother Ottmar had brought his young physician friend home for a visit. At that time, her reaction to him had been one of such indifference that she could not even remember subsequently what he looked like. Only now, when he was "summoned to cure" her, she found herself "unable to account to herself regarding the inward feeling" that permeated her. She feels powerless to resist surrendering herself completely to Alban in spirit, with the happy result that she believes herself cured of her nervous illness. The price of the cure is complete spiritual surrender to the young physician: "Only in this existence with him and in him can I truly live; and were it possible for him to withdraw from me in spirit completely, my self would become numb in deathly emptiness." Marie assures Adelgunde, however, that her spiritual union with Alban will not stand in the way of her marriage to Adelgunde's brother Hypolit; on the contrary, since Alban has become her "lord and master" it seems to her that "only through him" can she love her fiancé "more strongly and more deeply."

Marie's surrendering in spirit to Alban is mirrored by his belief in his mesmeristic domination of her, as revealed in his letter to another of his friends, Theobald, whose fiancée he had earlier cured of a nervous illness similar to Marie's (*FuN,* 169–74). From this letter we learn of Alban's attraction to Marie upon their first meeting and his accompanying jealousy about her engagement to Hypolit. Alban claims to Theobald that the attraction was not owing to Marie's admitted physical appeal but was instead "solely and only the immediate recognition of the secret spiritual relationship" between them. He attributed her apparent indifference toward him at that meeting to her engagement to Hypolit.

In the time between that first visit and his return to attempt a cure of Marie's nervous illness, Alban undertook to gain possession of her through the mesmeristic means of focusing his spiritual energies on her, thereby enabling him to appear to her in her dreams. He believes his activity produced Marie's nervous illness with the attendant dream visions. When, as he anticipated, he was summoned by her brother Ottmar to effect a cure, Marie recognized in him the man "who had appeared often to her in dreams in the aura of the ruling power as her master," so he reports (*FuN*, 173).[7] Marie's fatal swoon at the altar as she is about to wed Hypolit is owing, from Alban's perspective and her own, to their spiritual union. As Marie believed, should Alban withdraw from her spiritually it would be tantamount to rendering her dead. As Alban believed, he had gained complete spiritual mastery over her; therefore, he could presumably cause her to will to die. There is room to believe, however, that Marie's protestations to the contrary notwithstanding, her fatal swoon is caused by unconscious resistance to marrying Hypolit, or possibly to marrying at all. It is clear that at any rate her spiritual relationship with Alban is of overriding importance to her.

Marie's fatal swoon, moreover, was prefigured by a faint that seized her upon hearing about how Alban had once helped save the engagement of his friend Theobald and his fiancée Auguste. The fiancée's love for Theobald had been subverted by her infatuation with an Italian officer who was quartered in their home while Theobald was away studying at the university. On Alban's advice, Theobald regained Auguste's love by sitting at her bedside reminiscing out loud, as she slept, about their happy childhood together to dispel her nightmarish visions about the perils that endangered her Italian officer upon his return to the battlefield. Gradually, her thoughts returned to Theobald and away from the Italian.

Marie's faint occurs just as Ottmar, who is retelling what Alban had told him, has related that now " 'the real madness by which Auguste had been seized had left her and no obstacle stood in the way of the union of—' " (*FuN*, 160). Before Ottmar can add words like "the happy pair" his sister Marie swoons. It is as though the thought of marriage, or at least marriage to a childhood sweetheart instead of love from afar for an absent lover or spiritualistic mentor, is enough to make her faint.

"Der Magnetiseur" was followed by Hoffmann's fairy-tale masterpiece *Der goldne Topf,* which will be discussed in chapter 6. As in "Der Magnetiseur," the dimension of the miraculous in the succeeding story "Die Automate" ("The Mechanical Dolls"; January, 1814; published April 1814 in the *Zeitung für die elegante Welt,* then in *Die Serapionsbrüder,* vol. 3) is provided by belief in occult sciences. Ferdinand, a student, receives a prophecy from a mechanical doll done up as a fortune-telling Turk that in the very moment when he finds the beloved pictured in the amulet he wears around his neck, he will have lost her. The prophecy then comes true. On a journey Ferdinand happens into a village church where at that moment Professor X., the builder of the mechanical doll, is giving the beloved away in marriage to a Russian officer. Ferdinand is not upset over losing the beloved, however. Since she faints at the moment she sees him enter the church, he is comforted with the thought that while her body may belong to the officer, in spirit she is devoted to him.

On closer inspection, there is reason to doubt that Ferdinand's involvement with the beloved is anything but romantic fantasy, like the adventures of Hoffmann's enthusiast in the *Fantasiestücke*. Ferdinand and the beloved have never met. He has only seen her once before and heard her sing. More important, he relates the uncanny adventures he experiences to his fellow student and friend, Ludwig, who is not witness to those experiences and who has never seen the beloved. As is mostly the case in Hoffmann's tales, one way or another the reader is left to ponder whether the character's experiences are real or only imaginary.

Ghostly, devilish bloodlust provides the supernatural dimension in Hoffmann's next story, "Ignaz Denner" (May 1814). The gruesomeness of the piece is such that the publisher of the *Fantasiestücke*, Hoffmann's Bamberg friend Karl Friedrich Kunz, rejected it for publication in the fourth and final volume of that work. It found a home instead in the first volume (fall 1816) of Hoffmann's next collected tales, the *Nachtstücke* (*Nocturnal Pieces*), where its inclusion was most appropriate. The story's original title was "Der Revierjäger," because the central figure is a gamekeeper, Andres. For the *Nachtstücke*, though, Hoffmann used for the story's title the name of the sinister figure whose entry into the huntsman's life destroys his domestic happiness, resulting in the death of his wife and the younger of their two sons.

As Andres discovers in due course, the supposed merchant but secret robber chieftain Ignaz Denner who visits them on his way to the fair is actually his wife's father, whose secret aim is to obtain the blood of one of Andres's sons by butchering the child. Denner has inherited this bloodlust from his father, the still more sinister Italian doctor Trabacchio, grandfather of Andres's wife Giorgina. Indeed, Denner is following his father's example in the matter, because Trabacchio for many years kept himself young and vigorous by preparing an elixir from the blood of children he sired. Denner wishes to do the same now with his grandchildren, namely the two boys Andres has fathered with Giorgina. In the end, Andres manages to save his older son from the fate of his younger brother. His wife having died of grief over the younger son's murder at the hands of her father, Andres lives on at the end with the older son.

What did Hoffmann have in mind in concocting this horrifying tale of compulsive filicide? Is there a story behind the story here, as well as in

"Ritter Gluck," "Don Juan," and "Der Magnetiseur"? The driving force in the tale is the sinister great-grandfather's quest of eternal youth and vigor through siring children so that he can butcher them, a compulsion passed on to his son Denner.[8] Trabacchio and Denner, at the same time, are not merely sinister figures but also ghostly supernatural beings belonging to the realm of the fantastic. Through his marriage to Giorgina, Andres has come into contact with that realm. Had he not married at all, he would have avoided these horrors.

Hoffmann's characters tend to become involved in fantastic adventures that fulfill their dreams or secret wishes. From this perspective, at least, discovering that his wife, as wonderfully appealing and virtuous as she is, is the daughter and granddaughter of butchering devils may be seen as a welcome discovery for Andres. In the end, he is single again, with only the surviving son as his companion. He is not responsible for his wife's death, which is attributed to her father and grandfather. At the same time, the fantastic entry of Denner and Trabacchio into Andres's life may be a projection of his own feelings about having married and sired sons. Perhaps he secretly or unconsciously wishes that the devil might take them. Since Denner entered Andres's life nine months after the second son's birth, perhaps the devil fantasy reflects Andres's disappointment that the nine months' gestation had again produced a son, instead of a daughter he might dote on (the older son's name "Georg" may suggest that the first time around Andres wanted a Giorgina, a daughter, but got a son instead).

A father finds himself tempted to murder his infant son and his wife in Hoffmann's next story, "Die Abenteuer der Silvester-Nacht" ("Adventures of New Year's Eve," January 1815), which he substituted for "Ignaz Denner" as the concluding piece in the fourth and last volume (1815) of the *Fantasiestücke*. Here the temptation is still more plainly of devilish origin than the compulsions of Denner and his father Trabacchio. A temptress, Giulietta, serves the purposes of a certain Dapertutto (Mr. Everywhere), who seems engaged in the devil's chief work of trying to steal souls, here that of the young husband and father Erasmus Spikher. Spikher meets up with the seductive Italian femme fatale after he has taken a vacation from his wife and child, leaving them at home in Germany while he realizes his dream of traveling to Italy.

Murdering his wife and child is the price Giulietta exacts from Spikher if she is to be passionately and eternally his. Upon leaving her to return to the wife and child in Germany, Spikher gives Giulietta his mirror image. Once he is back in Germany she arrives to claim the higher price. Spikher withstands the temptation, but his wife and small son discover that he has lost his mirror image. The wife good-naturedly sends him packing, saying that once he finds the mirror image she will welcome him home.

This tale about Erasmus Spikher is a story within a story. Finding the Spikher manuscript is one of the New Year's Eve adventures experienced by Hoffmann's narrator, his enthusiast. The enthusiast's first adventure that evening was a humiliating reunion with a young woman he had passionately adored named Julia. At the party, she seemed about to become intimate with him when her ugly husband appeared and she rebuked the enthusiast for overindulging in drink, implying that in a state of inebriation he had been making improper advances to her. The second of the enthusiast's adventures that evening occurs when he flees the scene of his humiliation, seeks solace in a bar, and finds there the central figure, Peter Schlemihl, from a then just-published story by Hoffmann's literary friend, Adalbert Chamisso. Schlemihl is a fellow humiliated sufferer, having bargained away his shadow to the devil (in Chamisso's story *Peter Schlemihls wundersame Geschichte; Peter Schlemihl's Miraculous Tale,* 1814). The enthusiast and Schlemihl are joined by a small man who turns out to be Spikher.

The enthusiast's reaction to Spikher's manuscript confessing the humiliation of having given his mirror image to an Italian courtesan is to recognize in Spikher's Giulietta his own Julia, so that in the end he sees her as having been sent by the devil to tempt, torment, and humiliate him. If Julia was indeed the devil's agent, it is no wonder she held such great attraction for him. Giulietta, after all, almost brought Spikher to the point of murdering his wife and child. As Hoffmann's editor warns us about the enthusiast as narrator, however, and as we have seen for ourselves in the adventures he relates in "Don Juan," he is not always able to separate fact from fantasy in recounting his adventures. Certainly the enthusiast's encounter with the character drawn from the pages of fiction, Chamisso's Schlemihl, brands these New Year's Eve adventures as fantasy. And Erasmus Spikher is recognizable as an adaptation of the Schlemihl role that provides a closer parallel to the enthusiast's susceptibility to his former beloved Julia.

The enthusiast's imaginary reunion with his beloved is a revisiting of what he had felt and suffered earlier concerning his passion for her. On New Year's Eve one's thoughts turn to such memories as those of former loves, about what might have been or what a reunion would bring. As we know, while Hoffmann's readers in 1815 with few exceptions did not, his great romantic passion in Bamberg had been for his young voice pupil Julia Marc. The enthusiast's New Year's Eve adventures are secretly Hoffmann's self-humorous confession about his adoration of Julchen (in Italian, exactly the name Giulietta), about his dream that she would recognize and respond to his passion and his fear that it might end with his humiliation, and about his temptation to wish that his wife Mischa were out of the way so that he might be united with Julchen.[9]

In the story "Die Fermate" ("The Pause," February 1815; published fall 1815 in Fouqué's *Frauentaschenbuch* for 1816, then in *Die Serapionsbrüder*, vol. 1), which Hoffmann wrote just after completing "Die Abenteuer der Silvester-Nacht," the supernatural or miraculous element is provided simply by uncanny coincidence. Theodor, by now a thirtyish bachelor, finds in a painting at an exhibition in Berlin the depiction of a page from his own life. As he tells his bachelor friend Eduard when they have repaired to a wine restaurant after viewing the exhibition, he happened upon the same scene depicted in the painting when he was recently in Italy. Moreover, in his youth he had been involved with the two Italian women in the painting when, having just turned 19, he joined up with them as they toured Germany to give concerts.

Like the enthusiast's encounter with Julia in "Die Abenteuer der Silvester-Nacht," Theodor's youthful experience with Lauretta and Teresina had been a humiliating one. First with the soprano Lauretta, then with the alto Teresina, he suffered the embarrassment of discovering that instead of admiring his musical compositions and being · amorously attracted to him, they were only using him and making fun of him behind his back. Upon Lauretta, at least, to whom he was at first attracted, he succeeded in taking a form of revenge by cutting short the lengthened musical note she was singing, thereby ruining her chance to show off her voice to best advantage.

Fourteen years later in Rome Theodor witnessed the same thing happening to Lauretta again when he came upon the scene depicted in the painting by Johann Erdmann Hummel at the Berlin exhibition of 1814. In the painting an abbot with raised baton is waiting for the right moment to end the soprano's cadence. The abbot whom Theodor saw in the wine restaurant in Italy with Lauretta and Teresina confessed to Theodor that he had ended the trill prematurely, albeit in his case not to gain revenge, but on the contrary from looking too deeply into Lauretta's eyes as she sang.

Theodor left Rome without seeking to meet the two singers, explaining to Eduard that to become amorously involved with the women who have inspired one's music can only result in destroying that inspiration. Eduard, whose reaction to his friend's story is the comment "[s]trange but rather plausible," is left, like Hoffmann's readers, to ponder whether the uncanny coincidences that Theodor, after a few glasses of wine, has related actually happened or took place only in his imagination (*SB*, 74). The truth may be that Theodor experienced some such humiliation in late adolescence but meeting up with the two women in Italy years later is pure fantasy engendered by Hummel's painting.

"Die Fermate" was followed immediately by "Der Artushof" ("The Artushof," March 1815; published fall 1816 in Brockhaus's *Urania* for 1817, then in *Die Serapionsbrüder*). Here characters in a painting likewise play a role in the life of a young man. In this case, nothing uncanny or miraculous is involved, however. The lack of that element surely helps explain why, uncharacteristically for Hoffmann, the events are related straightforwardly, if quite humorously, by the narrator. The possibility that the story may be understood as fantasy on the part of one or more of the characters is thereby removed.

In this story, we clearly have a case of life imitating art. The resemblance of the old man and the youth to the figures in a painting at the Danzig stock exchange (the Artushof) results in the old man's mad belief that he painted the picture in question. To prove the truth of that insane claim (the paintings are more than two hundred years old), the man has dressed himself and the youth to look like the figures in the painting. Traugott, a young businessman at the exchange who finds himself powerfully attracted to the youth in the painting, discovers one day to his amazement that the two figures from the picture are standing near him. Traugott's subsequent discovery that the youth is actually the man's appealingly beautiful daughter leads him to break his engagement to his business partner Elias Roos's thoroughly domestic daughter Christina. Traugott sets off in search of the old painter Berklinger and his daughter Felizitas who have left their abode and, so Traugott believes, have gone off to Italy, the object of his own longing out of a sense of calling to be a painter himself.

While Traugott's infatuation with Felizitas saved him from marriage to Christina, his search for Felizitas in Rome results in his entering the role of bridegroom again, this time to an Italian girl, Dorina, in whom he thought he recognized Felizitas. Since Dorina has turned out to be someone else, Traugott comes to feel that marrying her would represent an act of infidelity to Felizitas as the source of his artistic inspiration. Devotion to Felizitas as his muse is therefore about to prevent him again from marrying when, having been called back to Danzig on business, he learns that Felizitas and her father did not go to Sorrento in Italy but have been staying at an estate named Sorrent outside Danzig, and that upon her father's death Felizitas married a criminal court official with whom she has had a number of children. Traugott's worship of her as his muse being therewith at an end (her name means happiness, but that meaning is related to the underlying one of fecundity), he declares his intention to marry Dorina upon his return to Rome.

Since Traugott's infatuation with Felizitas dated from the time of his impending marriage to Christina, we are left to wonder whether his attraction to Felizitas's image in the painting at the Artushof was motivated by desire to escape marriage to Christina, to whom he was not very much attracted, and whether similarly his ultimate worship of Felizitas then as his muse was motivated by unconscious avoidance of marriage altogether, considering that he was indeed strongly attracted to Dorina. Only when reality intervenes to destroy his image of Felizitas as his muse, replacing it with the one of her as married with children, does it appear that Traugott's defenses against marrying have finally been defeated.[10]

The role of bridegroom ends badly for the young man in Hoffmann's next story, "Der Sandmann" ("The Sandman," November, 1815; published fall 1816 in the first of the two volumes of *Nachtstücke*). The student Nathanael throws himself from the city hall tower shortly before he is to be wed to his distant cousin and foster sister Clara. Unlike Traugott in "Der Artushof," whose worship of Felizitas as his muse stood in the way of his marriage to her look-alike Dorina, Nathanael's planned marriage to Clara is subverted by his involvement with a sinister alchemist and builder of robots named Coppelius, a figure associated in Nathanael's mind with the Sandman, who, as his nurse told him when he was a child, is bent on stealing children's eyes.

As Nathanael writes to Clara from the university, he remembers that one evening, when he, still a child, was secretly observing his father and Coppelius conducting alchemistic experiments in the father's room, Coppelius discovered him hiding in the closet and threatened to take out his eyes and unscrew his limbs. Now that Nathanael is engaged to be married, Coppelius has reentered his life and, in the guise of an Italian named Coppola peddling optical instruments, engineers his infatuation with a robot named Olimpia that he and Nathanael's physics professor pass off as the professor's daughter. When Nathanael discovers that Coppelius has been deceiving him with the robot, he falls ill. Clara and his mother, though, nurse him back to health, and nothing appears to stand in the way of his marriage until, on the city hall tower with Clara, he sees Coppelius making his way toward the building. Surrendering to his fear of the sinister figure, Nathanael leaps to his death.[11]

Unlike "Der Artushof" but like most of Hoffmann's more fantastic tales, "Der Sandmann" is told by a not uninvolved narrator. In this case the narrator is someone who claims to have known Nathanael and presumably was his friend. The narrator, moreover, reports having been unsure how best to begin his story. He therefore starts it with an exchange of letters among Nathanael, Clara, and her brother Lothar about Nathanael's involvement with the sinister Coppelius. As a result, we learn first about Coppelius from Nathanael's perspective and then are exposed to Clara's contrary view that the sinister figure is surely a creature of her fiancé's fantasy. Most important, the narrator has put us on notice that the story might be told in more than one way, leaving us to wonder about the possibilities. Is the narrator telling it from a perspective like Nathanael's or like Clara's? Is the narrator telling the story as he imagines poor Nathanael must have experienced it rather than as it might have looked to an outside observer?[12]

Aside from the encounter with Coppelius from his childhood that Nathanael relates in his letter to Lothar (but "inadvertently" sent instead to Clara), his other involvements with Coppelius and the Italian Coppola concern his attraction to women. In particular, Nathanael believes that Coppelius is out to destroy his marital bliss with Clara. He makes that belief the subject of a love poem that he insists on reading to her and that she finds repulsive.[13] Having found Clara unreceptive to his poetic conviction that Coppelius will prevent their union, back at the university Nathanael falls victim to the fateful infatuation with Coppelius's robot Olimpia.[14]

In the end, it is not only Nathanael's belief that Coppelius is coming to get him but also his sudden association of Clara with the robot that causes his death. One interpretation is that, on the verge of marrying Clara, Nathanael sees her as another of Coppelius's robots, with which the sinister alchemist alias the Sandman is out to "steal his eyes."[15] Presumably in an effort to let the devilish Coppelius "take her," he attempts to throw the fiancée from the tower, toward which he sees his sinister persecutor approaching. It is only after Nathanael has been restrained from doing so by Clara's brother that he hurls himself instead. Hoffmann's reader is left to ponder whether Nathanael would have needed to kill himself along with Clara and why the student's fears about Coppelius are so intimately bound up with prospects of marrying.[16]

Hoffmann accorded "Der Sandmann" first place in his *Nachtstücke,* following it with the earlier story "Ignaz Denner" and its tale of crisis in the life of a husband and father. That story in turn was followed by one with the same theme, "Die Jesuiterkirche in G." ("The Church of the Jesuits in G.," May 1816). As we remember, in "Die Abenteuer der Sil-vester-Nacht," the story substituted for "Ignaz Denner" in the *Fantasie-stücke,* Erasmus Spikher was tempted to murder his wife and son in order to be united with the satanic seductress Giulietta, while in "Ignaz Den-ner" Andres's wife and son die as a consequence of his sinister father-in-law's blood lust. In "Die Jesuiterkirche," by contrast, the father is sus-pected of having done away with his wife and infant son, though in the end their fate remains unclear.

As in "Der Artushof," the fantastic element in "Die Jesuiterkirche" does not concern supernatural powers but only belief in the transcen-dent nature of artistic inspiration. The young German painter Berthold went to Italy to find himself as an artist and in the bargain found a wife. His crisis as an artist is owing to the unwelcome discovery, forced upon him by his artist friends, that the woman he has been depicting in his paintings exists in the flesh, in the person of the Neapolitan princess Angiola T. The painter is forced to see that his image of her did not come to him as a purely spiritual revelation but instead from having seen paintings of her done by an artist friend.[17] Berthold unconsciously had used those images of her as his own model. His emotional crisis is deepened when, in the confusion of a popular revolt touched off by the approach of Napoleon's army, he is cast into the romantic role of Angi-ola's rescuer. He accedes to her entreaties to marry her and carry her off to safety in his native Germany. After their marriage, he is at first no longer able to paint.

The fateful moment arrives after the princess has become pregnant with their first child. Berthold then finds himself unable to complete the painting of the Madonna and the baby Jesus with Elizabeth and her infant son John the Baptist with which he hoped to make a comeback. Whether Berthold in the end simply abandoned the wife and son or murdered them remains an object of conjecture for Hoffmann's narrator and for a Jesuit professor, with whom the narrator speculates about the mad painter's sudden disappearance.

For Hoffmann's readers the deeper question is why Berthold was only able to finish the painting of Mary and Elizabeth just before he either simply fled or committed suicide. The answer may lie in the fact that the painting depicts two women who like his wife Angiola have given

birth to sons. It is with this particular picture, not one on a subject irrel-
evant to his entry into fatherhood, that he experiences "painter's block,"
as we might say on the analogy of our present-day term "writer's block."
Before his wife's pregnancy, Berthold had done the images of Mary and
Jesus and was working on the image of Elizabeth. As one knows, in the
biblical tradition Jesus was fathered not by a man but spiritually by the
Holy Ghost. By contrast, although Elizabeth's conception of John the
Baptist was a miracle ordained by God, the child was indeed fathered in
the normal way. The—humorously ironic—point to Hoffmann's
"Jesuiterkirche in G." therefore may be that Angiola's conceiving a child
destroyed Berthold's last desperate clinging to his spiritualistic image of
her as his muse. Before the pregnancy, he envisioned her as the
Madonna with the spiritually sired Jesus. Upon recognizing his prospective paternity, however, he could see her as, at best, only Elizabeth with
the carnally sired John the Baptist. That subject he only succeeds in finishing—perhaps by way of sentimental farewell to the wife and child or
envisioning their reunion in an afterlife—when he is about to dispatch
himself or otherwise disappear finally and completely.

While "Die Jesuiterkirche in G." is about painter's block, so to speak,
Hoffmann's next story, "Das Sanctus" (September 1816), the last of the
four tales in the first volume of *Nachtstücke,* is about the related phenom-
enon one might call "singer's block." As though afflicted by a punishment from God, Bettina, a locally celebrated soprano, is visited with
that malady after she has cut short her participation in a mass, during
the Sanctus, to rush off to fill other singing engagements. Bettina's
complete loss of voice, though, is occasioned by the power of suggestion
in the jesting remark to her by Hoffmann's enthusiast, as she is leaving
the choir, that departing church before the Sanctus is sinful and will not
go unpunished.[18]

When Bettina later regains her voice, it is likewise through the power
of suggestion. The recovery happens after she overhears a story about a
Moorish girl Zulema, a convert to Christianity who took the name Julia
from whom the same loss of voice was lifted in the hour of her death and
transfiguration as a saintly martyr. Evidently attracted by the suggestive
power of the parallel between her affliction and that of Zulema–Julia,
Bettina is cured of her singer's block.

The story of how Bettina lost her voice and how the Moorish girl
regained hers is told by Hoffmann's enthusiast to two other devoted
admirers of her singing, her physician and the composer Johannes
Kreisler (like the enthusiast a figure recognizable to readers of the

Nachtstücke as being from Hoffmann's *Fantasiestücke*). While Bettina's loss of voice is factual, the enthusiast's account of how it happened is suspect as fantasy, a story made up to explain how that loss came about. Even if that story is true enough, the enthusiast tells the one about Zulema–Julia, which he claims to have read in an old book, in the knowledge that Bettina is eavesdropping in an adjoining room, so that the story is related "ad feminam." The enthusiast clearly means to effect a cure by enticing Bettina to be transported by a romantic image of herself as the converted Moorish girl. Indeed, the anecdote about his jesting threat to Bettina as she was leaving during the Sanctus may have been fabricated simply to facilitate that poetic identification. In any event, the enthusiast's appeal to fantasy works because three months later Bettina is singing again as gloriously as ever.

In "Rat Krespel" ("Councillor Krespel," September 1816; first published in fall 1817 in the *Frauentaschenbuch* for 1818, then in *Die Serapionsbrüder*, vol. 1), Hoffmann's next story and one of his most acclaimed, he provided a variation on the motif of singer's block. The soprano Antonia was prohibited from singing by her father, the lawyer and judicial official Krespel; or rather, her father conveyed to her the opinion of a physician that owing to a lung defect singing posed a mortal threat to her. The choice Krespel put to his daughter was between death, should she marry her fiancé—a composer who, Krespel insists, could hardly be expected to resist the temptation to have her sing his compositions—and life with her widower father who would guard her health as she comforted him in his approach toward old age. The truth of Krespel's belief that if Antonia married the composer she would sing again and that it would kill her appears confirmed by the uncanny coincidence that her early death happens during a night in which her father has a dream that she is singing to the accompaniment of the former fiancé.

Although Krespel offered Antonia a choice, he did not actually give her a chance to decide. He chose for her by taking her home with him and not informing her fiancé of their departure. Then, when the fiancé came to Krespel's house seeking his bride, Krespel had Antonia sing while he accompanied her madly on the violin in an effort to show the fiancé how flushed her cheeks became from the effort. When, confronted with the father's raving at him, the fiancé started to leave, Antonia swooned. On awakening and seeing her father ministering to her, she fell into a still deeper faint. Regaining consciousness after the second faint, she offered no resistance to the father's plan that she stay with him and refrain from singing. A melancholy sadness, though, took posses-

sion of her, as indicated a short time later by her surrender to the fantasy
that an old violin her father had bought "sang" with the sound of her
voice when Krespel played it. She begged him not to take that instrument apart, as he had done with all the other antique violins he bought,
in his effort to discover the secret of their superior sound.[19] Antonia's
fantasy seems to have betokened a suppressed yearning to sing again, as
she had sung to her composer fiancé's accompaniment before his disappearance. The fiancé's return did not occur in fact; it happened only in
Krespel's dream on the night Antonia died. It can well be imagined,
however, that Antonia died of a broken heart, perhaps dreaming the
same dream.

The story of Krespel and Antonia is narrated by a participant in the
action, a young lawyer who is recognizably one of Hoffmann's enthusiasts. Even before he has met Krespel, but on the basis of what he has
heard about him, the narrator casts him in his mind in the familiar operatic role of the parent or guardian who jealously chases away the pretty
daughter or ward's suitors. His subsequent involvement with Krespel
results in confirming that impression, so that when the narrator passes
through Krespel's town two years later on the very day Antonia is being
laid to rest, he immediately assumes that Krespel, out of jealous passion,
has murdered her. However, once the bereaved father has told him the
story of his ill-fated marriage to Antonia's mother, his learning about
the daughter's lung condition, and his life with the daughter afterward,
the narrator ends his report by saying that he left ashamed about his
belief that Krespel had murdered Antonia.[20]

Since there is reason to believe that Antonia withered away and died
of a broken heart and there are no grounds for believing that Krespel
murdered her, the narrator's shame over his mistaken belief is certainly
warranted. Yet even as told to the narrator by Krespel, the story implies
that the narrator's original impression that Krespel is like the jealous
father familiar from opera was not wrong. Krespel's actions to prevent
the daughter's marriage are understandable if perhaps not laudable,
assuming that Antonia indeed had a lung defect such that singing
would or might result in her death. His actions are even excusable if no
such condition existed but he only believed that it did based the physician's opinion.[21] There are hints in Krespel's account, however, that he
felt guilty about chasing away the fiancé. The last such hint is Krespel's
dream about the daughter singing to the fiancé's accompaniment the
night she died. The dream serves to justify Krespel's belief that singing
again would be the death of Antonia; it also suggests a need to believe

in that justification. In the dream, Krespel struggles to intervene, but a feeling that he is weighed down by lead prevents him from doing so. That leaden feeling in the dream may attest to a guilty sense that he should not have intervened in the engagement in the first place and that the daughter had continued to yearn to sing to the fiancé's accompaniment and be wed to him ever since the fateful evening. As we learn, even in his grief Krespel experiences the daughter's death as a liberation for himself, presumably because he no longer stands between Antonia and her grieving, longing for reunion with her fiancé. We can imagine that Krespel had secretly welcomed the physician's words about a lung defect as a justification for surrendering to his jealous passion for the daughter whom he met only at the moment he was to "lose" her, on the occasion of her engagement to the young composer.[22]

In "Rat Krespel" the only brushes with spiritualistic transcendence are the two uncanny coincidences of Krespel's dream on the night of his daughter's death and the narrator's return to Krespel's town at the hour of Antonia's burial. The supernatural element is even further limited in Hoffmann's next story, "Ein Fragment aus dem Leben dreier Freunde" ("A Fragment from the Lives of Three Friends," fall 1816; in *Der Wintergarten,* ed. Stephan Schütze, vol. 2 [Frankfurt a. M.: Wilmans, 1818], then in *Die Serapionsbrüder,* vol. 1). There is hardly anything uncanny about the three friends' discovery that they have courted the same girl, especially because they had been together when they first noticed her in the Berlin Tiergarten on the second day of Pentecost 1815. Similarly, the friend who weds the girl only jestingly claims that he had to marry to lay to rest the ghost of his unmarried aunt, who after being jilted had spent the rest of her life waiting in her bridal dress for the missing bridegroom in the house the nephew has inherited (one wonders whether Charles Dickens [1812–1870] had some knowledge of Hoffmann's tale, in view of the similar portrayal of the jilted bride in his novel *Great Expectations* [1861]).[23]

Romantic fantasy plays a role, however, as it inevitably does in Hoffmann's tales. The three young men notice the young woman not only because she is wondrously attractive but because she is shedding tears. They try to imagine the story behind the tears. When the three friends are reunited in the Tiergarten two years later to the day, they reminisce about having seen the young woman. Two of them, Marzell and Severin, tell of having had some short-lived involvement with her. Marzell, believing that her tears were over a disappointment in love, immediately lost interest in her when he discovered that instead the tears were over a hat she had ordered from Paris that had arrived in damaged condition. Severin then tells how the young woman, Paulina Asling, and her father humiliated him in public after he, imagining that her tears were over a suitor her father had tyrannically rejected, had sent her a note declaring his mystical devotion to her. Alexander, who has pretended that he alone of the three of them did not become involved with the young woman, and instead under the influence of his aunt's ghost has married someone else, then introduces Paulina as his wife when she arrives to greet him.

The four stories that comprise the second volume of Hoffmann's *Nachtstücke* (fall 1817), written from the winter of 1816 to the following fall, involve secular spiritualistic phenomena such as ghosts, somnambulism, and mesmerism rather more than the Christian elements of devilry and curse found in the four tales of the first volume. While the title of the second volume's lead story "Das öde Haus" ("The Empty House") suggests a ghost story, the eminently eligible, though quite narcissistic young aristocratic bachelor Theodor finds in the end that the house on Berlin's Unter den Linden that has attracted his attention is occupied by an older woman who had been jilted by another man.[24] Unlike Alexander's jilted aunt in the story just discussed, however, who was said to haunt the house he inherited, the jilted woman in the present story is not only quite alive but also using spiritualistic means in an attempt to make good her loss.

To his horror, Theodor finds that what has drawn him to the supposedly empty house is not his attraction to beautiful young Edmonde but the mesmeristic conjuring of her mad old aunt, Countess Angelika von S. Moreover, the aunt was attempting to "magnetize" not Theodor but Edmonde's father, Count von Z., who had spurned her to marry Angelika's younger sister. Although that conjuring had already resulted in the count's death, the aunt persists in trying to summon him. This discovery, which comes after a dinner party at which Theodor finally meets Edmonde who had appeared to him in his mirror, causes him to leave the beautiful niece and Berlin behind as he retreats to his estate in the countryside.[25]

In the end, Theodor associates Edmonde's appearance in his mirror with the mesmeristic conjurings of her aunt. Earlier, though, the image of the beautiful young countess in the mirror was linked in Theodor's mind to the warning of his nurse, when he was a boy, that if he persisted in admiring himself in the mirror the devil would one day appear therein. The mirror in which Edmonde appears to Theodor is one he bought from an Italian street peddler on Unter den Linden and used to peek at the window of the empty house while seeming to look in the opposite direction. In panic over seeing the beautiful young woman in the mirror one day in place of his own reflection, Theodor goes to a physician friend, Doctor K., to determine whether he is having hallucinations or perhaps even losing his mind. The doctor after first putting himself in magnetic (i.e., mesmeristic) rapport with his young patient declares that he, too, sees the young woman in the mirror. Subsequently the physician explains her appearance there by telling Theodor the story of the jilted countess who inhabits the empty house. (We may wonder whether that story is true or only invented by the doctor to dispel the patient's fear of insanity.)

Theodor tells his two friends, Lelio and Franz, about his adventure revolving around the empty house. As with a good number of Hoffmann's tales, the truth of the story is thus guaranteed only by someone who claims to have been involved in it. In this case, there is the odd circumstance that in telling the story Theodor refers to some notes, offering assurance perhaps that a form of documentation for the actuality of the events exists but at the same time leaving Lelio and Franz—and Hoffmann's readers—to wonder whether the need to refer to the notes does not suggest that Theodor has made up the story to boast in bachelorish fashion about having had a spiritualistic involvement with a beautiful young woman.[26]

The following tale in the second volume of *Nachtstücke,* "Das Majorat" ("The Entail"), is indeed a ghost story. A castle on the Baltic Sea coast is haunted by the ghost of a servant who murdered his master. The present owner of the castle Baron Roderich feels himself the special object of the servant's haunting, because he caused the servant's death, calling out to him, "Daniel, Daniel, what are you doing here at this hour?" when the sleepwalking servant was revisiting the scene of his crime (*FuN,* 554). Roderich's wife Seraphina, who has an hysterical, mortal fear of the ghost, dies in a sleighing accident, soon followed in death by her husband.

The story of the entail, which was established by Roderich's grandfather of the same name to stipulate that the castle be passed on according to the principle of primogeniture, is told by an elderly lawyer who has handled the family's legal affairs.[27] Oddly, the old man, who tells the story as he is recovering from a stroke, does not claim that what he relates is in fact true, only that it "could well have happened" ("eine merkwürdige Geschichte, die sich wohl zutragen konnte," *FuN,* 528). In the story, the lawyer assumes the role of exorcist of the baronial family's ghost, a role that involves in particular young Baroness Seraphina's belief that on their annual visit to the castle she is safe from the ghost only when the old lawyer is present. Considering that old Theodor suffered his stroke after receiving news of Baroness Seraphina's death in the sleighing accident, it is possible that his story about the entail is one he would like to believe or imagine is true, in view of his role in it as the beautiful Seraphina's special protector.[28]

The whole of "Das Majorat" is told in turn by one of Hoffmann's bachelor enthusiasts, the old bachelor lawyer's grandnephew and namesake, Theodor, himself a lawyer. Theodor's retelling of the great-uncle's story is preceded by one about his own involvement with Baroness Seraphina. He relates how, as a very young man, he became the object of an evidently adulterous passion on the part of Seraphina, herself at that time still only 19. Theodor was saved from requiting that passion first by his panic at his recognition of its adulterous nature and then by his great-uncle's care to rush off with him from the castle before the grandnephew could succumb to lover's folly. In telling his story in maturer bachelor years after revisiting the site on the Baltic coast, Theodor evidently enjoys the image of himself as the object of hysterical passion, as his bachelor great-uncle, too, seemingly did in relating his story about the entail and beautiful Seraphina's equally hysterical dependence on him as her protector.

Viewing the uncle's story as a romantic fabrication on his part explains a discrepancy in chronology. From his account, Seraphina had to have been married to Roderich in the 1760s, but she cannot even have been born yet at that time if in the 1790s when young Theodor meets her she is only 19. We may conclude that the uncle, envying the grandnephew his romantic involvement with the young baroness, fantasizes about a relationship with her from his earlier years when he was not yet an old man, if already middle-aged (like Hoffmann at the time of his romantic crisis over Julia Marc).[29]

Somnambulism, understood as out-of-body experiences, is the subject of the story "Das Gelübde" ("The Vow") that follows "Das Majorat" in the *Nachtstücke*. A young Polish countess, Hermenegilda, conceives a child with her fiancé, young Count Stanislaus, on a battlefield in northern Italy during the Napoleonic wars. The conception occurs at the same moment that, back on her father's estate in Poland, she is having intercourse in a pavilion with Stanislaus's look-alike cousin Xaver. At least, Hermenegilda believed that she was being wed to Stanislaus on the Italian battlefield when in fact she was engaged intimately with the cousin in Poland. Forced to accept that she conceived the child with Xaver instead, she looks upon him as having been an agent of the devil or the devil himself and vows never to show her face for fear it would attract the devil again. When Xaver discovers where she has gone to give birth and arrives to take the baby from her, she swoons and dies. The newborn dies in Xaver's arms as he flees with it, and he ends by retreating from the world in a Camuldensian monastery in Naples.

Hermenegilda's vision of her somnambulistic union with Stanislaus in Italy appears motivated by a need to suppress recognition that she has become physically attracted to the look-alike cousin. Her physical desire is in conflict with her virginal image of love as spiritual. She and Stanislaus, as young adolescents, had been hailed by their families and other Polish patriots as symbolizing Poland's dream of victory over the partitioning powers. When Stanislaus returned from the war that ended in General Tadeusz Kosciuszko's (1746–1817) defeat in 1794, Hermenegilda hysterically proclaimed to him that their union had to be postponed until the last enemy was driven from Polish soil, whereupon he in despair set off to seek an honorable death fighting in Italy. When Hermenegilda two years later surrenders to desire for the cousin, and indeed seduces him, she can do so only by imagining that she is not with Xaver in the pavilion but with Stanislaus on the battlefield.[30]

A vision likewise provides the element of the miraculous in the last of the *Nachtstücke,* "Das steinerne Herz" ("The Stone Heart"). Uncle Reutlinger faints when confronted with an image fulfilling his lifelong dream of spiritual union with the love of his youth, Julia. He awakens from his faint to discover that what he saw was actually his nephew, adopted son, and namesake Max with Julia's daughter, both of them dressed in period clothes from the time the uncle courted the mother. Young Max and Julia were attired that way in preparation for the annual party put on by Reutlinger in celebration of the bygone, gallant age of rococo in the previous (eighteenth) century when the uncle and the mother were young. Uncle Max had suffered an emotional crisis at the time of his courtship with Julia, in the wake of which he devoted himself to spiritualistic fantasies while she married another man. A second emotional crisis followed years later after his adoption of his younger brother's son, Max, about whose existence Reutlinger subsequently denied any knowledge until the nephew and Julia's youngest daughter, Julia, fell in love, whereupon the uncle vehemently opposed their union.

Reutlinger's seemingly insane opposition to the marriage is overcome as a result of the "vision" of the young couple as himself and the elder

Julia when they were young, presumably because following this vision-ary experience the uncle is able to believe that their marriage represents a fulfillment of his spiritualistic fantasies about himself and young Julia's mother—fantasies that may have been engendered at first by bachelorish avoidance of marriage and then by regret over having failed to marry the girl of his dreams. However Reutlinger's mad fantasies are understood, it is clear that "Das steinerne Herz" is at base a tender story about a young love that went unfulfilled but remained unforgotten.

Visionary experiences play an even greater role in another Hoffmann story that he completed while finishing the second volume of *Nachtstücke,* as the title of this tale, "Erscheinungen" ("Apparitions"), indicates. Hoff-mann wrote the story, set at the time of the allies' siege of French-held Dresden in late October and early November 1813, for a volume to bene-fit veterans (and their families) of the Wars of Liberation against Napoleon (*Gaben der Milde,* ed. Friedrich Wilhelm Gubitz, vol. 2 [Berlin, 1817, pp. 115–33], then in *Die Serapionsbrüder,* vol. 4). The tale, perhaps the most enigmatic of all of Hoffmann's stories and one of his shortest, is set on the night the French attempted to break out. It concerns the sudden appear-ance of two spies on the Elbe River bridge in Dresden, in whom the narra-tor recognizes a servant girl, Dorothea, from the inn where he is staying and an old beggar who frequents the bridge. Now they are identified for him as Russians, Popowicz and Agafia, who threaten to murder him so that he cannot betray them. Several days later, the narrator learns that the servant girl and the beggar have been arrested as spies.

There is every reason to assume that the story of these "apparitions" is pure fantasy. The tale is told to friends by Anselmus, the central figure in Hoffmann's *Der goldne Topf,* which is set in Dresden where Hoffmann was writing that story at the time of the action in the present tale. The occasion of Anselmus's storytelling is his and the friends' reminiscing about that last siege of Dresden. The friends' facial expressions as Ansel-mus prepares to tell them about his adventure with Agafia and Popow-icz indicate that they are expecting him to serve them up yet another fantastic tale. Moreover, Anselmus does not tell them directly what hap-pened but only the story as he told it to another friend on the second anniversary of the French attempt to break out of the allies' encir-clement of the city. Hoffmann's readers, like Anselmus's friends to whom he tells the story, are left to wonder whether he is simply spinning a yarn in which the servant girl Dorothea and the old beggar are trans-formed into Russian spies so that Anselmus can imagine himself caught up in the momentous events of those hours.

As Anselmus experienced it, or at least tells it, the adventure has an erotic dimension, with Dorothea–Agafia's emerging from the waters of the Elbe like a mermaid in response to "Popowicz's" conjuring and then trying to ensure that Anselmus does not betray them by seating herself on his lap, putting her arm around his neck, and threatening to murder him with her knife. Upon recognizing Dorothea in Agafia, Anselmus was reminded of how the innkeeper told him that the beautiful servant girl's imbecilic gaze was owing to the horrors of war she had witnessed. The girl's beauty and the aura of mystery surrounding her therefore may be seen as having engendered in Anselmus fantasies about an involvement with her as "Agafia." When Anselmus's friend, carried away by the image of Dorothea–Agafia, exclaimed sorrowfully that she and Popowicz then were recognized and executed, Anselmus smiled in a curious way and related that Agafia was saved and, several days after the capitulation, brought him a white "wedding bread" that she herself had baked. When, in turn, the friends to whom he is presently telling the story seek to learn more about the adventure, Anselmus does not oblige, perhaps simply because he does not want to admit that his Agafia adventure was a romantic fantasy inspired by his infatuation with the servant girl.

In a story that Hoffmann wrote presumably during the months following completion of the *Nachtstücke* in fall 1817, "Der Kampf der Sänger" ("The Troubadours' Contest"; first published fall 1818 in the Taschenbuch *Urania* for 1819, then in *Die Serapionsbrüder*, vol. 2), he returned to his earlier theme of involvements with the devil. In this case the medieval troubadour Heinrich von Ofterdingen accepts the aid of the devil to win the hand of a beautiful young widow, Countess Mathilda, who resides at the Wartburg Castle at the court of Landgrave Hermann of Thuringia. Heinrich impresses the countess with songs learned on the advice of the devil from the astrologer, sorcerer, and poet Klingsohr in Siebenbürgen at the court of Andreas II, king of Hungary (1205–1235).

As a result, the other troubadours challenge Heinrich to a singing contest, at which, filled with arrogant pride engendered in him by the devil's influence, he insults the Landgrave and his court. When Heinrich demands that his teacher Klingsohr be summoned to judge which of the troubadours is the best, the Landgrave decrees that Heinrich shall be pitted against one of the other troubadours drawn by lot, with the loser to be beheaded forthwith. In the end, through Klingsohr's magic a demonic spirit that has assumed Heinrich's form appears in his place at the fateful contest and, on being defeated in song by Wolframb, vanishes into thin air. The absent Heinrich thereby has lost the young widow Mathilda to Wolframb. In a letter to Wolframb later from the court of the king of Austria, however, he thanks his friend for having saved him from his involvement with satanic powers, believing now that it was not the beautiful countess who had awakened jealous desire in him but only an uncanny apparition.

Hoffmann's narrator tells the story of the troubadours at the Wartburg, as he explains at the outset, in order to bring into closer and sharper focus figures as depicted in a late-seventeenth-century chronicle (Johann Christoph Wagenseil's [1633–1705] *De sacri Romani imperii libera civitate Noribergensi commentatio* of 1697). The resulting depiction focuses on the contrast between Wolframb's true love of the beautiful Mathilda and Ofterdingen's emotional crisis over his attraction to the young, presumably no longer virginal, widow. Heinrich associates his attempts to win Mathilda with succumbing to satanic temptation and therefore experiences relief when Wolframb has won her away for good.[31]

The supernatural role in Hoffmann's subsequent tale, "Doge und Dogaresse" ("The Doge and the Dogaressa," completed probably in late fall 1817; first published in fall 1818 in *Taschenbuch, der Liebe und Freundschaft gewidmet* [*Pocketbook Dedicated to Love and Friendship*] for 1819, then in *Die Serapionsbrüder,* vol. 2), is dealt not to the devil or sorcerers but to the natural elements. The Adriatic Sea, to whom on Ascension Day, the Doge of Venice was traditionally wed, rises up to drown the Doge's young wife and admirer in a storm as they are fleeing the city after the Doge has been beheaded as the result of a failed political conspiracy. The implication is that the young lovers' death is an act of revenge on the part of the sea for the elderly bachelor Doge's having taken a young wife.

The sea's revenge appears misplaced, however, since the Doge's bachelor heart seems quite wed to the idea of becoming the husband of the Adriatic on Ascension Day, a ceremonial union that is prevented by the failure of the conspiracy that aimed at handing Falieri absolute power. The Doge's marriage to the young virgin Annunziata, indeed, occurs at the urging of the conspiracy's leader, Bodoeri, the beautiful girl's uncle and guardian. The old Doge's attraction to the girl is more avuncular than desirous, and he lives in some terror of being cuckolded by Annunziata's young admirers. In place of consummating the marriage, the Doge suggests to the young bride that she be content instead to ride the waves of the Adriatic "with the husband of the sea" (*SB,* 392).

Antonio, the young man who perishes in the end with Annunziata in the Adriatic, is attracted to her because, though he does not recognize it at first, she had saved him years earlier from endangerment by a snake. The relationship is encouraged by his former nurse, old Margareta, who plays the role of matchmaker, telling Antonio of the passionate desire that torments the Doge's young bride and arranging to make possible his entry to Annunziata's bedroom. Antonio is on his way there when the coup begins and Margareta's plan is thereby foiled for the moment.[32]

The tale of the Doge, Annunziata, and Antonio is told to two young enthusiasts at the 1816 exhibition of the Academy of Arts in Berlin by a stranger, an older man who claims to know the story behind a painting by Karl Wilhelm Kolbe (1781–1853) as being about Marino Falieri (ca. 1280–1355) who in advanced years was briefly Doge of Venice (1354–55). The motto on the frame of Kolbe's painting, depicting an old Doge with his young Dogaressa, suggests that the portrayal is the situation of an old man who despite his wealth and magnificence is unable to "satisfy the wishes of a heart full of yearning" (*SB,* 356). The motto, given both in Italian and German, reads "Oh, without love / To go upon the sea / With the husband of the sea, / Cannot give consolation." While the stranger claims to be providing a historical account, only part of what he tells is from recorded history about Marino Falieri; the love story about Antonio and Annunziata is of his own invention. The depiction of the Adriatic's fury as the woman spurned may thus be laid to the account of the stranger, whose story about the painting bears the stamp of bachelorish fantasies about the perils posed by erotic desire.

Chapter Five
Later Tales (1818–1822)

Already in such tales as "Ignaz Denner," "Der Kampf der Sänger," and "Doge und Dogaresse," Hoffmann used depiction of earlier times as part of the element of romantic transport. In the first two of those stories, though, the transcending of time and place was provided additionally, or even chiefly, by involvement of supernatural powers. In both cases contact with devil figures or the devil himself was depicted. A chief reason for the positive reception of Hoffmann's story "Meister Martin der Küfner und seine Gesellen" ("Master Martin the Cooper and His Journeymen," winter 1817–1818; published fall 1818 in *Taschenbuch zum geselligen Vergnügen* [*Pocketbook for Sociable Enjoyment*] for 1819, then in *Die Serapions-Brüder,* vol. 2) was its full dependence on poetic depiction of a bygone age without resort to supernatural elements as such.[1] In this tale the uncanny happening, if it can be called that, is the realization that a prophecy that seemed to refer to a cooper could be understood to refer to a silversmith.

The broadened understanding of the prophecy removes the obstacle to the marriage of Master Martin's daughter Rosa to her young suitor Friedrich, a silversmith. Such overcoming of a father's objection to a daughter's marriage was in Hoffmann's day a highly familiar plot element from contemporary stage farces and the comic opera. This tale exemplifies Hoffmann's application of his notion of romantic comic opera as expounded at the end of the dialogue "Der Dichter und der Komponist" (see chapter 3) to his storytelling. As we remember, for Hoffmann the romantic element in comic opera was to be provided by endowing figures familiar from everyday life with an element of the fantastic. Here that element of fantasy is achieved not only by setting the action in a bygone era—in this case, sixteenth-century Nuremberg—but also by the strange behavior of the widower father and the three young competitors for his pretty daughter's hand. Moreover, the narrator introduces the story as a product of his own daydreaming about life in Nuremberg at that time.

The fantastic dimension to Master Martin's actions concerns his insistence that, in view of the prophecy made by his aged grandmother at

Rosa's birth, the daughter must only wed a master cooper. That superstitious idea causes the three suitors—a nobleman, an artist, and a silversmith's apprentice—to pass themselves off to Master Martin as journeyman coopers in hopes of winning Rosa. In the process, each of the young men in turn comes to behave in such a peculiar way that he departs from Master Martin's service, giving up hope of marrying the pretty daughter. Master Martin's broadening of his interpretation of the prophecy about Rosa occurs after the three suitors have left and the last of them, the silversmith apprentice Friedrich, has sent Rosa his masterpiece, a silver goblet, as a farewell present before he leaves to take work in another city. As Master Martin now tells himself, the prophecy can be understood as referring to goblets as well as barrels since both serve to hold wine.

The odd behavior of the widower father and the three suitors can be tied to their "mad" passion for Rosa. Master Martin is so attracted to his old grandmother's prophecy because it tells him what he wishes to hear, that his adored daughter can only marry a man like him in the sense that the suitor will have the same trade. The old grandmother herself, on the threshold of death, may have been moved by a similar feeling in making the prophecy. Her great-granddaughter should marry a fine man and excellent cooper like her grandson, of whom we can imagine she was very proud. For Master Martin, having the daughter marry a cooper would mean that he would not be losing her but, more than just gaining a son, would have someone who could take over the business and let the widower father live with them and continue to enjoy his daughter's charming company.

The madness of the father's passion for the daughter is perhaps owing to the thought that he cannot, after all, marry her himself. The nobleman Konrad's attraction to Rosa is a mad passion because of their difference in social class; in the end he marries an aristocratic girl who is a Rosa look-alike. The artist Reinhold's passion for Rosa is a bit insane because as his name (connoting devotion to purity) suggests, his yearning is to paint her rather than marry her. Friedrich's passion for Rosa is the quieter one of a lover from afar with little hope of winning the beloved. Once Konrad and then Reinhold have left, Friedrich suddenly finds himself no longer the languishing unfavored suitor. At this point his dislike of the cooper's craft and yearning to return to silversmithing overwhelm him. With all three suitors gone, Master Martin is faced with the prospect that his adored daughter might wither on the vine, a thought related to his subsequent revelation about goblets holding wine as barrels do.

We have a widower father, pretty daughter, and three suitors, too, in the subsequent tale "Die Brautwahl" ("The Choice of a Bride"; fall 1818 or spring 1819; published in the *Berlinischer Taschenkalender* for 1820, then in *Die Serapions-Brüder,* vol. 3). Like "Meister Martin" this story has great affinities with stage farces and comic opera. Unlike Hoffmann's historical fantasies, "Die Brautwahl" is set in the Berlin of his day, so that the romantic element is not provided by the reader's transportation to a past time and place. Instead, supernatural happenings are introduced, albeit in this case with historical reference. The magic in the story is added by two figures returned from the dead, a goldsmith named Leonhard and a Jewish coiner named Lippold, who found mention in chronicles about sixteenth-century Berlin. These two revenants serve as go-betweens for the rivals, Leonhard for the old bachelor bureaucrat and bibliophile Tusmann and for the young artist Edmund Lehsen, and Lippold for the young Jewish millionaire Benjamin Dümmerl.

The evident obstacle to the triumph of young love here is the bureaucrat Voßwinkel's greed. He plans to marry his daughter Albertina to his bachelor friend Tusmann, who is almost three times her age (he 48, she 18), because being Voßwinkel's friend and an older man, Tusmann will not ask for much of a dowry and will not want a big wedding. When Tusmann, who had to be convinced to marry Albertina, appears to be losing his mind over the prospect of wedding the girl he has adored since the day of her birth, Voßwinkel is tempted by the possibility of marrying her off instead to the enormously wealthy young Dümmerl. Feeling guilty, though, that he could be tempted by greed to wed his daughter to a man she could not possibly love, Voßwinkel rejoices at word that the young painter Lehsen, with whom Albertina is in love, will be coming into a sizable inheritance. So as not to offend any of the three suitors, Voßwinkel agrees to a drawing for the bride modeled on the one in Shakespeare's *Merchant of Venice* (III, 2), once he has received assurance from the revenant magician Leonhard that the latter will ensure young Lehsen wins the bride.

The reactions of the three suitors to the prizes they draw are sufficient to characterize their nature as lovers regardless of the magical quality of two of the presents. Having drawn the gift of a magical one-volume limitless library, old Tusmann forgets all about Albertina, as does young Dümmerl when he receives a magical file that enables him to shave the edges of coins to collect gold without damaging the coins' protective markings. Lehsen, who receives the miniature portrait of Albertina as the token of his triumph, may not forget all about her; yet he goes off to Italy to paint, promising to return after a year, then fails to do so. For her part, Albertina does not seem to care about Lehsen's absence, because it enables her to make herself interesting at Berlin teas with talk about her artist fiancé off in Italy while she meanwhile enjoys the company of a new young man, Gloxin, who is preparing himself for a career in the Prussian judiciary.

Voßwinkel's joy over his daughter's new suitor Gloxin casts doubt on whether greed, disguised as frugality, was the deeper reason for his original plan to marry Albertina to his middle-aged friend Tusmann. Voßwinkel should be disappointed that the young painter Lehsen, supposed heir to the tidy sum of 80,000 Taler (more than 50 times Hoffmann's comfortable salary as a jurist at the time), has not returned to marry her as planned. Like Master Martin in the previous tale, Voßwinkel now would seem to be happy to see Albertina married at all.

The deeper motivation for Voßwinkel's original idea of having the daughter marry the friend may have been that it would be the next best thing to having her marry the widower father himself. Certainly, the prospect of marrying Albertina to Tusmann had the advantage for him that he would not be losing the daughter in the sense of being deprived of her charming company. The intervention by the magical figure Leonhard to save Tusmann from making a fool of himself by marrying a girl who was in effect his goddaughter and to get her engaged instead to young Lehsen may for that reason be considered to reflect Voßwinkel's guilt about a submerged possessive love of his daughter. Likewise the role of the other magical figure, the revenant Lippold, in his attempt to buy Albertina for young Dümmerl, may also be a sign of Voßwinkel's guilt. From this perspective Voßwinkel may be seen, like Hoffmann's Master Martin and like Councilor Krespel before him (see chapter 4), as the comic type of the older man romantically infatuated with an appealing young girl.

The motif of a father foolishly planning to marry his daughter to a friend his own age is found in another story written by Hoffmann at about the same time as "Die Brautwahl," "Der unheimliche Gast" ("The Uncanny Guest," end of 1818 or spring 1819; published 1819 in *Der Erzähler*, then in *Die Serapions-Brüder*, vol. 3). In this case, the friend is a former comrade in arms who became infatuated with the daughter when he saw her portrait one day while he and the father were serving together in the army.

Unlike Tusmann in "Die Brautwahl," Colonel von G.'s middle-aged friend, Count S—i, is anything but a reluctant suitor. So wildly dedicated is the passionate Italian to winning Angelika's hand that, after her father has promised her instead to young Moritz, a cavalry captain serving under the father, Count S—i resorts to mesmeristic means to transfer her affection from the young rival to himself. Count S—i, "the uncanny guest" referred to in the story's title, succeeds in winning Angelika as his bride after young Moritz is mistakenly reported to have died in combat; he does not, however, manage to make it to the altar. Dressed in his wedding suit and sitting in solitude on a bench in a grove of trees as the appointed hour arrives, he dies of a stroke. Young love then triumphs as Moritz, recovered from his wounds, returns from the war and he and Angelika are happily married.

As indicated, the miraculous or supernatural element in this story is provided by Count S—i's use of mesmerism to shift Angelika's love from the fiancé to himself. As we remember, in one of Hoffmann's first stories, "Der Magnetiseur," young Alban succeeded in a similar attempt where the aim was not to marry his friend's sister but to take spiritual possession of her. The case of Count S—i may be viewed in a similar light considering his fatal stroke on the wedding day. He is clearly Hoffmann's familiar type of the older man infatuated with an appealing young girl. The portrait of Angelika with which he fell in love was one made when she was at most 14. His passion to marry her may reflect a paternal or avuncular desire to enjoy her charming company, more than to mate with her, hence his evident and fatal psychosomatic crisis on the wedding day.

Angelika's susceptibility to the charms of the uncanny houseguest may be understood as owing less to mesmeristic influence, if any, than to her attachment to her adoring father and a crisis of passage from childhood to adulthood. At first repelled by the older man's passionate desire to wed her, Angelika becomes attracted to him during the absence of her father and young Moritz when their regiment is called back to service. Their absence provides Count S—i opportunity to replace the father and fiancé in Angelika's affections. She responds particularly to the older man as a substitute father. Granted, she accepts Count S—i's proposal of marriage only after she believes Moritz has died in combat, but she nevertheless seems quite happy about becoming the older man's bride.[2]

When Angelika and Moritz are married in the end, their union is accompanied by feelings of horror and relief regarding the revelation that Count S—i and Angelika's French companion and servant Marguerite used mesmeristic means to subvert their love, Marguerite's interest in the matter being her envy of her mistress as the object of the young cavalry officer's affections. To this extent there is a negative aspect to the story's happy ending. Angelika has escaped from a temptation to marry a man her father's age who had come to remind her of her father, and Moritz from surrender to the seductive appeal of Angelika's French servant girl into proper marital union with the beloved.

We encounter the motif of a bridegroom who dies in his wedding clothes before he reaches the altar in another of the stories written between the closing days of 1818 and spring 1819, "Die Bergwerke zu Falun" ("The Mines at Falun," winter 1818–1819; published in *Die Serapions-Brüder,* vol. 1), one of Hoffmann's best-known and most acclaimed tales.[3] Here Elis Fröbom, a young Swedish sailor turned miner, perishes in the cave-in of a mine on the morning of his wedding. The mine cave-in belongs to the realm of the uncanny, miraculous, or supernatural insofar it appears caused by a mysterious Queen of the Mines, about whom young Elis has had dreams and visions and whose blessing, that morning of the wedding, he goes to seek by descending alone into the mine. Elis's change of occupation from sailor to miner occurred in connection with these dreamlike, visionary experiences, which include not only the Queen of the Mines but the ghost of a miner named Torbern.[4]

Elis's compulsion to become a miner, which seems a result of supernatural influences, arises upon his return from a long voyage to discover that his old widowed mother has died. Life as a sailor appealed to him partly because it enabled him, following the death of his father in a shipwreck that Elis himself survived, to please his mother by bringing her gifts from foreign lands. His devotion to his mother helped him avoid the prostitutes indulged in by his seafaring mates upon reaching port. Now that his mother is gone, he experiences a crisis of emotion involving his encounter with a young prostitute, to whom he tries to relate as he did to his mother, giving her the present he had brought for the mother in place of accepting the girl's sexual favors.

Still troubled by images of the warmth, appeal, and humility of the gentle-spirited, melancholy prostitute, Elis has a dream. In the dream he is first attracted to an older woman and her young virgins, whom he sees below in the depths of a mine. Then he hears a voice telling him that there is still time to save himself if he will look up at the mine's opening. There a saving angel with a loving face smiles down at him. Pursuant to this dream, Elis, as though in a trance, follows the ghostly figure Torbern off to the mines at Falun.

The dream proves to be prophetic, or rather a prefiguration of Elis's emotional situation in Falun, where he becomes infatuated with the pretty daughter, Ulla, of his widower host and mentor Pehrson Dahlsjö. That infatuation produces a crisis in Elis as reflected in his hearing the ghostly Torbern rebuke him for devoting himself to mining not out of love of the craft but love of woman, the means to winning Ulla as his bride.[5] That Elis's guilt over his attraction to Ulla involves feelings of betrayal toward his dead mother is indicated subsequently when, having been tricked by Ulla's father into believing that she is about to be promised to another man, Elis rushes down into the mine and experiences a visionary encounter with the Queen of the Mines, to whom he swears his loyalty.[6] That same emotional situation of the man between two women, a virginal saving angel and a comforting maternal figure, is reflected then a final time when Elis goes down into the mine on his wedding day to ask the Queen's blessing of his union with Ulla. The ending thus is prefigured in the dream Elis had after his encounter with the prostitute at the outset. To surrender to his attraction to the Queen in the depths of the mine will mean his death, while up above Ulla yearns to be his angel of rescue.

In the story's epilogue Hoffmann perhaps offered a final, humorous hint that a mother's love was more comfortable for Elis than a woman's passion. Fifty years after he perished in the mine, Elis's corpse is discovered preserved in vitriolic water and looking, in his wedding clothes, just as he did on the day he was to be married. When Ulla, now an old woman who out of undying love for Elis never married, embraces his corpse it disintegrates in her arms, recalling how on their wedding day he had left her and disappeared into the mine.

As happens with Count S—i in "Der unheimliche Gast" and Elis in "Die Bergwerke zu Falun," who both die dressed as bridegrooms, being lucky in love can be unfortunate for some men. That would appear to be the humorously ironic point of another of Hoffmann's stories from this period, "Spielerglück" ("Gambler's Luck," winter 1818–1819; published in fall 1819 in the *Urania* for 1820, then in *Die Serapions-Brüder,* vol. 3). The supernatural element in this story is an uncanny relationship between good fortune at gambling and good fortune in love, a relationship that appears to bear out the saying that one cannot be lucky at both.

Baron Siegfried, who is quite a favorite with the young ladies and who has always refrained from gambling, is horrified to discover, in response to taunts and teasing about being too stingy to wager, that he seems unable to lose at the gaming tables. His fear about the compulsion to gamble is justified then by the tale a stranger tells him about a gambler, the Chevalier de Menars, and his ill-fated marriage to the daughter of another gambler. Menars, having succumbed to the passion to gamble, saw Angela as an angel of salvation from that temptation. After her father the old gambler Vertua had given Angela to Menars in marriage to settle a gaming debt, the husband succumbed again to the urge to gamble, to the point where, in the end, he loses her to another man in connection with a wager. Angela, however, dies of a broken heart at the very moment Menars loses her at the gaming table.[7]

The man who wins Angela in the end, only to fail to be able to "collect" on the wager in view of her death, is her former neighbor Duvernet who as a youth had adored her and lost her to Menars. There is thus reason to believe that "Spielerglück" is not ultimately about the gaming compulsion but about the other urge alluded to in the familiar saying. Like Menars, Angela's father, old Vertua, had looked upon the daughter as his angel of salvation from gambling. When she reached marriageable age, however, the gambling compulsion seized the father again as it had during his marriage to her mother. The relationship of the widower father to the daughter became much as it had been between him and his wife.

When Vertua uses Angela to pay his gaming debt to Menars he is "not losing a daughter but gaining a son," in the literal sense that the husband moves in with them. For both the widower father and the son-in-law, being lucky in love appears to mean having Angela as their "angel of rescue" from gambling, as the name she bears (which her father probably gave her) suggests. Being unlucky in love then means for them succumbing to erotic desire to possess her physically, which would explain their return to gambling, the father when Angela reaches marriageable age and the son-in-law after he has married her. If their image of Angela as saving angel is in the end a sublimation of the desire she awakens in them, then that unconscious tug of desire is their actual luck in love, thereby explaining why in their return to gambling they prove to be unlucky at it.

As Baron Siegfried learns at the end, the stranger who told him the story was none other than Menars himself, who died of a stroke immediately thereafter. As so often in Hoffmann's fantastic tales, there is thus no outside confirmation of the story's truth. The objective truth of Menars's account, however, is not as important as that he dies after having relived the story in his mind, or perhaps only envisioned it as having happened to him. Moreover, what matters ultimately is that the story is what Baron Siegfried needs and wants to hear to combat the temptation to gamble following his discovery that he seemingly cannot lose at it. Perhaps Hoffmann's ironic point is that Siegfried, who has been lucky in love in the sense that women are attracted to him without his succumbing to desire for them, might one day feel the tug of desire, causing him like Menars and old Vertua to become lucky in love in that unwanted sense and hence compelled to escape into gambling, at which he would then become unlucky.

A different form of sublimation of woman's love is indicated in an anecdote Hoffmann wrote during the same winter of 1818 to 1819, "Der Baron von B." ("The Baron von B.," January 1819; published in the *Allgemeine Musikalische Zeitung,* March 1819, then in *Die Serapions-Brüder,* vol. 3). Here the element of the fantastic is provided by the baron's self-delusion regarding his musical talent and accomplishments, of which he is entirely devoid, as the 16-year-old narrator discovers immediately when he arrives for a music lesson. Clearly, the baron is the comic type of the enthusiast who wishes to believe he is a great musician, music being considered the most sublime of the arts. He believes he is a master on the violin, commonly thought to be among the most heavenly and difficult of instruments. At the same time, the manner in which the Baron speaks to the youth about the difficulty of playing the violin suggests that violins, which are often thought to sing as though with a soprano's voice and which have somewhat the shape of a woman's proverbial hour-glass figure, are a substitute in the baron's life for involvement with women, as is indicated more strongly in Hoffmann's well-known earlier story "Rat Krespel" (see chapter 4).

The veiled theme of "Rat Krespel," a father's jealous passion, is the openly depicted, broadly comical subject of Hoffmann's tale after the manner of Boccaccio's *Decameron,* "Signor Formica" (March 1819; published fall 1819 in the *Taschenbuch zum geselligen Vergnügen* for 1820, then in *Die Serapions-Brüder,* vol. 4). The plot is that familiar from the commedia dell'arte and opera buffa about an older man's foolish enamorment of his daughter, niece, ward, or the like as being the obstacle to the girl's union with a suitor more properly her age. This role as the Pantalone figure is dealt in this story to the old bachelor Pasquale Capuzzi in Rome, who sets about to receive a papal dispensation to marry his niece, ward, and foster daughter Marianna. For her part, Marianna has fallen in love with young Antonio Scacciati, whose artistic mentor and adviser in love is the famous seventeenth-century Italian painter, poet, and satirist Salvator Rosa (1615–1673).

The fantastic element in the tale is the bizarre, extravagant nature of old Capuzzi's possessive jealousy, which causes him to attempt to marry Marianna to avoid losing her to a young suitor. Chastened in the end by a depiction of his death staged by Salvator Rosa, Capuzzi gives up his mad idea of marrying Marianna and settles instead for the promise of living with the young couple and thereby continuing to enjoy the niece's charming presence, which we may suspect was the underlying goal of his foolish passion anyway.[8] Salvator Rosa's rather cruel treatment of old Capuzzi and his identification with young Scacciati (his name means in Italian "those chased away") as the object of pretty Marianna's passion, together with his sense of horror at the thought of what faces the protégé as a married man, suggest that the humorous subject of the tale as a whole is bachelorish adoration of young maidens and a concomitant fear of becoming a prisoner of desire.[9]

Two young bachelor friends confront that prospect of marrying in one of Hoffmann's next tales, "Der Zusammenhang der Dinge" ("The Connection between Things," March 1819; published in February–March 1820 in the *Wiener Zeitschrift für Kunst, Literatur, Theater und Mode,* then in *Die Serapions-Brüder,* vol. 4). The sense of involvement with supernatural powers is provided by the uncanny coincidence, alluded to in the story's title, that one of the two young men, Euchar, rediscovers in a fandango dancer the girl whom he earlier had saved during his armed service. That discovery is all the more miraculous because it occurs as Euchar has become the object of passion of the beautiful aristocratic socialite, Countess Viktorina, on whom the other young man, Ludwig, has set his sights.[10]

In his romantic folly of pursuing a woman who is out to win someone else, Ludwig tells himself that his quest will be successful because, borrowing a phrase from Goethe's novel *Wilhelm Meisters Lehrjahre* (*Wilhelm Meister's Apprenticeship,* 1795–1796), it lies "in the connection between things." As it turns out, that comforting hope is indeed fulfilled by Euchar's rediscovery of the fandango dancer, leaving Viktorina to accept marriage to Ludwig, whom she rather despises. Since, however, we learn of Euchar's connection with Emmanuela only from his recounting of the experience in Viktorina's presence at a party, there is reason to think, as Viktorina appears to do, that Euchar has spun that yarn in unconscious reaction to the socialite's designs on him, a passion that he recognizes consciously only in the end. The humble and demure fandango dancer effectively affords Euchar, whose name from the Greek suggests he is thankful or favored, escape from Viktorina's passion. Viktorina's name, in turn, may mark her as having a Napoleonic passion for conquest. And Emmanuela's name, meaning "God is with us," fits her importance for Euchar as the answer to his unconscious prayer that he might avoid succumbing to Viktorina.

The devil makes a reappearance as the supernatural element in another Hoffmann story from the spring of 1819, "Aus dem Leben eines bekannten Mannes" ("From the Life of a Familiar Man"; published May 1819 in *Der Freimüthige,* then in *Die Serapions-Brüder,* vol. 3). The tale, based on an account in a sixteenth-century chronicle about the denunciation of a midwife as a witch, is offered by Hoffmann as a depiction of how the evil one was alive in the imaginations of Berliners toward the end of the period of Reformation (thus the title, in which the "familiar man" is the devil). The particular case in point is City Councilman Walter Lütkens's belief that the old midwife Barbara Roloffin who delivered his wife's child conspired with the devil to gain revenge on him by having the child born as a hideous changeling. The father's allegation is proven true in the end when, as the midwife is about to be burned at the stake, the devil appears and carries her off.

Beyond its avowed object of depiction, the anecdote may hint with veiled humor at a subterranean motivation for the father's denunciation of the midwife. The events are set in motion by the midwife's prediction that the pregnancy will produce a son, followed by a visit from the devil to the father to warn him that the midwife cannot be trusted. Then, when the child turns out to be indeed a son, but one who looks literally and figuratively like the devil, Lütkens denounces Barbara Roloffin as a witch in league with Satan. Hoffmann's reader is left to ponder what bothers Lütkens more: that the child is, as predicted, a son and therefore not a daughter; that the child is a changeling; or that the child looks as though he were sired by the devil, in which case Lütkens might imagine either that the devil slept with his wife, or that the wife was thinking of the devil when she conceived the child during intercourse with her husband.

Considering that the inciting incident in this chain of events is the midwife's prediction about the child's gender, and that in Hoffmann's tales the birth of sons as opposed to daughters tends to be associated with satanic involvements or actions (see for example "Ignaz Denner," "Die Abenteuer der Silvester-Nacht," and "Die Jesuiterkirche in G."), it is not amiss to judge that the councilman's wish was for a daughter and the disappointment of that wish amounted for him to having been cursed by the devil and his agents. The devil's visit to Lütkens, then, to tell him that the midwife could not be trusted, may be seen as occurring in answer to Lütkens's hope for a daughter, with the defeat of that hope leaving Lütkens angry both at the devil for having betrayed him by raising false hopes and at the midwife for having correctly predicted the birth of a son in the first place.

The birth of a daughter, as we have seen for example in "Rat Krespel," does not mean, however, that Hoffmann's fathers in that case necessarily fare better than those who sire sons. In "Das Fräulein von Scuderi" ("Mademoiselle de Scudèry," fall of 1818 or first half of 1819; published 1819 in the *Taschenbuch, der Liebe und Freundschaft gewidmet* for 1820, then in *Die Serapions-Brüder*, vol. 3), the widower Cardillac is the happy father of a daughter, Madelon, whom like Krespel he jealously guards, while at the same time, also like Krespel, he is the prisoner of a compulsive urge. As we remember, Krespel dissected old violins to discover the secret of their sound. Similarly, the goldsmith Cardillac repossesses the jewelry he has made for his customers, murdering them if necessary to recover his creations.[11] This mad compulsion, which largely provides the element of the fantastic in the present story, may be viewed as not unrelated to Cardillac's role, like Krespel's, as widower father to an appealing only daughter.

Cardillac blames his murderous compulsion on prenatal influence, namely his mother's attraction to a nobleman's necklace.[12] So great was the mother's fascination with the jeweled medallion that instead of encouraging or repelling the nobleman's amorous advances she grabbed instead for the necklace, strangling the would-be seducer in the process and falling to the ground with him in his dying embrace. Cardillac holds that bizarre incident—at the time, his mother was one month pregnant with him—responsible for his having had an irresistible urge to play with gold as a child. That urge resulted then in his becoming a great and much sought master at his craft and led ultimately to his reluctance to part with his creations and his compulsion to regain possession of them.

Cardillac gives this explanation to his apprentice, young Olivier Brusson, after the latter has chanced to witness his master's murder of one of his customers. The story Cardillac tells is intended to rehabilitate him in the eyes of the apprentice, whom, to keep him from going to the police, he has rehired and, more to the point, to whom he has promised the jealously adored daughter Madelon.[13] The goldsmith had chased Olivier away precisely because he noticed that the apprentice and the daughter were becoming enamored of one another.

The widower goldsmith's jealous possessiveness of the daughter is thus clear enough. We are left to wonder whether there is not a connection between that jealous love and his murderous compulsion. This possibility presents itself in view of Cardillac's focus on a particular type of customer, young aristocratic men like the officer Olivier saw Cardillac murder that fateful evening, who use the jewelry to procure the affections of young women. Cardillac's compulsion to retain or repossess the jewelry may therefore be seen as a need to avoid guilt as accomplice to seductions like that attempted with his mother and at the same time as secret horror at the prospect that young men might win away his jealously adored daughter by that means.[14]

Olivier tells his own story and relates the one he reports Cardillac told to him after he himself stands accused in the death of his master. In the end, Olivier is absolved of that guilt when one of Cardillac's intended victims, Count Miossens, comes forward to confess that he slew the goldsmith in self-defense as the latter was attempting to murder him.[15] That confession, though, does not absolve Olivier of guilt for failing to tell the police about seeing Cardillac commit murder. Olivier's justification for that sin of omission is that of a young man in love. He did not denounce Cardillac to the police because of the terrible effect he believed it would have on Madelon, his intended. Perhaps more to the point, however, is that Olivier seemed tacitly to agree not to report the murder in exchange for Cardillac's offer of Madelon as his bride.

To this point, we have made no mention of the title role, a fanciful portrayal of the historical personage Madeleine de Scudéry (1607–1701), a female writer and leading figure in the literary movement (ca. 1625–1645) known as preciosity (*préciosité*) that devoted itself to combating coarseness in manners and speech and to promoting elegance and nobility of spirit in the French language.[16] In Hoffmann's story Mlle de Scudéry, as a woman now in her 70s, becomes involved first when she receives a casket with finely worked jeweled bracelets and a necklace with a note, purportedly from jewel thieves. The note applauds the witty couplet she had produced at the court of King Louis XIV saying that "[a] lover who is afraid of robbers is not worthy of love." As she later discovers, the jewelry and note are from Cardillac, delivered to her by the goldsmith himself shortly before he is slain by his intended victim Count Miossens. Her involvement then continues after Cardillac's death as she is moved to take his orphaned daughter Madelon into her house to save her from being arrested with her fiancé Olivier. Mlle de Scudéry's poetic proclivities characteristic of *préciosité* show themselves in her romantic identification with Madelon and in her conviction of the fiancé's innocence, in whom she subsequently recognizes the boy she had adopted earlier.[17]

This latter, poetic coincidence makes it seem as though the aging spinster author has been granted a role in one of her novels as a form of recompense for lack of romantic fulfillment in her personal life. Toward the end, Mlle de Scudéry jestingly calls attention to her unmarried status in making her plea to the king for Olivier's release, dressing up in black as though she, Madelon's new "mother," were Cardillac's widow mourning the murderous goldsmith's death. Cardillac's gift of jewels was motivated not by romantic attraction, however, but by the thought that he could thereby defeat his compulsion in view of his veneration of her as a paragon of womanly virtue. At the same time, what pleased him in her couplet was surely the implication that his murderous repossession of his jewelry was excusable, since she was saying that being a lover means taking risks such as being murdered by a jewel thief.

Devotion to scientific discovery replaces romantic passion in one of Hoffmann's tales from these months, "Haimatochare" (first half of 1819; published June 1819 in *Der Freimüthige oder Unterhaltungsblatt für gebildete, unbefangene Leser*). This story in epistolary form is told chiefly through correspondence between the main figures, the British biologists Broughton and Menzies. The two bachelor bosom friends end by killing each other in a duel over the louselike specimen referred to in the story's title. The element of fantasy is provided not by anything supernatural but simply by the bizarre nature of the jealous passion to claim discoverer's rights to the scientific "find."

Fantasy enters in particularly in the bachelor scientists' writing to each other about the creature as though it were a woman, referring to it as a female island inhabitant ("Insulanerin"). There is thus room to suspect that the specimen is a substitute object for romantic jealousy and envy, the more so because we learn that one of the two men, Menzies, is being pursued by another female island inhabitant, Kahumanu, the wife of King Teimotu of O-Wahu (Oahu) in the Hawaiian Islands, where the two Britishers have gone to conduct their research. The bachelors' horror in the face of such adulterous passion, we may suspect, suffices to cause them to retreat to the relative safety of professional jealousy, a refuge that in the end proves deadly. As we ponder the nature of the passion that leads to double homicide in the duel, we are left with the image of Kahumanu's grief over Menzies's loss, grief she expresses by boring a shark's tooth into her buttock. That image may not be unrelated to the name Menzies gives to the louselike creature, the other female island inhabitant that simultaneously entered his life. "Haimatochare" means in Greek "one who enjoys blood."[18]

Fantasy and the supernatural are intertwined in "Eine Spukge-schichte" ("A Ghost Story"), also from the first half of 1819 (published in *Die Serapions-Brüder,* vol. 2). This brief tale is recounted by Cyprian, among Hoffmann's Serapion brethren the one most devoted to spiritu-alistic phenomena. In the story, the presence of a ghostly figure from folk superstition, "The White Woman," is demonstrated by the uncanny floating of a saucer through the air. The floating saucer convinces young Adelgunde's family that her claim to have seen the ghost and developed a spiritual rapport with it is valid. To disabuse the daughter of what they saw as adolescent imaginings the parents had secretly moved the clocks in the house back an hour, so that when the daughter claimed, as she did each evening, that the White Woman appeared to her at precisely nine o'clock, it would actually already be ten o'clock. At the appointed hour (eight on the clocks, but actually nine), the ghost signals its pres-ence to the assembled family members via the floating saucer. The par-ents are horrified, so much so that the mother dies shortly of a nervous ailment, and the father seeks and finds death on the battlefield at Waterloo in the allies' defeat of Napoleon.

The uncanny floating saucer does not terrify Adelgunde, of course, since it bears out the truth of her seemingly fantastic claim to having become the White Woman's protégée. That her elderly French gov-erness also fails to be horrified is surprising, unless we assume that out of devotion to or romantic identification with her young charge she has come to believe in the ghost, too. Adelgunde's older sister Auguste, meanwhile, is taken ill as a result of witnessing the saucer's flight but then finds refuge in the belief that she herself is the ghostly White Woman. Here we may see an instance of what is now called sibling rivalry, for the older sister has gone the younger sister one better by claiming not merely to have come under the ghost's protection but indeed to be the ghost itself. This mad belief, moreover, brings us back to the story's beginning, with Adelgunde's claim to her girlfriends, at the party celebrating her 14th birthday, that she was going to appear to them as the White Woman, then instead claimed, to the horror of all but one of the friends, that the ghostly figure had appeared to her. Since when that friend tried to convince Adelgunde that she was letting her imagination run away with her, Adelgunde fainted, we may suspect that on the occasion of her birthday Adelgunde was moved to make herself interesting to her friends, to cast herself in the romantic role of a maiden involved with a supernatural being. This would assume, of course, that Adelgunde's involvement with the ghost happened only in her imagination, a view contrary to Cyprian's telling of the story. Yet from his account it is clear that he was not an eyewitness to what he relates but has it secondhand. Still more revealingly with regard to the possible narrative irony involved, another of the Serapion brethren, Ottmar, suggests after hearing the story that "Adelgunde's imagination infected her father, mother, and sister [and] that the saucer was floating around only in her imagination" (*SB,* 327).

In the course of 1819 and the first half of 1820, Hoffmann wrote a story, "Die Irrungen" ("The Mistakes"; published fall 1820 in the *Berlinischer Taschenkalender* for 1821), that rivals his seven fairy tales (see chapter 6) in its use of magic and fantasy. In a hotel room in the Berlin of Hoffmann's time, a beautiful magical princess arrives to claim from an eminently eligible young bachelor aristocrat, Baron Theodor von S., the small sky-blue purse she lost in the Tiergarten. That encounter, as Baron Theodor experiences it, ends with the young beauty taking a small surgical knife from the purse and opening an artery in his arm, whereupon she ties that arm to her arm and flies away with him.

"Die Irrungen" ends with an almost equally fantastic encounter. The princess leads Baron Theodor to a voluptuous sofa, throws herself into his arms with passionate kisses, and tells him she will be his if he will succeed in liberating Greece from the Turks. Should he fail and be captured, so she tells him, he will need the courage to face death by impalement or by having gun powder poured in his ears and lit. At this prospect, Baron Theodor runs off, leaving the narrator to promise a continuation the following year should he learn anything further, a promise that Hoffmann subsequently fulfilled with the continuation entitled "Die Geheimnisse." The princess's pursuit of the young Prussian aristocrat amounts to a case of mistaken identity, for she believes him to be the young freedom fighter Teodoros Capitanaki whom she passionately adores as the hero destined to liberate her Greek homeland, as foretold by her horoscope.

Theodor's fantastic involvement with the mysterious Greek princess comes as though in answer to his secret image of himself as a Greek prince. That fanciful belief—one that his bachelor uncle, his deceased mother's brother Baron Achatius von F., finds ludicrous—stems from the love Baron Theodor's maternal grandfather as a young man conceived for a pretty Greek girl, a peddler of flowers and fruits, whom he encountered on his travels. The grandfather's passion had been such that he brought the girl home to his estate in Mecklenburg and had a life-sized portrait painted of her. Baron Theodor's mother then, when she was seven, conceived the fantastic belief that she was the daughter of the father's earlier love, the Greek girl, who Baron Theodor's mother imagined was in reality a princess. The mother's girlhood fantasy was revived when she gave birth to Theodor, her first child, in whom she was thereby enabled to see a Greek prince and to instill that belief in the son.

The infatuation with the Greek flower girl that seized Theodor's grandfather finds a comically grotesque counterpart in the jealous passion for Theodor's Greek princess exhibited by the princess's putative guardian, a gnomish former clerk in the Prussian bureaucracy with the ridiculous name Schnüspelpold, who lost his position out of an irresistible urge to travel, a trait he shares with Theodor's deceased grandfather. Of greater significance perhaps is that Schnüspelpold's relationship to his beautiful ward bears comparison to Theodor's with his mother as supposed Greek princess, since the 16-year-old maiden's role is largely to mother the middle-aged guardian, taking him to the confectioner's for sweets and caring for him when he has suffered an injury.

The gnomic guardian's possessiveness toward his beautiful ward appears to involve suppressed and sublimated erotic desire, particularly as regards the nature of the magical pigtail that he wears screwed on for his outings with her. The pigtail has a compartment for the napkin, knife, and spoon Schnüspelpold uses for eating sweets when he and the princess are out. It bends and curls in eel-like fashion as he walks proudly with his stately ward. At the confectioner's one day the pigtail becomes aroused by the piano playing with which Baron Theodor attempts to attract the princess's romantic attention. The pigtail's state of arousal is such that it invades the space on which the princess is sitting, causing her to leap up.

Baron Theodor's fantastic involvement with the Greek princess alternates with his attraction to another young woman who belongs to familiar reality. Amalia Simson is the daughter of a rich Jewish banker with a villa in Berlin's famous and fashionable Tiergarten district. Young Theodor had been courting her quite heavily just before the first of his magical encounters with the exotic princess. When he begins again to come under Amalia's spell and consequently goes in search of more suitable lodgings, he stumbles as though by fate or magic upon the room where the princess and Schnüspelpold are staying and from which Theodor flees in horror after the princess's challenge to his courage on the sofa. For her part, Amalia is convinced that Theodor's Greek princess is in reality the daughter of a Jewish scholar from Smyrna who has come to Berlin for discussions with fellow experts on the Koran.

The impression that the Greek princess's entry into Baron Theodor's life is intimately bound up with his attraction to Amalia finds further support in the story's continuation, "Die Geheimnisse" ("The Secrets," June 1821; published fall 1821 in the *Berlinischer Taschenkalender* for 1822). After Theodor's paleness and distraction resulting from the fright he experienced on hearing the Greek princess's challenges to his manhood have made him attractive to all the young society girls, he comes again under Amalia's coquettish spell, only to be soon reminded of his passion for the magical beloved by a note from her. After a series of efforts to find and impress the princess have failed, Theodor's attraction to pretty young women gains the upper hand again. This happens first with a cousin, Fräulein von T., then again with Amalia. Both times the beginnings of romantic intimacy are halted by slaps on his cheek by the invisible hand of the magical beloved. Theodor's involvement with Amalia is put to a definitive end when, following Schnüspelpold's advice, he hurls a Jewish curse at her father, believing that the latter is conspiring to see that Theodor, being an eligible young aristocrat, marries the daughter.

Schnüspelpold's denunciation of Simson to Theodor amounts to projection of guilt, since the ugly, dwarfish ex-bureaucratic employee is himself conspiring to wed the 22-year-old dandyish aristocrat to the magical princess. The sequel's title, "Geheimnisse," refers chiefly to the secrets surrounding Schnüspelpold's relationship with the beautiful 16-year-old ward. In a dreamlike appearance to Theodor on St. Bartholomew's Night, Schnüspelpold tells him that he was present at the princess's birth in Greece and was made her godfather; returned to become her guardian when she was 12; and four years later brought her to Berlin to marry her to Theodor who being descended from a Greek princess is eligible to fulfill the horoscope according to which the goddaughter is supposed to marry a Greek prince.

The greatest of the secrets is that Schnüspelpold, as he tells Theodor, has seized upon him as the way to avoid having the princess marry the hero Teodoros Capitanaki, for whom she is actually supposed to be destined. The reason for the deceit is evidently that in his jealous passion, which is as much that of a spoiled little boy as of a tyrannical guardian, Schnüspelpold wants the beautiful ward to marry a man who will actually be only a pretended lover and husband. When Schnüspelpold reentered the girl's life as she was on the threshold of adolescence, he tried to divert her from involvement with the opposite sex by giving her a clay "teraphim" doll that looked like a cute young man. When that doll immediately turned to dust at her touch, he learned from a prophet

named Sifur about Theodor's birth in Mecklenburg six years before the
princess's birth. Sifur made for Schnüspelpold a little cork doll to look
like Theodor that the princess was content to play with on her lap until
she reached age 16, at which time she came into possession of a mysterious "talisman" that gave her power over Schnüspelpold, therefore making it urgent for him to get her married to the false bridegroom.
Schnüspelpold's disparaging reference to Theodor as a "cork stopper"
(*korkstöpsel; SB,* 205) toward the story's end is a final hint that the godfather is preoccupied with the goddaughter's awakening sexual desire,
which threatens him with the loss of her charming company and maternal ministrations.

Hoffmann's use of shifting narrative perspectives, more elaborate in
"Die Geheimnisse" than in any other of his tales, makes abundantly
clear that we are to understand the story as a poetic fantasy. At the
beginning of this sequel to "Die Irrungen," Hoffmann has himself visiting Schnüspelpold to find out more about the Greek princess, indeed in
the—disappointed—hope of meeting her there. Moreover, Hoffmann
relates that he discovered in Schnüspelpold his double, who hands over
to him the beautiful princess's little sky-blue purse, which to Hoffmann's disappointment does not contain her surgical knife and so forth
but instead only little leaves of paper that, in the handwriting of the
various characters, tell the rest of the story.

Hoffmann's playful identification with Schnüspelpold suggests that
he self-humorously depicts himself here in the role of madly jealous godfather and guardian, similar to his infatuation with Julchen Marc.
Young Baron Theodor, meanwhile, whom the princess aided by her
nurse and godmother Aponomeria ultimately recognizes as an impostor,
does not serve simply as a vehicle for satirizing contemporary social life
in the Prussian capital. He is Hoffmann's familiar type of the young
man eager enough to please the ladies, yet in whom the stirrings of
desire give rise to fantastic involvements with magical beloveds.

The effects of a father's jealous possessiveness in trying to make his
daughter's gender abhorrent to her is the subject of "Die Marquise de la
Pivardiere," which Hoffmann probably wrote in late summer 1820
between "Die Irrungen" and "Die Geheimnisse" (published late in 1820
in the *Taschenbuch zum geselligen Vergnügen* for 1821). The widower Chevalier Chauvelin raises his daughter to believe that love only makes fools of
women and that in marriage husband and wife should remain passion-
less. When the daughter Franziska finally marries at age 28, three years
after the father's death, she weds a man she believes shares that convic-

tion, only to discover later that he has been deceiving her with another woman and that love, therefore, has made a fool of her after all.

Franziska appears to have learned from that mistake when she later encounters her first love, Charost, whom her father had chased away and who then entered a monastery and became a monk. Love makes a fool of her once again, however, because Charost has become enthusiastically dedicated to celibacy and the life of the spirit and is unreceptive to Franziska's yearning in middle age to return to the passion of their youth. To make matters worse, she and the monk, who are taken to be lovers, stand accused of her husband's murder until it is discovered that he is not dead but only contrived to disappear. During the time of their accusal, Franziska sublimated her desire by viewing Charost as a martyr and blaming herself for having sinned with him in spirit. Even her passion for Charost when she was a girl of 16 had made a fool of her, because it turned out that he was an all too easily discouraged lover quite content to escape from romantic disappointment to monastic celibacy.

Franziska's passionate, sensual nature shows itself in her fiery eyes, and her appeal to men was evident immediately upon her introduction to society. Precisely that appeal, inherited evidently from her dead mother, had awakened her father's jealous possessiveness in the first place. He preached abhorrence of her sex and avoidance of passion in marriage with a view to keeping her charming company for himself, as he did until his death, with the unhappy result for her that her passion was doomed to remain frustrated.

The depiction of wildly passionate women, like Franziska and like the Greek princess in "Die Irrungen" and "Die Geheimnisse," continues in another story from these months, "Die Räuber" (winter 1820–1821; published fall 1821 in the *Rheinisches Taschenbuch* [*Rhenish Pocketbook*] for 1822). In this case the passionate woman is Amalia von T., niece and foster daughter of old Count Maximilian von C., who lives at his castle in the forests of Bohemia. The beautiful young countess has conceived a mad, hysterical devotion to her absent stepbrother Karl, who had left to study at the university then ended up as head of a band of robbers. The seeming brush with supernatural forces is provided here by the uncanny coincidence of names and relationships between the members of Count Maximilian's family and the characters in the then already famous play by Friedrich Schiller (1759–1805), *Die Räuber* (1781).[19]

The decisive difference in the family relationships between Schiller's play and Hoffmann's story is that while in the play the young lovers Karl Moor and Amalia von Edelreich are cousins and hence marriage between them would have been acceptable at that time and place, the Karl and Amalia in the story are half-siblings and their union is therefore forbidden (the man who sired Amalia was Karl's mother's first love, with whom she had conceived Karl). That insurmountable obstacle to the acceptable fulfillment of Amalia's passion for Karl, a passion dating from when she was 12 and he was leaving to become a student, renders her love from afar that much more romantic and wildly passionate. As in Schiller's play, Karl here has a younger brother named Franz who is envious of Karl's position as the object of Amalia's passion, with whom Franz became infatuated at the same time she conceived her adolescent passion for Karl. Amalia's widower uncle, meanwhile, hopes that she will overcome her incestuous passion for Karl and marry Franz, which would keep the uncle from losing her charming presence at his castle.[20]

This sexually supercharged counterpart to the constellation of main characters in Schiller's play forms the object of horrified fascination for two young travelers, Hartmann and Willibald, as announced in the subtitle of the Hoffmann story, "Abenteuer zweier Freunde auf einem Schloße in Böhmen" ("Adventure of Two Friends at a Castle in Bohemia"). Their uncanny encounter with persons as though taken from Schiller's play, yet consumed with mad sexual passion, evidently serves them unconsciously as a cautionary example of how love can render one insane. In any case, the adventure at the Bohemian castle forms the content, in subsequent years, of the two friends' conversation whenever they, now rising young bureaucrats in the Prussian capital and evidently still bachelors, meet in the evening to drink wine.

A connection between erotic passion and insanity, as manifested in a young woman's hysteria, is the subject of another of Hoffmann's tales from the winter of 1820 to 1821, "Vampirismus" ("Vampirism"; published in *Die Serapions-Brüder*, vol. 4). The title under which the story has become known but that did not originate with Hoffmann is misleading, since Baroness Aurelia appears seized by a compulsion not to suck blood but to eat flesh.[21] Moreover, she is not returned from the dead but on the contrary is suspected of eating the flesh of corpses. Erotic passion and hysteria are involved when her ghoulish compulsion occurs in connection with her first pregnancy; and the actual object of her unnatural hunger appears to be the flesh of her husband, an urge she presumably resists by eating from bodies of the dead.[22] The compulsion is seemingly triggered by her physician's talk about unnatural appetites and compulsions of pregnant women that he concludes with the example of the blacksmith's wife who murdered her husband, implicitly out of a compulsion to eat his flesh. A possible explanation, though not offered by the physician, is that pregnant women either become wildly desirous or resent having been impregnated or both. Aurelia's ghoulish compulsion, though, appears to have its origins farther back in her experiences resulting from her mother's affair with an executioner's son who had deceived her into believing he was a wealthy aristocrat.[23]

We may suspect that things are not quite as they seem regarding Aurelia, however. There is no direct evidence that her mother had engaged in such activity with her lover. To be sure, on the day Aurelia and Hyppolit are to be wed, the mother is found dead on her way to his family's graveyard; but she may have been drawn there out of unrequited love for Hyppolit's deceased widower father, a possibility supported by the deathlike seizure she experienced upon meeting and coming into physical contact with the son Hyppolit. That is to say, the mother desires Aurelia's marriage to Hyppolit as compensation for her own disappointed hope of marrying Hyppolit's father. Likewise, Aurelia's nocturnal visits to the graveyard later, when she is pregnant, may have to do with her fear that the mother, who according to Aurelia had tried to pander her to the executioner's son, would return from the grave to oppress her anew. At any rate, it is the mother's ill treatment of her, whether real or imagined, that is the object of Aurelia's hysteria in her marriage to Hyppolit. Therefore, when Hyppolit, following his nightmarish, patently fantastic graveyard vision of Aurelia in a crowd of female ghouls, accuses her and she reacts by sinking her teeth into his chest, she may be seen as acting out of hysterical despair that he could think her capable of such a reprehensible passion.

As is mostly the case in Hoffmann's tales, and as we have just seen in "Die Räuber," "Die Irrungen," and "Die Geheimnisse," mad passion or hysteria on the part of women serves as the object of terror experienced by young men in connection with becoming attracted to the fairer gender. Such would appear to be the case in "Vampirismus" as well. Count Hyppolit enjoys a peaceful existence on the estate inherited from his father until Aurelia and her mother, a distant relative who had been the object of disapproval and revulsion over the shameful affair with the executioner's son, come to visit. Hyppolit's ensuing fantastic experiences as Aurelia's husband may be seen to confirm his unconscious worst fears about surrender to desire for women. We learn that he had avoided the idea of marriage until Aurelia's mother came calling with the appealing daughter he immediately found irresistible.

Bachelor fears about involvement with passionate women are the subject, too, of "Der Elementargeist" ("The Elemental Spirit"; published fall 1821 in the *Taschenbuch zum geselligen Vergnügen* for 1822), written probably in the first half of 1821. The middle-aged career Prussian military officer Viktor von S. becomes romantically if unconsciously attracted to Baroness Aurora von E., who has nursed him back to health after a nasty fall from his horse as he rode past her husband's estate while returning home from the defeat of Napoleon at Waterloo in June 1815.

The fantastic dimension to the story is provided by Viktor's discovery that his host's wife is in reality an elemental spirit, a salamander with whom Viktor, as a young officer, had had a spiritualistic liaison. In other words, it is as though Aurora had supernaturally caused Viktor to fall from his horse as he passed her estate so that she might attempt to resume their acquaintance. Their relationship had broken off after the salamander—like the devil's agent Biondetta in "Le Diable amoureux" ("The Devil in Love," 1772) by Jacques Cazotte (1719–1792), which Viktor had been reading—asked him whether he was prepared to give up blessedness in the afterlife in order to be united with her.[24] Persuaded by his friend and comrade in arms, Albert von B. who finds him at Aurora's estate, that he has become the object of an adulterous passion (to which Albert himself feels not impervious), Viktor agrees to depart for the barracks at Potsdam. First, however, he gains assurance that his attraction to his host's wife is owing to an earlier spiritual liaison by hurling at her the oath he had used to conjure the salamander. He convinces himself on the basis of the woman's resulting faint that she is indeed secretly the salamander "Aurora" from the time of his first—and presumably last—experience of romantic love.

The story of Viktor's involvement with the elemental spirit in his youth is told by him to Albert to explain and excuse his attraction to his host's wife. From what Viktor tells, it is clear enough that the fantastic romantic involvement was a product of the young officer's belated first erotic contact with women, which led him immediately to yearn instead for encounters with passionate female elemental spirits such as Cazotte had depicted in his fantastic story. Having been placed by the fall from his horse in the position, eminently conducive to romance, of patient to nurse and sensing in Aurora the smoldering embers of a middle-aged woman's desire unsatisfied by her husband, Viktor once again finds himself attracted by a member of the opposite sex. As before he explains that attraction to himself as resulting not from desire for women but from a yearning for spiritualistic union. We are not surprised that Aurora's faint proves to Viktor that his intimation was right and she is secretly an elemental spirit. We are not necessarily convinced, however, that the host's wife actually is a salamander, considering that having a cabalistic oath bellowed at her as Viktor does, when she is expecting sweet words of farewell, is sufficient in itself to cause the poor woman to faint.[25]

While the Belgian wife in "Der Elementargeist" may not have been a salamander after all, fateful spiritualistic influences at the time of a child's conception do have a palpable, indeed biological effect in "Die Doppelt-gänger" ("The Doubles," July 1821; published 1822 in *Die Feierstunden*). After two friends, Prince Remigius and his prime minister Count von Törny, marry two young women, Princess Angela and her bosom friend, respectively, the princess and her friend simultaneously give birth to sons, both of whom look like the count. The reason the two baby boys are indistinguishable is evidently that while at the time of conception the princess was sleeping with the prince she was imagining it was with the count, her friend's husband. The fateful consequence of this uncanny birth of the look-alike sons Deodatus Schwendy and George Haberland is that Princess Angela's niece, with whom the doubles are both in love, renounces marriage altogether because she cannot tell the two young men apart and enters a convent. Deodatus, Prince Remigius's son, inher-its the throne, while Haberland, Count von Törny's son and a painter, comforts himself with the thought that Natalia represented for him not a woman but art itself and happily goes off to Italy with his artist friend Berthold to paint.

Both young doubles find renunciation less than painful because they conceive of their passion for the beautiful and erotically appealing Natalia as spiritual, insofar as she seems to them an incarnation of an ideal that had been with them since boyhood. In his spiritualistic view of his attraction to Natalia, George is bothered by the recognition that he fell in love with her in a fashion all too familiar from novelistic romance, namely as he was painting her portrait. Moreover, once he finds his love requited by Natalia, he makes himself quite scarce, leaving the field to Deodatus, whom Natalia, then unaware of the look-alike's existence, mistakes for George. Deodatus, meanwhile, to his great surprise and amazement finds himself to be the object of her passion. In the end, Natalia rejects marriage because she is in love with George but could never be sure it was not Deodatus; Deodatus discovers that he was not really the object of her passion; and George finds that marriage to her would have been a mistake since she represented for him an ideal of art, and therefore resumption of his artistic friendship with Berthold is to be preferred. Even Princess Angela who in her mad hysteria was bent on seeing her pretty niece married to the son she had borne who resembled her girlfriend's husband seems not very disappointed to have Natalia share her fate of spending the rest of her life in a convent.

While these young people in "Die Doppelgänger" renounce marriage, Eugenius in "Datura fastuosa (Der schöne Stechapfel)" ("The Beautiful Thorn-Apple," completed July 1821; published posthumously fall 1822 in *Taschenbuch der Liebe und Freundschaft gewidmet* for 1823), marries all right but enters into the marriage with the understanding that the union will not be consummated. The young botanist Eugenius, upon the death of his mentor Professor Helms, accepts a proposal of marriage from his teacher's elderly widow so that he may continue to live in her house and pursue his research as before.[26] Only after he finds himself coming under the spell of the beautiful exotic seductress Gabriela who demands that he poison the widow, and after Frau Helms instead dies of natural causes, does Eugenius recognize that he has been attracted all along to the widow's highly appealing 16-year-old foster daughter Gretchen, with whom his relationship had been one of working together in the greenhouse and teaching her about the care and nurturing of flowers.[27]

Eugenius's receptivity to the elderly widow's proposal of marriage arises from his earlier disappointed adolescent infatuation with another young girl he met in the Helms household, the professor's grandniece, whom he adored from afar and who married a young physician. Escape into a marriage that is really no marriage fails to extinguish Eugenius's erotic desire, as is shown by his susceptibility to the charms of the seductress Gabriela. With Gabriela, however, his experience of rejection or betrayal with the professor's grandniece is repeated when he discovers that Gabriela is having an affair with a sinister Spanish Jesuit, Fernando Valies, whom she serves as a veritable satanic agent.[28]

Eugenius's attraction all along to Frau Helms's foster daughter Gretchen and his unconscious panic about that attraction is indicated by his delight over becoming, through the marriage to Frau Helms, the pretty maiden's foster father. He had not thought of marrying her until, with Frau Helms's death, the specter of having to move out of the house arises again as before. Only the contrast between Gabriela's perfidious seductivity and Gretchen's quite opposite loyal devotion enables Eugenius in the end to enter into a more legitimate marriage.[29]

With his next to last completed tale, "Meister Johannes Wacht" ("Master Johannes Wacht," April–June 1822; published posthumously 1823 in *Geschichten, Märchen und Sagen*), Hoffmann returned to the theme of a father's love for a daughter, as found in such earlier stories as "Rat Krespel" and "Meister Martin der Küfner und seine Gesellen." This time, however, the jealous, possessive nature of the father's love is not hidden or submerged but is very much out in the open. It is the bizarre quality of Master Wacht's passion for Nanni that provides the element of the fantastic in this story devoid of magic, miracle, spiritualistic visions, or anything at all supernatural.

Wacht's objection to Nanni's marriage to the promising young lawyer Jonathan Engelbrecht is understandable as motivated by his desire for her to wed a master craftsman like himself and by his fear that her marriage to a man in the professions will produce an estrangement between himself and the daughter because of her accompanying rise in social status. The madness of his passion for the daughter exhibits itself in his bizarre plan to marry her to Jonathan's deranged brother Sebastian simply because the latter, like Wacht, is a master craftsman.

Wacht's emotions in the matter are complicated by the circumstance that Sebastian is his foster son, whom he raised together with his two daughters Nanni and Rettel. Wacht had wanted to take in Sebastian's brother Jonathan as well, the other orphaned son of his best friend Engelbrecht, after his own beloved son Johannes died in an heroic attempt to rescue people from a fire; but Jonathan was given instead to a lawyer, though he so regularly visited Wacht's home as to be virtually a member of the family after all. Johannes, had he lived, would not have been eligible to marry either Rettel or Nanni, his biological siblings. Wacht's paternal relationship with his deceased friend's two sons creates the possibility for the daughters to marry within the family, so to speak, and for the widower father consequently to envy them that eligibility as regards Nanni, the favorite younger daughter who reminds Wacht so much of his beloved deceased wife.

Wacht's objection to the idea of Nanni marrying Jonathan is rendered all the more irrational by the circumstance that Wacht himself had married above his station and that Nanni's innate refinement, which so attracts him, is clearly inherited from her mother. Wacht is cured of his folly in the end by his awe at Jonathan's generosity of spirit in not only forgiving Sebastian for having tried to murder him but moreover in using his skill as a lawyer to arrange for the brother's pardon and achievement of the status of master carpenter. The secret reason for the widower's change of heart in giving his consent to Nanni's union with Jonathan, though, may be that with the approach of Rettel's happy marriage he cannot bear to see the adored younger daughter disappointed in love.[30]

The central figure in Hoffmann's last completed story, "Die Genesung" ("The Recovery," April–June 1822; published posthumously July 1822 in *Der Zuschauer*), is the bachelor uncle, not the widower father, of an appealing young woman. Here we may speak of a seemingly miraculous, not merely fantastic, dimension to the tale. Uncle Siegfried, who has succumbed to the mad belief that Nature has taken the green out of springtime as punishment for humanity's profanation of her gifts, is uncannily cured through mesmeristic means. Out of gratitude to the niece's beloved, a young physician, the elderly aristocratic uncle makes Dr. O . . . , a commoner, the administrator of his estate, thereby providing him sufficient means and status to render him eligible to marry the niece, Wilhelmina von S.

Uncle Siegfried's gratitude and generosity, however, are also motivated by self-interest, since the bridegroom and bride will live with him on his estate and he will not lose the charming presence and company of the beloved niece. Indeed, the uncle's bizarre belief about Nature's punishment may have been occasioned by his need to return to his estate and the resulting prospect of separation from Wilhelmina. Moreover, the role of green in his *idée fixe* calls to mind that color's association not only with springtime and renewal but relatedly with hope and specifically with love, as in certain expressions common in Hoffmann's time, such as *ich bin dir grün,* for "I love you," and *die grüne Seite,* for the left side of the body, where the heart is.

The setting of "Meister Johannes Wacht" and "Die Genesung" in Bamberg (the former tale explicitly so, the latter only implicitly) and their common focus on an older man's adoration of an appealing young woman suggest that Hoffmann, as he dictated these last two tales on his deathbed, was reminiscing about the infatuation with Julchen Marc that had immediately preceded and largely precipitated his entering a career as teller of tales.

Chapter Six
The Seven Fairy Tales

Hoffmann considered seven of his stories to belong to a particular genre, the *Märchen* or fairy tale. The distinguishing feature in his mind was surely the dominant role of the magical and miraculous in these works as contrasted with a more episodic, incidental, interventional function of these elements, and in some cases their complete absence, in his other short fiction. In particular, the magical personages in these seven stories are depicted as existing within the framework of a supernatural realm, about which a good deal of information is conveyed, invariably in the form of a story within the story.

This establishment of the magical realm against a familiar, everyday world is a basic distinguishing feature between Hoffmann's *Märchen* and other artistic fairy tales, or *Kunstmärchen,* on the one hand, and literary folk fairy tales, or *Volksmärchen,* on the other. The *Märchen* in Goethe's *Unterhaltungen deutscher Ausgewanderten* (*Conversations of German Emigrants,* 1795) and Klingsohr's *Märchen* in Novalis's *Heinrich von Ofterdingen* (1802) both are set wholly in magical realms so that the action may convey an entirely allegorical or symbolic import. In Ludwig Tieck's stories with magical elements, notably "Der blonde Eckbert" ("Blond Eckbert," 1797), "Der Runenberg" ("The Rune Mountain," 1802), and "Die Elfen" ("The Elves," 1811), which exerted a considerable influence on Hoffmann's concept of fantastic fiction generally, the existence of the spirit realm remains largely unexplained and mysterious (these stories were collected in the first volume of Tieck's *Phantasus,* 1812).

In other German Romantic fiction of this type, the identification of the realm from which magical or miraculous happenings emanate is indeed clear; but at the same time there is no story within the story about that realm. Thus, in Fouqué's *Undine* (1811)—which was a major influence otherwise on Hoffmann's first *Märchen, Der goldne Topf,* and out of which he and Fouqué created an opera—the mermaid heroine is a creature from the realm of elemental spirits in search of a soul. However, little else about that realm as such is related or depicted. Meanwhile, in Chamisso's *Peter Schlemihl* (1814) the supernatural power is the Christian devil; and in Joseph von Eichendorff's "Das Marmorbild" (1819) it is that of the heathen love goddess Venus, identified from a pious perspective as being a satanic agent.

In the literary folk fairy tale, too, as known from the classic collections of Giambattista Basile (ca. 1575–1632), Charles Perrault (1628–1703), and the Grimm brothers Jacob (1785–1863) and Wilhelm (1786–1859), the action is set not in a magical realm but in the more familiar world of everyday experience—in which magical happenings occur. In contrast to Hoffmann's *Märchen,* there is no story within the story to explain or describe the existence of a spirit world. As we remember, in famous stories such as "Snow White" and "Sleeping Beauty," we are dealing simply with magical curses or conjurings on the part of older women with supernatural powers of unspecified origin, whereas in "Cinderella" the same power is used for good rather than for evil purposes. In other well-known stories, such as "Beauty and the Beast" or "The Frog Prince," which involve magical transformations, the focus is so much on the reversal of the metamorphosis that the question of the magic that produced it is hardly raised or only as a seeming afterthought.

A chief difference between Hoffmann's *Märchen* and the literary folk fairy tale is the surprise, awe, or anxiety registered by the characters when confronted by emanations from the spirit realm. As we know, in the literary folk fairy tale the characters do not act as though the magic they encounter is anything out of the ordinary. They would not think of such occurrences as magical. While they live in an otherwise familiar realm, magical happenings are very much a part of that reality. In philosophical, allegorical, or symbolical fairy tales like those by Goethe and Novalis, the characters likewise do not show the least surprise at magical phenomena for the similar reason that they live totally within a spiritual realm.

Registering anxiety in the face of seemingly transcendental experiences is not a feature separating Hoffmann's *Märchen* from his other fiction, however. As we have seen, the characters in his tales not uncommonly fear for their sanity in connection with their encounters with a spirit realm. This feature, indeed, is the one Hoffmann's *Märchen* have most in common with Tieck's, Fouqué's, Chamisso's, and Eichendorff's magical tales referred to earlier. In Hoffmann's *Märchen,* however, as opposed to his other tales and to the magical or fantastic tales of his German Romantic contemporaries, there is a manifest requirement that, as in the literary folk fairy tale, the ending be a happy one in which good triumphs over evil.[1]

The magical realm in Hoffmann's first *Märchen, Der goldne Topf* (completed March 1814; published fall 1814 as the third of the four volumes of *Fantasiestücke*), is that found in Fouqué's *Undine,* namely the realm of elemental spirits. A fire sprite whose natural form is that of a salamander has been banished from the spirit realm as punishment for having mated with a snake against the wishes of the realm's ruler, the spirit prince Phosphorus, who sired the snake with a fire lily. The salamander has been condemned to live as an archivist named Lindhorst in Dresden in Germany until such time as he has succeeded in marrying his three serpentine daughters to young men of the town. The first of the three daughters to wed is Serpentina, with whom a young university student, Anselmus, falls in love. They are transported to a magical spirit realm called Atlantis where they marry and presumably live happily ever after.

Anselmus's union with Serpentina is a happy ending because he was blissfully enchanted by her from the moment she first appeared to him, in her elemental form as a small snake. He saw her among the leaves of an elder tree by the banks of the Elbe River in Dresden on Ascension Day. During the course of the following summer, he yearned in vain for the little snake with the beautiful blue eyes and heavenly singing voice to reappear to him in the elder tree. With the approach of autumn, he learns from the archivist Lindhorst, for whom he had agreed to copy manuscripts, that the appealing snake is named Serpentina and is Lindhorst's daughter. In the course of his subsequent work for Lindhorst that following fall, Serpentina appears to Anselmus in human form to declare her love for him. Anselmus's devotion to Serpentina wavers when he is seized by fear that this involvement with a being from the spirit realm indicates that he is losing his mind. His doubt about his love for Serpentina is punished by imprisonment in a glass bottle on a shelf in Lindhorst's library, from which torment he is released by a renewal of his faith in his devotion to the magical beloved. Upon his release from the glass bottle he is transported to Serpentina's spirit homeland Atlantis.[2]

Anselmus's lapse in his devotion to Serpentina is occasioned by the attention paid to him by the appealing daughter of his older schoolmaster friend, Vice-Principal Paulmann. Veronica Paulmann, a blossoming maiden of 16, sets her cap on Anselmus from the moment she hears that Anselmus, as a result of his work for Lindhorst, has excellent prospects of achieving the coveted rank of councilor to the royal court (*Hofrat*). Veronica immediately consults a fortune-teller, Frau Rauerin, recommended by her girlfriends for her usually favorable predictions about marriage prospects. To her dismay, Veronica hears from the fortune-teller that Anselmus is in love with Serpentina, whereupon Veronica enlists the old woman's aid in attempting to win him away from the supernatural beloved with magical means. Aided by this magic, Veronica succeeds briefly in turning Anselmus's head as he pays a visit to her one morning that fall, only to have him then return to his love for Serpentina and disappear with her from Dresden. Veronica grieves that winter over the loss of her dream of marrying Anselmus and becoming Frau Hofrat but then finds a substitute in the young bookkeeper Heerbrand, who in the meantime has himself been named to the coveted rank, with its elevated social status.

Anselmus is not only a young man whom two young women are out to marry, he is also a pawn in a related struggle between two magical beings—the salamander alias archivist Lindhorst and Frau Rauerin alias an old woman apple peddler.[3] Lindhorst's interest in Anselmus, as we have seen, is to wed him to Serpentina so that he will then have only two daughters to marry off before being allowed to return to his spirit homeland. Frau Rauerin, meanwhile, is out to defeat Lindhorst's plan. Even before Veronica enlists her aid in winning Anselmus, she appears to him in Lindhorst's door knocker to prevent him from reporting for work there. She then enables Veronica to produce a little metal mirror with which Veronica can turn Anselmus's thoughts to her mesmeristically.[4] Finally, Frau Rauerin makes a last attempt to prevent Anselmus's union with Serpentina when she battles Lindhorst in his library as Anselmus watches from inside a glass bottle on the shelf. Lindhorst's defeat of her in that struggle is the signal for Serpentina to appear and for Anselmus to be liberated from the bottle and blissfully plunge into the spirit beloved's arms.

While Frau Rauerin does not belong to a spirit realm as such, her struggle with Lindhorst shows her to be a creature of the nether world, understood as a cross between the realm of earth sprites or gnomes and that of the devil. She uses soil from pots as her weapon against Lindhorst's salamandric flames, and it is revealed that she is the offspring of a union between a root vegetable and a dragon's feather, the latter calling to mind the representation of the devil in Revelations as a dragon. Already in her first appearance, she may be seen as associated with infernal temptation insofar as she is peddling apples like the serpent in the biblical story of the Fall. Her role as apple peddler may be seen at the same time as anticipating her later role as fortune-teller and mentor in Veronica's quest to marry Anselmus if one thinks of Eve's temptation of Adam as erotic seduction. From this perspective, the apple woman's enigmatic warning to Anselmus that he will soon fall "into the crystal" ("ins Kristall bald dein Fall—ins Kristall!" *FuN,* 179) may be understood as not a curse but a prophecy of the outcome Frau Rauerin seeks but that fails to happen. She aims to have him marry a girl of the sort for whom she prophesies marital bliss, hence the reference to crystal as an allusion to the practice of fortune-telling with crystal balls, wherein the girl's intended would appear as a sign that her wish will be fulfilled.

Since the apple woman appears to utter her warning in anger at Anselmus's absent-minded overturning of her apple baskets in his haste, she seems more likely to be foretelling that Anselmus will come to a bad end. As a fortune-teller alias magical being, she may be presumed to foresee his imprisonment in the glass bottle, perhaps even his union with Serpentina, which from Frau Rauerin's perspective is a bad or at least unwanted end for him. It can be assumed that the apple peddler knows that he is headed to the amusement park to meet young women, and she perhaps recognizes him as the type of young student with his head in the clouds. She does not demand money from him; it is he who in his horror and embarrassment over his clumsiness tosses her his purse and thereby loses his chance to try to strike up polite conversation with the girls at Linke's Bad. In her identity as Frau Rauerin, the last thing the peddler woman wants is to prevent him from meeting young women.

Hoffmann's reader is introduced first to the little snake alias Serpentina, and only afterwards to Veronica. However, it soon becomes clear that Anselmus has known Veronica for a good while before the little snake and her two sisters appear to him in the elder tree, under which he seated himself to smoke his pipe to console himself over the missed opportunity to see the girls at the amusement park. Once he has encountered the little snake, Anselmus thinks no more of those girls; at the same time, he begins to notice Veronica and feel an attraction to her. Moreover, he notices for the first time that Veronica has blue eyes, as did the little snake he saw shortly before in the elder tree.

If we view Anselmus as the romantic dreamer, then we can see his visionary experiences with Serpentina as a reflex and sublimation of his attraction to Veronica, an attraction that rises to the level of his consciousness only after he has encountered a sublimation of it. From this perspective, Veronica has the misfortune of setting her cap on a romantic dreamer who is for that reason not the marrying type or is so only when it comes to marriage with spirits. At the same time, we may suspect that she is attracted to him precisely because he is a romantic dreamer, which would explain her psychic ability to know what he is dreaming. That also explains why, at the end, she alone among Dres-

den's nonspirit residents seems to know what has happened to Anselmus. To the bewilderment of her father and her fiancé Heerbrand, she
reports that Anselmus has married the green snake who is "much more
beautiful and richer" than she (*FuN*, 249). Most significant, though, is
that as a token of her forswearing of any further employment of satanic
arts, she asks her fiancé to deposit the fragments of her little metal mirror in the Elbe River from the bridge. It was there, if Anselmus's "fellow
prisoners" in glass bottles are to be believed, that he was standing when
last seen in Dresden. The implication is that, unknown to himself,
Anselmus in plunging into Serpentina's arms was actually leaping to his
death from the bridge.[5]

Such a reading of the tale suggests itself, too, from the playfully ironic
tone in which *Der goldne Topf* is narrated, most notable in the frequent
asides to the reader that culminate in the narrator's confession of the difficulty he encountered in envisioning Anselmus's bliss with Serpentina in
Atlantis. The concluding rhetorical question that Lindhorst puts to the
storyteller—"Is Anselmus's bliss, all told, anything else than living in
poetry, to which the sacred harmony of all beings reveals itself to be
nature's deepest secret?" (*FuN*, 255)—may be answered in the affirma-
tive as well as in the expected negative. Anselmus's bliss, which we know
only from the storyteller's vision of it as experienced under the influence
of Lindhorst's magical alcoholic punch, was by definition living in poetry
on the storyteller's part. As for Anselmus himself, his bliss was a matter
not only of living in poetry but—albeit unconsciously—dying for it.[6]

The magical realm in Hoffmann's second fairy tale, "Nußknacker
und Mausekönig" ("The Nutcracker and the King of Mice," completed
November 1816; published fall 1816 in the volume of *Kinder-Mährchen*
by Fouqué, Hoffmann, and Contessa; then in *Die Serapionsbrüder*, vol. 1),
is that in which the events related in literary folk fairy tales take place. A
handsome young man has been transformed into an ugly nutcracker
doll by a woman seeking to take revenge on a king with a beautiful
daughter. The young man can only be restored to his human form
through the brave devotion of a young woman who will assist the nutcracker in defeating the woman's son. We may recognize in this story
elements of such familiar fairy tales as "Sleeping Beauty," namely the
woman's taking revenge on a king with a beautiful daughter, and
"Beauty and the Beast," in which the beautiful daughter becomes
devoted to the creature despite his ugliness.

A chief difference between Hoffmann's nutcracker story and literary
folk fairy tales is that, as in *Der goldne Topf*, the central figure receives an

explanation of the magical realm's entry into his or her life from another character in the story. Seven-year-old Marie Stahlbaum hears the "Märchen von der harten Nuß" ("Fairy Tale about the Hard Nut") from her godfather Droßelmeier as she is recovering from a nasty cut she received when she fell against a glass cabinet in her parents' living room. The wound resulted from her witnessing, alone and at the stroke of midnight, a pitched battle between the nutcracker doll, which she and her siblings had just received that evening as a Christmas present from her father, and a hideous mouse with seven heads, each with a small crown. When the King of Mice appeared to be winning the battle and Marie took off a slipper to hurl at him, she fell against the cabinet.

On hearing from Marie about her magical adventure, Godfather Droßelmeier tells her a story in which it is revealed that the nutcracker doll is really his nephew who even before his transformation possessed an uncanny ability for cracking hard nuts with his teeth. The King of Mice is the son of the Queen of Mice, Frau Mauserinks, who is out to take revenge on Princess Pirlipat's father for having ordered that all of the mice in his castle be killed. Droßelmeier's nephew was transformed into an ugly nutcracker doll by Frau Mauserinks when, after having restored Princess Pirlipat's beauty by cracking a notoriously hard nut named Krakatuk, he rendered himself vulnerable to that evil spell by failing to fulfill the last requirement, that after having restored the princess's beauty he take seven steps backward before looking up at her.

Strikingly, Droßelmeier's tale includes Droßelmeier himself and casts the nutcracker as his handsome young nephew. That part of the idea for the tale is clearly related to the exchange that had occurred Christmas Eve between the godfather and goddaughter about the nutcracker doll's ugliness. Droßelmeier teasingly asked how Marie could possibly take such an ugly creature into her devoted care, whereupon she asked whether the godfather, if he were done up so nicely as the nutcracker doll, would look as good. In the tale he tells, Droßelmeier's role is first to find the hard nut and then to discover, in the nephew, someone who can crack it. The nephew's role is the romantic one of the handsome young man who rescues a beautiful princess from an evil spell. In Princess Pirlipat, Droßelmeier provides a role with which Marie can identify in a negative way. The princess refuses to wed young Droßelmeier when she sees that he has been turned into an ugly nutcracker doll. More important, the godfather provides the goddaughter with a positive role most appealing to her imagination, that of angel of rescue for the handsome young man whom Frau Mauserinks turned into a nutcracker.[7]

Marie's role as angel of rescue was suggested to Godfather Dro-ßelmeier in part by his having seen how, on Christmas Eve, the god-daughter took the nutcracker into her care when her brother had broken the doll's jaw by using it to crack a nut that was too big and hard. A twinge of envy surely seized the adoring godfather at that moment. Marie, meanwhile, devoted herself to caring for the injured doll. Her ensuing magical adventure at midnight that evening can be seen as the fulfillment of a wish that the nutcracker doll might be in reality a brave young man who would try to protect her against mice—stereotypically an object of terror or revulsion for her as a young girl—and to whose aid she would come should he encounter mortal danger on her behalf in combating the mice.[8]

After hearing her godfather's fairy tale about the hard nut, in which it is told that her nutcracker is Droßelmeier's nephew, Marie is hesitant to pick up the doll, which she now sees as a handsome young man. At the same time, she envisions herself, like beautiful young Princess Pirli-pat in that tale, as the object of attack from Frau Mauserinks and her son, the seven-headed King of Mice. Marie's ensuing magical adven-tures concern visits to her bedroom by the King of Mice to extort for-feits from her and her aiding Nutcracker in obtaining a sword with which to slay the mouse. After Nutcracker has defeated the villain, he transports Marie, via the sleeve in her father's overcoat, to his magical realm of dolls. There Marie falls asleep and awakens back home at her parents' house in Berlin. Her identification with Princess Pirlipat from her godfather's tale is then revealed when she talks out loud to herself one day about how, if she were Pirlipat, she would not reject young Droßelmeier because he has been turned into an ugly nutcracker doll.[9]

It is that declaration by seven-year-old Marie about the difference between herself and Princess Pirlipat that brings about the fairy-tale end-ing in which young Droßelmeier appears at her father's door to ask for her hand in marriage. The godfather's nephew explains that her declaration has just restored him to human form. That declaration of love for the ugly nutcracker doll, at the same time, produced a loud cry from Godfather Droßelmeier, who at that moment was in the living room with Marie working on the family's clock. There resulted an explosive jolt as well that caused Marie to fall off her chair in a faint, from which she recovers to learn that young Droßelmeier is at the door wishing to see her.

Hoffmann's readers are left to ponder the connection between the goddaughter's declaration of love for "Dear Mr. Droßelmeier," as she addresses the nutcracker in her reverie; the godfather's reaction; and the nephew's magical arrival. Since the nephew entered Marie's imagination as a character in the godfather's tale, we are perhaps to understand that the godfather's excitement over Marie's declaration of love to "Herr Droßelmeier" results from his embarrassed delight that he has indeed succeeded in getting the adored goddaughter to fantasize about marriage to the imaginary nephew who embodies for the godfather a younger, handsome self.[10]

As we have seen, the magical realm to which Marie is introduced in "Nußknacker und Mausekönig" is a romantic fantasy of her own making partly inspired by the tale told to her by her adoring godfather Droßelmeier. In all likelihood, the name Droßelmeier, as well as the story's inciting incident, was inspired by the Grimm fairy tale "König Droßelbart" (no. 52) in which a young king tames the pride of a haughty princess after she has rejected him as insufficiently handsome, ridiculing his chin and beard as making him look like a bird, the Droßel, or thrush. In Hoffmann's next tale, "Das fremde Kind" for the following year's volume of *Kinder-Mährchen* by Contessa, Fouqué, and Hoffmann (then included in *Die Serapionsbrüder*, vol. 2), the fantastic adventures of little Felix and Christlieb owe their inspiration to pious tales for children like those appended by the Grimm brothers at the end of their *Kinder- und Hausmärchen* (*Children's and Household Tales*, 1812; 1815; see seventh, definitive edition of 1857). This shift from romantic to pious fairy tale was surely in response to the criticism that Hoffmann's nutcracker story was more for adults than for children and that he was incapable of writing a proper children's fairy tale.

Felix and Christlieb von Brakel, a brother and sister of school age or approaching it, encounter a magical child while playing in the woods on their parents' estate. Like the nutcracker in the previous story, this magical playmate, known to the siblings as the Strange Child, is threatened by an evil adversary, in this case a gnome or earth-spirit named Pepser. The gnome, having adopted the alias Pepasilio to veil his identity, became prime minister to the Strange Child's mother in her kingdom. Pepasilio rebelled, causing that paradisiacal realm to be forever separated from the earth. The child tells Felix and Christlieb that his sojourn on earth must now end, since the gnome is master there. Sadly, they cannot join him in his return to his mother's kingdom because unlike him they are unable to fly.

The siblings' encounter with the Strange Child occurs as they and their parents are anticipating the arrival of a tutor whom a rich relative, Count Cyprianus von Brakel, is sending out to their modest estate so that the children might receive some schooling that the count considers proper to the family's social standing and in keeping with the latest fashion. In the tutor, Master Ink, the children discover the Strange Child's adversary, the Gnome Pepser, who was punished for his rebellion by being transformed into a fly. Even after Felix and Christlieb's father has chased off Master Ink with a flyswatter, the children are no longer able to find and communicate with the Strange Child. The children's father then soon dies, as though in punishment for having chased away the tutor.

Felix and Christlieb's encounters with the Strange Child are identified as fantasy insofar as the brother refers to the magical playmate as belonging to his sex, while the sister sees the child as a girl. The entry of the child into their lives occurs in connection with their anxiety about having their idyllic rural childhood disturbed or ended by the arrival of the tutor. Master Ink represents for them the specter of growing up and assuming a proper station in society. Their father, Thaddeus von Brakel, has not met that challenge fully, to judge from his impoverishment and deep financial indebtedness to Cousin Cyprianus. As the father reveals to Felix and Christlieb shortly before his death, when he was their age the Strange Child appeared to him as well. What Thaddeus von Brakel is saying to them is perhaps that he understands their sorrow at the prospect of leaving their childhood behind. The father's ensuing death can be seen as having been hastened by feelings of guilt that he had not provided better for his family and the recognition that his failure had resulted from his own reluctance to bid farewell to childhood bliss.

Following the father's death, hard-hearted Cousin Cyprianus chases Thaddeus's widow and the children from their estate. When their mother collapses on a bridge as they are on their way to seek refuge with other relatives, the Strange Child appears once more to Felix and Christlieb to comfort them. That last appearance of the magical playmate may be understood as a final indication that their encounters with the Strange Child are fantasies engendered by their emotional crisis.

The magical realm depicted in Hoffmann's fourth *Märchen, Klein Zaches genannt Zinnober (Little Zachary Named Cinnabar,* completed November 1818; published late 1818 or early 1819), is that of the French *conte des fées,* from which our English name for the genre of fairy tale comes. The worker of magic is a fairy, Rosabelverde (alias Canoness Rosengrünschön), reminiscent of such figures as the fairy godmother in "Cinderella," in particular the French version by Perrault. Here, however, the fairy has taken pity not on a beautiful girl being mistreated by her stepmother but on an ugly changeling who has been rejected by his own birth mother, a poor peasant woman.[11] Rosabelverde's magic being insufficient to transform Little Zachary into a handsome young fellow, she has to settle for providing his originally bald head with three magical hairs that will cause people to believe he has all the positive attributes and accomplishments of those around him. Since Little Zachary cannot be beautiful, wonderful, and successful in his own right, the fairy endows him with the automatic ability to "deck oneself out in foreign plumes" (*sich mit fremden Federn schmücken*), meaning to plagiarize, in this case in an extended sense.[12]

Little Zachary, although he has the title role, is not the central figure in the story. Indeed, he is inwardly at least as revolting as is his outer appearance. Our interest is chiefly directed instead toward a handsome dreamy youth, Balthasar, a student at the—imaginary—University of Kerepes. The gnomish changeling enters Balthasar's life on the very day Balthasar's friend and fellow student Fabian has accused him of being in love with pretty Candida, the daughter of their science professor Mosch Terpin. It is not until the next afternoon, however, that Little Zachary's magical hairs come into play. The occasion is a tea at the professor's house at which Balthasar has mustered the courage to admit to himself that he is in love with Candida and to confess that love in a poem he recites. When he finishes the recitation, the praise of those present is heaped not on him but on the ugly little changeling instead, of whom Candida becomes instantly enamored and whom the professor welcomes as his prospective son-in-law.

In his lover's dismay and disappointment, Balthasar himself finds access to the realm of magic in the sorcerer Prosper Alpanus, like Rosabelverde a character from the pages of French *contes des fées* such as those of Marie-Catherine Le Jumel de Barneville, Countess d'Aulnoy (ca. 1650–1705). Alpanus and Rosabelverde test their magical powers against each other when they sit down together for coffee. As a result of the fairy's visit to him, Alpanus is able to provide Balthasar with the magical means to defeat the spell that Little Zachary has worked on Candida, her father, and everyone else who has come into contact with him. Balthasar is thus able to wed his beloved, while her father is dismayed that Little Zachary, who seemed such a good match for the daughter and a benefactor for himself, has been unmasked as an impostor, so to speak.

The magical business in *Klein Zaches* clearly is a vehicle for Hoffmann to indulge in humorous if also occasionally biting satire on greed, false ambition, corruptibility, and vanity in contemporary life.[13] At the same time, the magical happenings can be seen as involving romantic fantasy as well. Particularly striking in this regard is that as soon as Balthasar has had to admit to himself that he is in love with Candida, a magical rival for her arrives on the scene in the person of Little Zachary. Moreover, as mentioned earlier, the magic of the changeling's hairs comes most strikingly into play at the moment when Balthasar is confessing that love to Candida with his poem. Balthasar's public rather than private declaration of love suggests either that by confessing it publicly he feels less likely to be rejected or that winning applause for the poem is his primary goal or both. Little Zachary's receiving the applause and thereby winning the girl's devotion can be understood as a magical fulfillment of what Balthasar was after, an indication that flattering his vanity was the overriding passion. Only when Balthasar finds himself rejected in favor of the ugly changeling does he seem spurred to ardent passion as opposed to vanity; this quality is found in a number of the younger bachelors in Hoffmann's tales and is not unrelated to their flight from erotic attraction into fantasy.

The same connection between vanity and sublimation of desire can be seen in Balthasar's rushing from Mosch Terpin's lectures on science out to the forest to commune with nature. In the lectures, Balthasar was horrified at the professor's probing into nature's sacred mysteries. At the same time, he was hiding from himself his attraction to the professor's pretty daughter. We can imagine that in the dreamy young student's unconscious the professor's way of relating to nature was associated with fantasies about how Mosch Terpin, as widower father, related to the creature of nature, his pretty daughter, in his own household. What Balthasar was repressing, in any case, was awareness of a desire to live with Candida himself as her husband.[14]

A young man's vanity as reflecting flight from desire is more clearly the subject of Hoffmann's next fairy tale, *Prinzessin Brambilla* (*Princess Brambilla,* completed 1820; published fall 1820, with the date 1821). In Rome, the pretty Italian seamstress Giacinta Soardi has set her cap on marrying her longtime boyfriend, the actor Giglio Fava, whose vanity is an obstacle to that aim. He admires and adores himself so much in his roles as languishing lover on stage that he continues the same role off-stage, rendering him unfit to become a bridegroom and husband. Giglio's vanity leads to his involvement with a magical realm reminiscent of *The Arabian Nights* and French *contes merveilleux* inspired by it, such as Anthony Hamilton's (1645–1719) *Les quatre Facardins* (1715), as well as mythical representations of the Creation such as those of the mystical nature philosopher (*naturphilosoph*) Gotthilf Heinrich Schubert. Thus, Giglio becomes passionately enamored of a magical princess named Brambilla, who in turn stands in symbolic relationship with a mythical Queen Mystilis.[15]

Queen Mystilis is born in a primeval spring (the *Urdarquelle*), the same body of water into which King Ophioch and his queen Liris had looked in order to cure his melancholy and her compulsive laughter by seeing their inverted reflections in the water. Mystilis seems to be the product in some way of those cures, which were followed by the king and queen finding happiness in their marriage for the first time and repairing to bed together. After Ophioch and Liris had died, Mystilis emerged from the lake as a baby girl whose immediate compulsive passion for making nets resulted in her being turned into a porcelain doll. The breaking of that evil spell is dependent on finding an "I" or self who can create its "not-I." In the end, it is the actor Giglio who achieves that feat. Through his action the spell on Queen Mystilis is broken, and she grows instantly to the gigantic proportions of an earth or nature goddess.

Princess Brambilla, meanwhile, is out to marry the Assyrian prince Cornelio Chiapperi, who in turn ardently wishes to marry her. The obstacle to that union is the actor Giglio, who is in love with Brambilla and ultimately convinces himself that he is Chiapperi and has slain Giglio. The problem for Giglio, though, is that he finds himself unable to distinguish the exotic beloved Brambilla from the pretty seamstress Giacinta. In the end, he simply has to give up and surrender himself to "Princess Brambilla," even if he cannot be sure that the beautiful beloved in question is not Giacinta instead. As it turns out, the girl of his dreams is indeed Giacinta and has been so all along.[16]

For her part, Giacinta has an exotic man of her dreams, as well, namely the same Assyrian prince Cornelio Chiapperi of whom Giglio's dream beloved Brambilla is enamored. Giacinta accepts Giglio as her bridegroom only after he has turned himself into Chiapperi by doing away with Giglio in a duel—that is, by believing that he has done so in acting out such combat. Actually Giacinta, as Brambilla, has required of Giglio that he cease playing the languishing stage lover that so flatters his vanity, as outwardly manifested by his dress as a stage prince, and embrace instead the role of comedian, by donning ludicrous attire appropriate to the role of the captain in the commedia dell'arte.[17] As Giglio comes to recognize, the only way he can cure himself of the "dualism" regarding himself and the girl of his dreams is for his "I" to create its "not-I," in other words for the stage lover Giglio to turn himself into a comedian. In the end Giglio becomes a bridegroom and husband. To his former vain bachelor self such a development perhaps was equated, unconsciously, with the dreaded prospect of becoming a comedian. Out of fear of being caught by Giacinta he escaped into fantasies about her imaginary look-alike Brambilla. His double identity suggests as much, Giglio meaning lily in Italian and Chiapperi being a name made from the verb for being caught or trapped (*chiappere*).[18]

Ultimately, Giglio is of course trapped by his own romantic attraction to Giacinta as sublimated in fantasies about Princess Brambilla. Giacinta is aided in catching Giglio, however, by two older men, the theater impresario Celionati and his friend Ruffiamonte, helped in turn by the theater tailor Bescapi and Giacinta's old housekeeper Beatrice. Celionati and Ruffiamonte bring Giglio to the point of proposing marriage to Giacinta; their names, indeed, may be understood as indicating that role, Celionati suggesting a meaning in Italian such as born of heaven or born of jest, recalling perhaps depictions of Cupid as a roguish winged infant in eighteenth-century rococo paintings, and Ruffiamonte suggesting connection with Italian *ruffiano* (pimp or go-between). Bescapi's role as tailor is to aid in getting Giglio to dress as a comedian instead of a romantic tragedian as part of the process of rendering him fit to wed Giacinta. Beatrice, as her name meaning "she who makes happy" suggests, is Giacinta's confidante and helper in affairs of the heart, a stock role for older women in traditional comedy as reflected for example in that of the procuress (*ruffiana*) in the commedia dell'arte.

It is Celionati, together with Ruffiamonte, who relates the mythical story about King Ophioch, Queen Liris, and the Urdarquelle that culminates in Mystilis's transformation into a porcelain doll because of her compulsive net making. Breaking that spell requires capturing a motley bird in nets the ladies in Celionati's Pistoja Palace have made, together with successful creation by an "I" of its "not-I." In the end, it is Giglio of course who fulfills those requirements, while Giacinta is identified not only with the imaginary Brambilla but also with the mythical Mystilis. Like Mystilis, we are presumably to understand, Giacinta was programmed from birth, that is biologically, to snare a man in her nets. By the same token, we may imagine, Giglio was destined willy-nilly, or biologically, to become a prisoner of Giacinta's and his own desire (the prisoner of love having been represented in emblematic tradition of the sixteenth through eighteenth centuries as a bird in a cage). In the doting eyes of the middle-aged bachelors Celionati and Ruffiamonte, Giacinta is an incarnation of the goddess of love, to judge from their fantasy about Queen Mystilis and her explosive swelling to cosmic proportions upon Giglio's surrender to desire for the pretty seamstress.[19]

With the capriccio *Prinzessin Brambilla*, as with the novella "Signor Formica" written the year before, Hoffmann sought to make clear to his readers his aim of combining Italian humor, as exemplified in Boccaccio's *Decameron* and in the commedia dell'arte, with German humor, especially its inclination to veiled irony. To that end, in *Prinzessin Brambilla* Hoffmann has Celionati engage in discussions of humor, at the Cafe Greco, with a German artist friend Reinhold and other German painters living in Rome. For Celionati the danger is that Germans will be too serious minded to understand the ironic jest involved in his project of getting Giglio to the altar with Giacinta. In the end, Celionati's idea of humor is fulfilled in Giglio and Giacinta's jesting about courtship and marriage, both as a team performing on stage in the commedia dell'arte and in their lives offstage as a happily married couple.[20]

Like *Prinzessin Brambilla,* Hoffmann's next to last fairy tale, "Die Königsbraut" ("The King's Bride," written spring 1821; published toward the end of that year in *Die Serapionsbrüder,* vol. 4), concerns a young man whose vanity, in this case his imagining himself to be a poet, stands in the way of his marrying. The young man in question, Amandus von Nebelstern, is not the central figure, however. Instead, it is his intended, Anna von Zabelthau, who for her part becomes enthralled by a magical creature. Anna's fantastic adventure follows upon her discovering in her vegetable garden to which she is uncommonly devoted a carrot that has grown through a ring. Reacting to her widower father's claim that the unusual find means that an elemental spirit, an earth sprite, wishes to court her, Anna prefers to believe that the suitor is instead one Daucus Carota, who is king in the realm of vegetables.

The widower father's interpretation of his daughter's finding results from his preoccupation with literature about elemental spirits. His devotion to that study concerns his hope that he might sufficiently purify himself of all baser desires to dare to marry an air sprite or sylph. The father, Dapsul von Zabelthau, at first warns Anna about her having become the object of a gnome's attentions, earth sprites being the basest of the elemental spirits. Once Dapsul has met Daucus Carota, however, he changes his mind and warms to the idea that he and his daughter might simultaneously marry elemental spirits in a double wedding. Bothered though by Anna's contrary belief that Daucus Carota is not the gnome Corduanspitz, but instead the Vegetable King, Dapsul seeks to disenchant her by unmasking Daucus for her as writhing in a cesspool of filth and ugliness. When Dapsul then tries to do away with the unwanted carrot-shaped suitor entirely by cooking him in a pot in Anna's kitchen, the result is her transformation into a carrot and the father into a poisonous mushroom. She and her father remain transformed until the carrot suitor who has retreated to his underground realm beckons for her to put the ring back on him by pushing his carrot tip up through the ground. Therewith the original situation is restored and Anna's magical adventure ends.

What then of Anna's young neighbor, Amandus von Nebelstern, whom she wanted to marry before her discovery of the carrot grown through the ring? The carrot appeared after Amandus had left to study at the university and Anna had written to him that her father had no objection to their marrying. The reply she received from Amandus, with whom she had not previously raised the subject of marriage, was not as she wished, he seeming to be completely consumed with fancying himself a poet. Worse still, even when Anna writes to inform Amandus that she has met and fallen in love with Daucus Carota and plans to wed him instead, Amandus does not rush home and rid himself of the rival. In the end, he returns only in response to Anna's call for him to rescue her from Daucus, whom she now portrays to him as an evil sorcerer. Instead of saving Anna, however, Amandus on his return strikes up a friendship with Daucus, who holds out to him the prospect of becoming his court poet. Anna succeeds in landing Amandus as her bridegroom only after, faced with Amandus's recital of his poetry, Daucus has fled to his underground realm, Anna has returned the ring to him, and Amandus has been cured of fancying himself a poet as a result of Anna's inadvertently hitting him in the head with her garden spade.

Hoffmann's readers are left to wonder what is signified by Anna's adventure with the carrot. Finding in her kitchen garden a carrot grown through a ring would understandably delight a girl who since childhood has been a passionate gardener.[21] The find, though, happens when Anna, at 16, has reached marriageable age, is entertaining thoughts of wedding the neighbor boy Amandus, and has just had cold water thrown on that desire by his letter in response to her overtures. Her dream of marrying, we may understand, is reflected in the carrot with the ring around it. The carrot calls to mind the ring finger with a wedding ring on it as token of the physical and spiritual consummation of the union.

Dapsul's parallel dream of marrying a sylph may be understood as related to his situation as widower father to a pretty daughter who has reached marriageable age. At the outset, when Anna goes to her father about her desire to marry Amandus, he speaks darkly about a danger or peril that Amandus must confront if he is to wed her. Nonetheless, Dapsul seems to accept the inevitability of their union when he humorously remarks that since her intended's name is a Latin gerund, Amandus clearly is "one who in this matter shall and must" (*SB*, 952). At the same time, Dapsul speaks as though the thing is one of indifference to him, asking only that Anna inform him of the wedding date.

Once Anna has found the carrot with the ring in her garden, Dapsul is quick to see in her discovery a confirmation of his foretelling that Amandus would have to overcome some peril if he is to wed Anna. When Dapsul now identifies that peril as the desire of a gnome to wed her, he is interpreting the carrot with the ring around it in connection with his dream of wedding an elemental spirit himself. It is perhaps not amiss to infer that Dapsul's dream of marrying a sprite is a sublimation engendered by an embarrassed, repressed romantic infatuation with his nubile daughter. Seen this way, Dapsul's interpretation of Anna's find as indicating an earth sprite wants to wed her suggests perhaps his guilt over that gnomish urge in himself, an interpretation that is all the more likely considering that the ring around the carrot may be the one, so we learn, that Dapsul gave her when she was a little girl. Dapsul's gnomish guilt may be reflected, too, in his subsequent identification of the carrot as "Tsilmenech" alias "Corduanspitz," an earth sprite who reputedly was able purify himself sufficiently to maintain a spiritual union in Cordova, Spain, with the abbess Magdalena de la Croix from her 12th year (the onset of her nubility?) onward. By contrast, while Dapsul is able to refrain from eating breakfast in his effort to purify himself of baser urges so that he might dare to wed his sylph "Nehahilah," his resolve always weakens by the time of the noon meal, which he takes with his pretty daughter.[22]

The miraculous realm in the last of Hoffmann's seven fairy tales, *Meister Floh* (*Master Flea,* completed March 1822 and published that same spring), is of a mythical, primeval sort. A leech prince kisses the beautiful Princess Gemaheh on the neck with a blood-sucking bite as she lies sleeping at Famagusta (on Cyprus, where famous temples to the Greek love goddess Aphrodite are located). The princess dies as a result of the bite, and her corpse is carried away through the air by the Genius Thetel.

Two Dutch scientists, Leuwenhoeck and Swammerdamm, observe her abduction through their telescopes, then rediscover her in a tulip with their microscopes. They revive her with the bite of a flea, on whose bites she then is dependent for remaining alive. Master Flea, however, escapes from Leuwenhoeck's flea circus, whereupon Leuwenhoeck attempts to recapture him, while Princess Gemaheh, in her alias as the magical Dutch beauty Dörtje Elwerdink, tries to gain possession of Master Flea herself to be independent of Leuwenhoeck. Because Master Flea has sought refuge with a rich bachelor in Frankfurt am Main, Gemaheh alias Dörtje tries to seduce the bachelor in order to seize the flea.

Hoffmann focuses our interest, however, not on the magical princess or the magical flea but on the 36-year-old bachelor Peregrinus Tyß. We meet him at the outset as he eagerly waits on Christmas Eve for his housekeeper and former nursemaid to finish preparing his Christmas tree and the toys that he has spent the day buying for himself. After he has had a chance to play with the toys, just as he did when he was a child, he packs them up and delivers them, as he does every Christmas Eve, to a poor family with young children. While he is on this charitable errand the seductively beautiful magical princess Gemaheh alias Dörtje enters his life, fainting in his arms and begging him to carry her to her lodgings. To Peregrinus's panicked astonishment, home for her means his own house. Unknowingly, Peregrinus had brought Master Flea home in one of the toys he purchased for his Christmas. Dörtje, perceiving this, contrives to get Peregrinus to bring her home in hopes that she might manage to gain possession of the life-sustaining flea. The middle-aged bachelor's ensuing involvement with the seductive beauty concerns her continuing efforts to capture him and his protégé Master Flea. In the end, Peregrinus is saved from succumbing to Dörtje's charms by meeting and falling in love with the daughter of the poor couple to whom he had brought the toys that Christmas Eve, Röschen Lämmerhirt.[23]

Peregrinus is helped in avoiding Dörtje's snares by the interventions of a friend from his student days at the University of Jena, George Pepusch, who is himself in love with Dörtje. Pepusch's attraction to her has primeval origins, in view of his mythical identity as the Thistle Zeherit, he having fallen in love with her in her mythical identity as Princess Gamaheh. More recently, Pepusch's passion for the magical beauty is owing to his infatuation with her as a singer in Leuwenhoeck's flea circus, a singer whose popularity resulted in her being given the name Aline, Queen of Golconda, the heroine in a then-popular opera of the same name by Henri Montan Berton (1767–1844; *Aline, Reine de*

Golconde, 1803). Whenever it seems that Dörtje (alias Gamaheh alias Aline) is about to have her way with Peregrinus, Pepusch arrives as if on cue to lay claim to her. Pepusch indeed wins Dörtje in the end. On the morning after Peregrinus and Röschen's wedding night, they find Dörtje, as a Dutch tulip, wound around Pepusch's wilted blossom as a *cactus grandiflorus.* Now in no danger of being captured since Dörtje–Gemaheh is no longer around to yearn for his life-sustaining bites, Master Flea remains attached to Peregrinus as guardian spirit of his family and household.

The losers in the bizarre struggle over the mythical princess and the flea are the Dutch scientists Leuwenhoeck and Swammerdamm. Leuwenhoeck never regains possession of Master Flea and hence not Dörtje either. Swammerdamm early on lost out to Leuwenhoeck because of the latter's possession of the life-sustaining flea; and his attempt to win Dörtje after all by taking a room in Peregrinus's house as a certain "Herr Swammer" likewise comes to naught. Toward the end, the mythical leech prince and the Genius Thetel enter the fray under (satirically appropriate) French aliases, the former as a customs official, the latter as a ballet dancer. In a sense, Peregrinus's old housekeeper Aline loses out, too, when Peregrinus marries Röschen; for after her initial scolding of Peregrinus for bringing home a seductively clad beauty, the housekeeper herself became vicariously taken with the young woman, especially upon discovering that they shared the same name, Aline being the name under which Dörtje introduced herself to Peregrinus as he was carrying her home that fateful Christmas Eve.[24]

The sharing of the name Aline between the ugly housekeeper and the seductive beauty may hold the key to understanding them as creatures of Peregrinus's fantasy. As we remember, it was Peregrinus's magical friend George Pepusch who encountered the mythical Princess Gamaheh alias Dörtje Elwerdink under that name. If we view Pepusch as Peregrinus's image of himself from his student days, then we can understand that he might endow his phantom housekeeper with the name Aline because he is in no danger of succumbing to her romantically. That would explain why the other, wildly appealing Aline appears to him that Christmas Eve attired as a stage princess, and also why this happens as he is about to leave the scene of domestic happiness at the Lämmerhirts. That evening, we may imagine, he is feeling a twinge of remorse that he has not married and started a family. Marriage, however, is associated in his mind with surrendering to passion for a woman, hence the specter of an infatuation like that which he, as Pepusch, experienced as a student with the singer Aline. That specter in turn might produce a yearning for an appealing but not threateningly seductive girl like the one Peregrinus marries in the end, Röschen Lämmerhirt. Peregrinus's ultimate discovery that the Lämmerhirts have just such a daughter thus comes as though in answer to a prayer. The name Lämmerhirt meaning shepherd calls to mind—especially in the context of Peregrinus's Christmas adventure—Christ as savior, while according at the same time with Röschen's nonthreatening nature, she being indeed as gentle as a lamb.

Chapter Seven
The Two Novels

Hoffmann's fame is as a master of the fantastic tale, of which his seven fairy tales can be considered a subgenre. His few attempts at drama were mostly early and came to naught. As he himself recognized, he had no appreciable talent for writing verse. But what of Hoffmann as novelist? When still a student at the university in his native Königsberg he made two attempts at the genre, the completed manuscript "Cornaro" that he unsuccessfully submitted for publication and the presumably abortive effort he entitled "Der Geheimnisvolle." When he later was launching himself in earnest as an author, following the contract with Kunz for the *Fantasiestücke,* the idea of succeeding as a novelist surfaced again in the spring of 1814 in Leipzig just after Hoffmann had lost his position as conductor with Joseph Seconda's theater company.

Considering that he had at that time just completed his fairy-tale masterpiece *Der goldne Topf,* with which he himself was extremely pleased, it is surprising that he now returned to the idea of writing novels. Practical considerations surely played a large part. His financial situation was quite desperate. Novel writing must have seemed to offer the prospect of quicker and larger monetary gain than producing the fourth and last volume of *Fantasiestücke.* It may have been, too, that he wished to see whether the fantastic mode of his shorter fiction could be adapted to the novel.[1]

The result of this attempt was *Die Elixiere des Teufels (The Devil's Elixirs,* 2 vols.; 1815, 1816). As the title indicates, the element of the fantastic or supernatural has to do—at least ostensibly—with the influence of the devil. The story of the young monk Medardus resembles those of the saints. Indeed, he sees himself experiencing temptation like that which afflicted St. Anthony (ca. 250–356) in the desert. The temptation occurs after he has been charged with the care of one of the bottles of wine with which, it is claimed, the devil had tempted Anthony. In Medardus's case the temptation is to lust after St. Rosalia as she is depicted in a painting that hangs near the confessionals in his Capuchin monastery in Germany. As fate, or perhaps the devil, would have it, Medardus meets up with a living counterpart to the depicted saint in the person of a young aristocratic woman, Aurelia, whom he yearns to possess. His lust leads him out into the world, where he is tormented by encounters with doubles who either inflame that lust or rebuke him for it. After one of these doubles murders Aurelia, Medardus's thoughts turn to union with her in heaven as St. Rosalia. Thus, in the end it is as though St. Rosalia as Aurelia had been sent by God to test the young monk's faith and obedience to his oath of celibacy.

Beyond its parallel to the saints' lives, Medardus's story is also one involving a family curse and its removal. The story of the curse begins with one of Medardus's ancestors, a young Italian painter named Francesko who was apprenticed to the famous Leonardo da Vinci (1452–1519). The curse, if it may be called that, is a confounding of fleshly lust with holy inspiration, which compels Francesko the Painter to portray St. Rosalia as Venus, leads him to believe that his Venus-like consort was in league with the devil, and causes him to turn to visions of St. Rosalia praying for him in heaven. A similar compulsion to fleshly lust and blasphemy has afflicted Francesko the Painter's male descendants in a direct line to Medardus, including Medardus's father Franz (called Francesko), his grandfather Paolo Francesko, and his great-grandfather Francesko the Foundling. With Medardus's return to his monastery and devotion to the hope of being united in heaven with Aurelia as St. Rosalia, an end to the family curse will finally be at hand, since he will then not father any children.

Aside from the temptations of the devil and the workings of the family curse, Medardus's adventures involve his struggle with mental illness. In particular, his encounters with doubles project his sense that he is losing his mind since the doubles themselves appear subject to insanity. The chief double figure, the libertine Count Viktorin, whose identity Medardus assumes after he has caused Viktorin to plunge from a cliff, seems crazed by lust. The other figure in whom Medardus finds a ghostly double, young Hermogen, appears to have lost his sanity over his self-appointed role as protector of his sister Aurelia's virtue against the seductions of Viktorin, and hence of Medardus as Viktorin's impersonator. When Medardus subsequently succumbs to temporary insanity, it is at the moment when his double, presumably in the person of either Viktorin or Hermogen, challenges him for the physical possession of Aurelia on the day that she and Medardus are to be wed. And Medardus's ultimate dedication to the vision of his union with Aurelia as St. Rosalia in heaven comes after the lust-crazed double has murdered Aurelia as she is about to become a bride of Christ as a Cistercian nun.[2]

Medardus's difficulties with lust and erotic desire began well before his encounters with his ghostly doubles, however. As Franz, a 16-year-old pupil at the monastery school, he experienced a crisis of embarrassment over his attraction to his music teacher's sister. The origin of the attraction was erotic in nature, stemming from his having seen the girl in a state of undress one day when he arrived for his lesson. The youth's embarrassment came when her girlfriends noticed him distractedly kissing a glove she had dropped. Franz's memory of the incident surfaces as the monastery's prior, Leonhardus, asks him about his knowledge of and feelings about sexuality in view of Franz's intention to become a priest. Recalling the ridicule he suffered for his mooning over the girl, Franz begs the prior to allow him to take orders and to complete the novitiate in much less time than normally required. At his subsequent investiture as Medardus, he sees or imagines that he sees the girl sitting melancholy and tearful in the congregation.

The crisis of erotic desire for Medardus comes then five years later. He has begun to doubt his calling as a monk, to resent having locked himself away in a monastery, and, through self-glorification as a preacher, to relieve that doubt and compensate himself for having renounced the world. One day in the confessional he hears a young woman declare her sinful love for him. As the girl confesses, Medardus gazes at the painting of St. Rosalia, whom he assumes the veiled young woman must resemble. The experience of having heard the confession of love and having envisioned the young woman as looking like the depiction of St. Rosalia leaves Medardus no peace. He is contemplating flight from the monastery to search for the girl when Prior Leonhardus asks him to accept a mission to Rome. If desire tormented Medardus inside the monastery, on the outside he is beset by seemingly endless encounters with lust, madness, corruption, and other dangers and evils, so that in the end he is happy to return to the peace and security of cloistered life. Final peace, as we have seen, is then brought to him by visions of union with Aurelia, the girl in the confessional, as St. Rosalia in heaven.

Medardus's struggle with erotic desire has its origins, too, in his mother's raising him to believe that he was especially chosen by God for a saintly life. She told how a miraculous child, seemingly the Baby Jesus, had been brought to play with him when he was an infant and how he was destined to expiate unspecified sins of his father.[3] As part of her vision of a saintly life for young Franz, she brought him to her friend, the abbess of a Cistercian convent, so that he could attend the neighboring Capuchin monastery school. The abbess appears to share the mother's vision for her son and is there to admonish him when he later surrenders to the temptation of blasphemous self-glorification in his preaching. At the same time, though, the godmother appears to feel an erotic attraction to the boy, as least so Medardus remembers sensing when he was first introduced to her.

Medardus's subsequent infatuation with the painting depicting St. Rosalia also may be understood as erotic in nature, particularly in view of what we learn about the painting's origin from the parchment about his ancestors and the family curse. In doing the portrayal of St. Rosalia, on commission from a Capuchin monastery near Rome, his ancestor Francesko the Painter used for the face that of a girl with whom he had fallen secretly, unconsciously, and guiltily in love at Leonardo da Vinci's atelier and for the body depictions of the goddess of love, Venus. The inspiration for the painting having been in that sense impure and the aim blasphemous, Medardus's attraction to that portrayal of St. Rosalia may be seen to have involved similar urges.

As Medardus tells us, he relates his story as a form of penance for having surrendered to satanic temptation. We are therefore left to decide whether we wish to believe that his extravagant adventures actually happened or are products of his fantasy. The first of his memoir's seven chapters or sections, entitled "Die Jahre der Kindheit und das Klosterleben" ("The Childhood Years and Life in the Monastery"), do not contain any clearly supernatural adventures, which Medardus experiences only beginning with the second chapter, "Der Eintritt in die Welt" ("The Entry into the World"). Considering that we are dealing with a memoir, it is appropriate to consider the possibility that the fantastic adventures Medardus relates represent his imaginings about what he would have encountered should he have left the security of the monastery. Meanwhile, precisely that fear of what would happen to him has kept him from actually venturing beyond the monastery's walls. Viewed this way, Medardus's account of his mad, sinful adventures serves him as a rationalization for remaining in the monastery and renouncing life on the outside. The story of his childhood and his becoming a monk, then, show us why monastic life suits him. The experience of erotic desire fills him with panic and guilt, desire he sublimates through dreams of being united in heaven with St. Rosalia as she is depicted in the painting.[4]

One of the countless puzzles posed for Hoffmann's readers by *Die Elixiere des Teufels* is why Medardus did not include his ancestor Francesko the Painter's parchment in his memoir. After Medardus was given the manuscript at the Capuchin monastery near Rome, he himself recognized that he found confirmed there much of what he had intimated about himself and his ancestry. Perhaps we are to understand that the prior of that monastery did not allow Medardus to keep the parchment. However, Hoffmann's editor of Medardus's memoir had it available to him for insertion at the point where, as Medardus relates, he received the parchment to read. Perhaps we are to understand that Medardus did not wish to reveal or admit to himself that the inspiration for the painting that catapulted him into his wild adventures was not a vision of St. Rosalia, but instead one of Venus's body with the face of a girl with whom the painter had been unconsciously and guiltily infatuated. Medardus would not wish to have to think or have us recognize that the effect of the painting on him had been rather sensual than spiritual, hence his belief that he was hearing St. Rosalia incarnate, in the person of Aurelia, declaring her sinful passion for him in the confessional. Moreover, the ancestor Francesko's infatuation with the girl in Leonardo da Vinci's atelier may be seen to parallel Medardus's first embarrassed, guilty experience of erotic desire after seeing his music teacher's sister in a state of undress.

It is indeed the memoir's editor, not Medardus himself, who declares that what is recounted in the parchment is essential for a proper understanding of the memoir. The editor, however, does not say exactly what is in the parchment that makes it so important. Since in the novel's subtitle, "Nachgelassene Papiere des Bruders Medardus eines Kapuziners / Herausgegeben von dem Verfasser der Fantasiestücke in Callots Manier" ("Posthumous Papers of Brother Medardus, a Capuchin / Edited by the Author of the Fantasy-Pieces in Callot's Manner"), the editor of the memoir is identified with Hoffmann and his enthusiast from the earlier work, we can imagine that for the editor the story surrounding the painting of St. Rosalia is of paramount importance. Here, as elsewhere in Hoffmann's tales, we find the cautionary theme that an artist should not physically consummate his passion for the woman who is the inspiration for his art. Francesko, in the end, embraces the belief that the girl from Leonardo's atelier, with whom he sired a child once she had grown to Venus-like voluptuousness and had reentered his life, was an agent sent by the devil to tempt him. After she has died in childbirth, Francesko has a vision of St. Rosalia interceding for him in heaven and wanders off, absent-mindedly leaving behind in a cave the son to whom the woman had given birth. Here we recognize the motif, familiar in Hoffmann's tales from "Ignaz Denner" to "Meister Johannes Wacht," that fathers react to sons as being of satanic origin, whereas daughters are angelic objects of adoration and infatuation. For Hoffmann's enthusiast then, as fictive author of the *Fantasiestücke* and fictive editor of the *Elixiere des Teufels,* the moral of Francesko's story is that artists should not wed their muses and the lesson of Medardus's memoir is that, by the same token, one should not profane art by succumbing to lust for women depicted in paintings.

Hoffmann, as we know, was very much an art lover himself. The role of the enthusiast he created with his *Fantasiestücke,* though, was one hardly devoid of irony and indeed a case of self-humorous depiction. Hoffmann's own perspective on Medardus's memoir, as distinguished from that of his enthusiast, is perhaps hinted at in the anecdote told in the novel by a court physician (volume 1, chapter 4). In that anecdote, an eccentric British bachelor named Ewson never quite admits to himself that his strange inability to tear himself away from the German inn where he was staying resulted from his having fallen dotingly in love with the innkeeper's daughters. We may indeed suspect that the anecdote is one of Hoffmann's fanciful depictions of his infatuation with his music pupil Julchen Marc. Medardus's crisis over the St. Rosalia painting, at any rate, appears to represent a suppression of awareness of that crisis's connection with his earlier embarrassment about mooning over the concert master's sister.

An ironic epilogue to Medardus's memoir is provided at the novel's end by Pater Spiridion's account of Medardus's death. According to that account, Medardus expired on the same day and at the same hour that Aurelia was murdered, namely at noon on 5 September (4 September, the date on which Medardus's death throes begin, is St. Rosalia's day). In his report, which Pater Spiridion writes he is making "to the greater glory of God,"[5] Medardus's death is recounted almost as that of a saint, certainly as a death at which St. Rosalia was present in spirit. At the same time, the account Pater Spiridion gives serves as a suitably pious end to Medardus's memoir as a monkish love story. The truth of the report is dubious on several grounds other than the uncanny happenings related therein. At the beginning of the second half of Medardus's memoir (volume 2, chapter 1), he appears to be referring to himself when he speaks of "a monk grown gray who in his dark cell thinks of the sunny time of his love" (*ET/KM,* 153). The impression is thus given that Medardus is writing his memoir in old age, or at least in much later years, meaning that he could not very well have died on the first anniversary of Rosalia's death, as Pater Spiridion claims. We can on that count believe Spiridion when he declares that he has not read Medardus's memoir. At the same time, that declaration is suspect as a deceit to make it seem impossible that Spiridion has tailored the happenings in his report to fit the story contained in the memoir in order to render those occurrences the more uncanny. In all likelihood, Hoffmann means for us to understand that Spiridion's claim not to have read the memoir, like his report as a whole, is intended to serve "the greater glory of God" by providing a piously miraculous ending to the account of a life that it would be best monks not read at all. As Hoffmann's editor indeed reports in his foreword, he received the manuscript from a prior who, while evidently not having known Medardus, was familiar with the memoir's contents since he remarked to the editor that the manuscript really should have been burned.

Unlike *Die Elixiere des Teufels,* Hoffmann's other published novel, *Lebens-Ansichten des Katers Murr,* remained unfinished. The first two volumes appeared in 1819 and 1821, respectively. The writing of the projected third and concluding volume was prevented by Hoffmann's death. Also unlike the earlier novel with its many supernatural adventures, *Kater Murr* has no element of the miraculous, nor even the fantastic. To be sure, the title role belongs to a tomcat gifted with speech; but that is no more than a convention of the literary genre of the fable. Like animals in the fable, Tomcat Murr and his feline and canine friends come by their gift of speech naturally, not requiring a witch's spell as with Hoffmann's title role in the earlier "Nachricht von den neuesten Schicksalen des Hundes Berganza" or even a bump on the head from a coconut like the educated ape Milo in the subsequent humorously satirical piece "Nachricht von einem gebildeten jungen Mann" (1814 in the *AMZ,* then in vol. 4 of the *Fantasiestücke*). Even in the other half of this double novel referred to in the subtitle ("nebst fragmentarischer Biographie des Kapellmeisters Johannes Kreisler in zufälligen Makulaturblättern"), nothing of a clearly supernatural sort occurs in this "biography" of the young romantic composer Johannes Kreisler.

However, the Kreisler biography has a decidedly fantastic character in a novelistic sense. Among the chief figures are two aristocratic Neapolitan brothers, the elder of whom, Antonio, poisoned his beloved Angela because he suspected her of deceiving him with the younger brother Hektor. Then there is the organ builder Master Abraham, rescuer of a young Italian girl, Chiara, from her impresario Severino, who was abusing her by having her serve as the invisible maiden in his clairvoyant seances. Finally, there is the equally sham court, Sieghartshof, of

Prince Irenäus, who recently lost his lands in the political reshuffling in Germany at the Congress of Vienna (1815) following the defeat of Napoleon. Prince Irenäus's daughter Hedwiga inclines to hysteria and is subject to cataleptic seizures, while her brother Ignaz, heir to a throne that actually no longer exists, is an out-and-out imbecile. The prince himself, in whom the son's idiocy is somewhat prefigured, appears the dupe of a woman in his court circle, a widow named Counciloress Benzon with whom he has maintained an undefined liaison.[6]

The main interest in the Kreisler biography lies of course not with any of the figures just described but with the still young, thirtyish composer himself and his beloved, Counciloress Benzon's 16-year-old daughter Julia. The story of their love is the actual novel and is a romantic depiction of erotic desire sublimated through devotion to a dream of transcendent longing. That is to say, the story of Julia and Kreisler's passion is, and is intended to be, the stuff of a romantic novel par excellence. The other more ordinary and mundane novelistic elements referred to earlier serve as a contrasting backdrop to the sublime love between the romantic composer and the blossoming virginal maiden.[7]

The most jarring of these contrasts is that between Kreisler's love of Julia and the lusting after her on the part of the Neapolitan prince Hektor who has the role here of a veritable Don Juan, only more arrogant and sinister. Hektor, who has come from Naples to Sieghartshof to marry Princess Hedwiga, is drawn to Hedwiga's friend Julia by the same quality of her virginal innocence and purity as is the romantic composer Kreisler, though, in Hektor's case, like Mozart's Don Giovanni (Hoffmann's favorite opera, it seems), because of the challenge thereby posed to his powers of seduction.

Hektor's intended, Princess Hedwiga, meanwhile, envies Julia that innocence and purity that both awakens Hektor's satanic lust and inspires in the composer Kreisler a dream of transcendent love. Hedwiga, though herself presumably likewise still a virgin, lost her innocence regarding the power of lust already as a three-year-old when the painter Leonhard Ettlinger succumbed to madness over his attraction to her mother Princess Maria whose portrait he had been commissioned to do. Now 16, like her companion Julia, Hedwiga is obsessed with the thought of herself and Julia as objects of male lust, principally on the part of the libertine Hektor, but on the part of Kreisler as well, in whom she hysterically sees a potential reincarnation of the portraitist Ettlinger driven mad by a conflict between lust and a dream of transcendent love.

Julia's mother, Counciloress Benzon, too, may be seen to envy her daughter as the object of Kreisler's sublime, transcendent passion, insofar as she herself earlier had a role as his confidante. At any rate, she has no use for the budding love between Kreisler and Julia because it might stand in the way of her plan to wed Julia to Prince Irenäus's imbecilic son and heir Ignaz. That cold-hearted plan, in turn, is meant to compensate Counciloress Benzon for having been Prince Irenäus's mistress without thereby achieving actual regal status. Her role as spoiler of romantic bliss extends as well to her putative involvement in the disappearance of Master Abraham's young wife Chiara. There also remains the mystery surrounding Counciloress Benzon's possible relationship with Hektor and Antonio's beloved Angela, the latter being possibly her daughter fathered by Prince Irenäus. What seems clear is that the counciloress is the type of the older woman whose passion is now to avenge herself for disappointments in love suffered as a younger woman.

Master Abraham has the contrasting role of encouraging the sublime love between Julia and Kreisler as their self-appointed confidant. Abraham sees in that love a parallel to his own dream of transcendent union with his lost young bride Chiara. Indeed, he seeks in the fulfillment of Kreisler and Julia's sublime devotion to one another a sign that he and Chiara will find each other again in a similar transcendent union, a token that he and his erstwhile "invisible maiden" will be reunited spiritually.

From Abraham's account of his life and relationship with Chiara, some doubt is cast on the spiritual purity of that love. To be sure, Abraham first fell in love with Chiara sight unseen in her role as the invisible maiden in the sham spiritualistic seances presided over by the charlatan Severino. Abraham believed her voice to be that of a spirit rather than a woman of flesh and blood. The conflict in that passion for Chiara begins with his discovery that she is not a spirit but a young girl whom Severino has abused by hiding her in a cramped space to aid him in deceiving his public. In Abraham's account the enormity of this abuse appears somewhat exaggerated. Abraham, in any case, passionately embraced the romantic role of Chiara's rescuer, while at the same time avoiding the possibility of becoming her suitor by departing and leaving her behind in the care of others. For her part Chiara, however, yearned to resume the role of invisible maiden and sought out Abraham in the hope that he would use her in that fashion and take her in to live with him. The specter of becoming a second Severino, an abuser of innocent young girls, and of having her serve as his housekeeper greatly troubles Abraham. His guilt about using and cohabiting with Chiara leads to his marrying her, only to have her then mysteriously taken from him. Abraham's subsequent dream of union with Chiara is thus a return to his original passion for her as a spirit, a dream of transcendent love now motivated by a guilty sense of himself as a Severino, an abuser of young maidens (such as the would-be ones portrayed in *opera buffa* and the *commedia dell'arte*[8]).

While Master Abraham's dream of transcendent union with Chiara is endangered by the specter of abuse, the competition of the two Neapolitan brothers Hektor and Antonio for Angela's love involved hot-blooded jealous passion and murderous lust. Believing that Angela had deceived him with Hektor, Antonio poisoned her, whereupon he was mortally wounded by Hektor. When he did not die from the wound, Antonio attributed the recovery to the dead beloved, declaring that Angela in heaven had worked a saintly miracle. Turning his crime of murdering her to his advantage and aggrandizement, Antonio became a monk, taking the name Cyprianus and touring Europe to proclaim the miracle that had been wrought on him. Both Antonio's jealous love in poisoning Angela and the hypocrisy of his claim to have been the object of a holy miracle brought about by her contrast sharply with Kreisler's transcendent passion for Julia.

Antonio, as the monk Cyprianus, serves as a cautionary figure for Kreisler. Like the monk Medardus's libertine double in Hoffmann's earlier novel, Antonio murders the beloved out of jealous passion, whereupon, like Medardus himself, Antonio as Cyprianus devotes himself to visions of the slain beloved as a saint specially devoted to him. Kreisler finds the revelations about Cyprianus so horrifying because, we may surmise, he senses that his dream of transcendent love with Julia similarly might have its origins in erotic passion that could lead to murderous jealousy. Such self-identification would help explain why Kreisler, immediately after learning Cyprianus's story, removes himself precipitously and mysteriously from the vicinity and also from Julia and why he fails to return for Princess Maria's name day later despite Master Abraham's plea that he do so.

Earlier, Princess Hedwiga had tried unsuccessfully to make herself romantically interesting to Kreisler by telling him the story about the painter Ettlinger and claiming that Kreisler reminded her of him.[9] Kreisler rejected that identification and its implication that he could be seized by such madness. Cyprianus's story, however, appears to hit home with Kreisler, perhaps because of the monk's attempt to believe and make others understand that he was the special object of a female saint's devotion, when secretly he had murdered her out of jealous passion. That is to say, lust has guiltily and self-deceivingly masqueraded as transcendence for Cyprianus. Even Master Abraham's passion for Chiara involved a problematical intermingling of erotic desire and transcendent yearning. Kreisler perhaps sensed that intermingling, which would help explain his failure to heed Abraham's plea to return for the name day celebration.

The love interest in *Kater Murr*, of course, rests not with the tomcat's autobiography but with the Kreisler story, and ultimately with the still-young composer's passion for Julia. That is not to say, though, that love is not a theme in the tomcat story. Murr displays proclivities with which tomcats are popularly credited. Early on, he attempts to mate at first sight with the female cat Miesmies on a rooftop, only to be prevented by her tomcat brothers from doing so. He discovers that he has fallen in love and attempts cures for lovesickness he finds in Ovid's *Ars amatoria* (*Publius Ovidius Naso,* 43 B.C.–ca. 17 A.D.). The cures having failed, he woos and wins Miesmies, then soon sours on love when she begins to be unfaithful to him. Later, when he and Miesmies, having reconciled, are at a dance together, he becomes infatuated with a young female kitten Mina only to suffer the embarrassment of hearing from Miesmies that Mina is their daughter. Still later, Murr is foolish enough to become enamored of an elegant greyhound bitch Minona, who quickly cools his ardor by literally dousing him with cold water.[10]

As Murr's experience with Minona suggests, dogs in the tomcat autobiography have a higher standing in the society of canines and felines. Dogs are proverbially man's best friend, a connection that is shown to pay off in Murr's world. Cats, by contrast, are loners, and in this depiction suffer the consequences of not being as well connected socially as the dogs. Human society, Hoffmann may be suggesting in this satirical depiction, is "for the dogs." No self-respecting cat should want to be a part of it. Murr's experiences with human society come chiefly through his friendship with just such a well-connected dog Ponto. The name, suggesting bridge, may refer to that function of his friendship with Murr, but more obviously to his role as carrier of messages between aristocrats engaged in adulterous affairs (he is a pontifex of a different sort than the Pope as pontifex maximus, the bridge maker between God and humanity). While dogs are associated with established society, it is the tomcats, as outsiders, who have formed a fraternal society, the "Katzburschenschaft," which Murr is invited to join but that he, with his independent spirit, quickly finds uncongenial (this depiction of course gently satirizes the patriotic student societies of Hoffmann's day that promoted a mixture of national and democratic ideals, the latter largely inspired by the French Revolutionary slogan "Liberty, Equality, Fraternity").[11]

In the last installment of the Kreisler biography as we have it, which by fictive happenstance occurs first among those installments in this unfinished whimsical double novel, Master Abraham tells the composer Kreisler that he is going off on a journey and leaves his tomcat Murr in Kreisler's care. At the end of the second of the projected three parts of *Kater Murr,* we learn that the third part is to contain the tomcat's views about life that came to him while he was living with Kreisler, together with further fragmentary installments of the Kreisler biography. Regarding these installments we are left completely in the dark. We do not know whether they would carry the story of Kreisler's life forward from the moment of Abraham's handing over of the tomcat to him or whether they would simply fill in gaps of the story left to that point. Certainly, a number of mysteries remain, especially those surrounding the Counciloress Benzon's role in the disappearance of Abraham's invisible maiden Chiara and the parentage of Angela, of Princess Hedwiga, and possibly even of Kreisler's beloved Julia.[12]

What we do have of the Kreisler biography is owing to the literary tomcat Murr insofar as he happened to use pages from that work as blotting paper for the manuscript of his autobiography, then forgot to remove them when he gave the manuscript to a friend, who in turn gave it to Hoffmann in hopes the latter would find a publisher for it. Since Hoffmann, in his editorial preface speaks of this friend as someone with whom he is "of one heart and soul," and we are reminded in the editor's postscript at the end of part 2 that Murr went to live with Kreisler, it is reasonable to assume that the friend who brought Hoffmann the manuscript was the romantic composer, his fictive alter ego. Because the postscript also brings word of the tomcat's death, and in such a way as to indicate that by that time Murr was living with Hoffmann himself, we have the possible implication of an identity of Hoffmann with Master Abraham, to whom Murr was to be given back once Abraham returned from his journey. In other words, Hoffmann is not only, as we obviously know, the creator of the figures of Murr, Kreisler, and Abraham; he also hints at an identification of himself with them.

Viewed in this way, the literary tomcat Murr may be a self-humorous image of Hoffmann as a writer, exhibiting all due authorial vanity; the romantic composer Kreisler, as has been often observed, a novelistic recasting of Hoffmann's passion for Julchen Marc; and Master Abraham a second humorous self-image as the older man foolishly devoted to a dream of transcendent young love. Or, expressed somewhat differently, Kreisler's story is fancifully that of Hoffmann up through the Bamberg years, until his adored Julchen was married off to an unworthy suitor; the Murr story is largely Hoffmann in his subsequent career as an author; and Master Abraham, as friend and protector of both, is Hoffmann the poetic conjurer, devotee of a transcendence that exists only in the mind in romantic transport and fantasy.

From Hoffmann's correspondence, it appears that at the time he was finishing *Kater Murr* he planned to turn from tales to writing novels. The reasons for that plan are unclear and may have been largely financial. His debts at his favorite wine house were considerable, despite a good salary and an already quite healthy income from his writings, probably at least equal to his salary. Perhaps he sensed that the vogue of the supernatural was in decline, that greater realism in fiction was demanded, at least as regards depictions of magical or miraculous happenings. He may simply have wanted to devote himself more fully to humorously satirical depictions, such as those more common or obvious in his later tales and in *Kater Murr*.

Clearly, he did not intend to turn himself into a Walter Scott and write historical novels. A more likely model, at least in certain respects, would have been his early idol and older contemporary Jean Paul Friedrich Richter, as evidenced by the whimsically humorous title of the novel he planned to write after Kater Murr, "Johannes Schnellpfeffers Flitterwochen vor der Hochzeit" ("John Quickpepper's Honeymoon before the Marriage"). That title may indicate, too, that Hoffmann planned to draw—as he had always done, and never more completely than in *Kater Murr*—on his own life experiences, in this case the spring of 1802 in Posen when he was breaking his engagement to his cousin Minna Doerffer and courting Michalina Rorer, whom, as we know, he then wed that summer.

Conclusion

Hoffmann's fiction, from its first appearance on the literary scene, has fascinated us with its intermingling of fantasy and reality. He was himself intent on calling this feature to his readers' attention. As we have seen, his introduction of the fantastic into familiar everyday life was intended to fill us with a sense of being transported to or coming into contact with a miraculous, transcendent realm. That feeling of transcendence, in turn, would arise because of our inner yearning for a higher existence.

For Hoffmann, such yearning was the source of our sense of the poetic and our capacity to fantasize. We respond to fantasy, and fantasize ourselves, out of romantic longing. Hoffmann therefore believed in and championed the power of comic as well as sublime fantasy to fill us with a sense of transcendent delight.

In the piece that may be considered Hoffmann's last will and testament in poetic matters, the fictional dialogue "Des Vetters Eckfenster" ("The Cousin's Corner Window," 1822; in *Der Zuschauer*, 23 April–4 May, nos. 49–54) dictated on his deathbed, he focused attention once again on the power of fantasy to lend a transcendent quality to familiar scenes from everyday life. The dialogue is reported by the cousin of a dying author after a visit to the infirm relative. From his wheelchair at a window in his apartment overlooking the marketplace, the author uses his powers of imagination to sketch the life circumstances of various figures as they make their purchases.

Surprisingly from what we know of Hoffmann as teller of tales, there is nothing especially fantastic in these imaginings. The point is rather that the mere sight of these figures is enough to set the author's powers of fantasy to work and thereby to produce for himself and the cousin, as well as Hoffmann's readers of course, the experience of a romantic transcendence through fantasizing along with the author. Seeing the figures in a poetic way means imagining lives to go with the figures' outer appearances.[1]

"Des Vetters Eckfenster" reminds us of connections between Hoffmann's profession of jurist and his literary career. A judge is called upon to look beyond appearances, even to imagine the story behind the case as presented. Moreover, jurists are aware that events may be reported and understood from varying viewpoints, in which emotions and imaginings play no small role. Hoffmann came from a family of jurists and practiced that profession for most of his adult life. It is little wonder therefore that as an author he exhibited a proclivity for shifting narrative perspectives that leave his readers to judge matters for themselves.

The jurist's need to evaluate testimony in relation to motives and facts, in turn, is not unlike the psychiatric physician's concern to assess the mental state of patients. It is therefore understandable that Hoffmann became fascinated with the study of mental illness and depicted it and insanity in his fiction. That fascination was not limited to Hoffmann; it had become common in German literature beginning with Goethe's *Werther*.

Hoffmann's love of the theater can be seen as related to his profession as jurist and his interest in psychiatric medicine. Portrayal of passion, especially of the more extreme or violent sort, is pretty much the stuff of theater. Certainly German drama as heavily influenced by Shakespeare, following the lead of Lessing, Goethe, and Schiller, tended particularly in that direction. The theater audience directly and vividly witnesses the expression of these passions, much as a judge or psychiatrist might, and is challenged to understand them. At the same time, the poetic nature of the depiction and the aura of the stage produces, as Hoffmann repeatedly emphasized, a feeling of transcendence to a miraculous realm.

As we know, Hoffmann himself had no particular talent for writing plays. He did, though, have a gift for caricature not only in his fiction but as a graphic artist as well. As he stressed repeatedly, writing involves transformation of reality in the mind's eye. Depiction of the miraculous has to be graphic to transport us. Hoffmann's specialty was ironic or comic fantasy that produces a feeling of transcendence through the element of the eccentric, the bizarre, the extravagant—qualities that for him were synonymous with the fantastic.

Hoffmann's love of the fantastic colored not only his passion for the theater, his graphic art, even his opinions as a jurist, and hence his fiction, but also his interest in music. As we have seen, while music was for him the language of transcendence per se and instrumental music and romantic opera seria its epitome, in actuality he was more a devotee of comic opera, witnessed by his esteem for Mozart's *Don Giovanni* as the opera of all operas and his own *Undine*. While transcendence was the stuff of romanticism, for Hoffmann fantasy was the means to that transcendence. It was opera buffa, however sublimely conceived, that was his passion and provided the inspiration for his fiction.

Transcendence has been the theme in Hoffmann's fiction that has attracted interest from critics of a platonic persuasion. Few readers of

Hoffmann would contest that depiction, or expression, of a yearning for transcendence is central to his poetic works. The question remains only whether Hoffmann believed in the existence of spirit realms or any sort of transcendence beyond.

Other critics, including Marxists, focus on Hoffmann's depictions of contemporary society, claiming him as a forerunner of the realism toward which European literature turned shortly after his death. For these critics, Hoffmann's use of fantasy was secondary, either an escape from life in the society of his time or an indirectly satirical distortion of that social reality. The question is whether social depiction is the main thing or a backdrop against which to contrast the element of the miraculous or fantastic.

There is also the bizarre, often quite mad, behavior of the characters in Hoffmann's fiction. As we have noted, this element caught the attention of psychoanalysts and critics interested in psychoanalytic theory early on. Hoffmann clearly invites us to fathom the origins of these mental and emotional disturbances. The question is whether psychoanalytic theory, whether Freudian, Jungian, or another variety, is applicable here. Was Hoffmann a forerunner of psychoanalysis in his understanding of the workings of the human psyche? Did he have such an understanding or was his anticipation of psychoanalysis an unconscious matter, explainable by virtue of those theories' claim to universal applicability as "natural law"? Did he indeed, as the present account has depicted him, have other models from depictions of sexual passion in classical traditions of European literature, especially those familiar from the commedia dell'arte by way of opera buffa?

Hoffmann's fiction is nothing if not filled with enigmas, horrors, and uncanny happenings deliberately and avowedly aimed at producing in the reader a feeling of vertigo and a fear that the world is becoming unhinged. This element has attracted interest among critics writing from an existentialist viewpoint. Social alienation, too, and lack of belief in a supreme power providing for order in the moral and psychic universe are among Hoffmann's themes.

The puzzles posed by Hoffmann ensure that his fiction will be variously interpreted. As recent interest in theories about the understanding of texts has made us especially aware, response to what we read is subjective, conditioned for example by our temperament, experience of life, ideological enthusiasms, and intellectual interests.

Hoffmann's connections to the literature and intellectual life of his times and of earlier periods were many and varied. A prolific writer, he made extensive use of material wherever he found it. He is therefore potentially an attractive subject for deconstructionist theory, with its interest in relationship between texts or intertextuality.

Being very much a man of his times, Hoffmann deserves further study by feminist critics for the role of women as depicted in his works. There is also the question of his many seemingly misogynistic declarations, whether meant seriously or only in jest, and if in jest to what end or purpose?

In recent decades, literary scholarship has included a greater emphasis on understanding authors in the context of their times. That direction has culminated most recently in a "new historicism" seen by some as a revival of the passion for facts that was the cry of the positivism that characterized literary studies a century ago. The danger is of course that literary works of genius will be swallowed up by oceans of information about the life and times of the authors and their contemporaries. There is, at the same time, a potential gain in the understanding of a world classic like Hoffmann. As romantic and fantastic as his writings are, they need to be seen in relation to the politics, economics, society, and culture of his day and of the periods that went before and have come after.

Like many with extraordinary powers of invention, however, Hoffmann was as much a man at odds with his times as a creature of them. Most important, he was most intimately connected with traditions in the literary and poetic arts. A poetic genius, he had the closest bond with manifestations of like genius. To understand and appreciate his works, we need to see him chiefly in the context of European literary traditions dating from Homer, traditions in which Hoffmann's fiction itself became a milestone and significant influence.

Notes and References

Chapter One

1. *Briefwechsel: Erläutert von Hans von Müller und Friedrich Schnapp,* ed. Friedrich Schnapp, 3 vols. (Munich: Winkler, 1967–1969), vol. 1, 52, letter of 12 January 1795.

2. For fuller information about Hoffmann's work in the Prussian judiciary, see E. T. A. Hoffmann, *Juristische Arbeiten,* ed. Friedrich Schnapp (Munich: Winkler, 1973).

3. For important information about Hoffmann as musician, see Gerhard Allroggen, *E. T. A. Hoffmanns Kompositionen: Ein chronologisch-thematisches Verzeichnis seiner musikalischen Werke mit einer Einführung* (Regensburg: Bosse, 1970).

4. Friedrich Schnapp, *E. T. A. Hoffmann in Aufzeichnungen seiner Freunde und Bekannten: Eine Sammlung* (Munich: Winkler, 1974), 83–84.

5. For discussions of Hoffmann as musician, see Friedrich Schnapp, "Der Musiker E. T. A. Hoffmann," *Mitteilungen der E. T. A. Hoffmann-Gesellschaft* 25 (1979): 1–23, and Norbert Miller, "E. T. A. Hoffmann und die Musik," in *Zu E. T. A. Hoffmann: LGW-Interpretationen,* ed. Steven Paul Scher (Stuttgart: Klett, 1981), 182–98. Reprinted from *Akzente* 24 (1977): 114–35.

6. For a study on these Warsaw years see J[an] Kosim, "Ernst Theodor Amadeus Hoffmann in Warschau 1804–1807," *Zeitschrift für Slawistik* 24 (1979): 615–36; also in an expanded version posthumously in *Mitteilungen der E. T. A. Hoffmann-Gesellschaft* 37 (1991): 1–35.

7. For further information about Kunz see Wulf Segebrecht, "Weinhändler, Buchhändler, Literat: Vor 200 Jahren wurde Carl Friedrich Kunz geboren," *Mitteilungen der E. T. A. Hoffmann-Gesellschaft* 31 (1985): 59–68.

8. For a study regarding the influence of psychiatric literature on Hoffmann's tales, see Friedhelm Auhuber, *In einem fernen dunklen Spiegel: E. T. A. Hoffmanns Poetisierung der Medizin* (Opladen: Westdeutscher Verlag, 1986).

9. An incisive analysis of the relation between Hoffmann's turn to satire and his work on the investigative commission is given by the jurist Ulrich Mückenberger, "Phantasie und Gerechtigkeitssinn: Der Dichter und Jurist E. T. A. Hoffmann," *Neue Rundschau* 100, 2 (1989): 163–86. The effectiveness of Hoffmann's efforts to hold up to ridicule the Prussian government's suppression of political opinions as opposed to actions is discussed by Marko Pavlyshyn, "Interpretations of Word as Act: The Debate on Hoffmann's *Meister Floh,*" *Seminar: A Journal of Germanic Studies* 17 (1981): 196–204.

Chapter Two

1. Anon., *Morgenblatt für gebildete Stände* 9, 2 (1815), Literaturblatt 4: 14–15.

2. Anon. [F. G. Wetzel], *Heidelbergische Jahrbücher* 8, 2 (1815), no. 66: 1051.

3. Anon., *Leipziger Literatur-Zeitung*, 2 June 1815, col. 1064.

4. Anon. [Karl Ludwig Woltmann], *Jenaische Allgemeine Literatur-Zeitung* 12, 4 (1815), no. 232, col. 422.

5. Anon., *Allgemeine Literatur-Zeitung* [Halle] (1815), no. 134, col. 294.

6. Anon., *Literarisches Conversations-Blatt* (1821), no. 68: 270–71.

7. Anon., *Morgenblatt für gebildete Stände* 12, 2 (1818), Literaturblatt 19: 74.

8. Anon. [Konrad Schwenk], *Hermes oder kritisches Jahrbuch der Literatur* 2 (1820): 211.

9. Anon., *Allgemeine Literatur-Zeitung* [Halle] (1822), no. 57, cols. 454–55.

10. *Rahel: Ein Buch des Andenkens an ihre Freunde,* ed. Karl August Varnhagen von Ense, vol. 3 (Berlin: Dunker & Humblot, 1834), 13–15, entry dated February 1820.

11. Anon., *Zeitung für die elegante Welt* (1818), no. 216, cols. 1741–42.

12. Anon. [Theresa Huber], *Morgenblatt für gebildete Stände* 13, 1 (1819), Literaturblatt 7: 25.

13. Anon. [Konrad Schwenk], "Über E. T. W. Hoffmann's Schriften," *Hermes oder kritisches Jahrbuch der Literatur* 3 (1823): 86–143; here 119.

14. Anon., *Heidelberger Jahrbücher* 14 (1821), no. 6: 102.

15. Anon., *Zeitung für die elegante Welt* (1819), no. 216, col. 1723.

16. Anon. [Konrad Schwenk], *Hermes oder kritisches Jahrbuch der Literatur* 2 (1820): 217.

17. Anon., *Heidelberger Jahrbücher* 14 (1821), no. 6: 101.

18. Anon. [Wilhelm Müller], *Literarisches Conversations-Blatt* (1821), no. 275: 1099.

19. Anon., *Leipziger Literatur-Zeitung* (1821), no. 267, col. 2136.

20. Anon., *Heidelberger Jahrbücher* 14 (1821), no. 78: 1231–32.

21. Anon., *Morgenblatt für gebildete Stände* 15, 4 (1821), Literaturblatt 100: 397.

22. Anon., *Literarisches Conversations-Blatt* (1825), no. 211: 842.

23. Anon., *Zeitung für die elegante Welt* (1819), no. 54, col. 427.

24. Anon. [Friedrich von Gruenthal], *Morgenblatt für gebildete Stände* 14, 1 (1820), Literaturblatt 12: 45.

25. Ludwig Börne, "Humoralpathologie [1820]," in *Sämtliche Schriften,* ed. Inge Rippman and Peter Rippman (Darmstadt: Melzer, 1964), vol. 2, 450–56; here 453.

26.   Anon., *Allgemeine Literatur-Zeitung* [Halle] (1822), vol. 1, no. 123, col. 105.

27.   Börne, "Humoralpathologie," 451.

28.   Heinrich Heine, "Briefe aus Berlin," in *Heinrich Heine. Historisch-kritische Gesamtausgabe der Werke,* ed. Manfred Windfuhr, vol. 6, ed. Jost Hermand (Hamburg: Hoffmann und Campe, 1973), 51–52, in third letter, dated 7 June 1822.

29.   Anon., *Heidelberger Jahrbücher* 14 (1821), no. 75: 1187.

30.   Anon., *Blackwood's Edinburgh Magazine* 16, 2 (1824): 57.

31.   Ibid., 58.

32.   Robert Pearse Gillies, Introduction, *German Stories: Selected from the Works of Hoffmann, de la Motte Fouqué, Pichler, Kruse and Others* (Edinburgh: Blackwell; London: Cadell, 1826), ix.

33.   Walter Scott, "On the Supernatural in Fictitious Composition; and particularly on the Works of Ernest Theodore William Hoffman [sic]," *The Foreign Quarterly Review* 1, 1 (1827): 61–98; on Hoffmann esp. 74–98, here 72.

34.   Ibid., 97.

35.   Thomas Carlyle, "E. T. W. Hoffmann [1827]," in *The Work of Thomas Carlyle in Thirty Volumes: Centenary Edition,* vol. 22 (London: Chapman and Hall, 1898), 3–21; here 20. For a discussion of Hoffmann's reception in England, see Wulf Segebrecht, "E. T. A. Hoffmann and English Literature," in *Deutsche Romantik and English Romanticism: Papers from the University of Houston Third Symposium on Literature and the Arts: "English and German Romanticism: Cross-Currents and Controversy,"* ed. Theodore G. Gish and Sandra G. Frieden (Munich: Fink, 1984), 52–66.

36.   For a discussion of the decisive influence of Scott's review, see Gerhard R. Kaiser, " 'impossible to subject tales of this nature to criticism': Walter Scotts Kritik als Schlüssel zur Wirkungsgeschichte E. T. A. Hoffmanns im 19. Jahrhundert," in *Kontroversen, alte und neue: Akten des VII. Internationalen Germanisten-Kongresses Göttingen 1985,* ed. Albrecht Schöne, vol. 9: *Deutsche Literatur in der Weltliteratur,* ed. Franz Norbert Mennemeier and Conrad Wiedemann (Tübingen: Niemeyer, 1986), 35–47.

37.   Johann Wolfgang Goethe, review "German Romance. Volume IV. Edinburgh 1827," *Ueber Kunst und Altertum,* 6 (1828), as quoted in Friedrich Schnapp, comp., *E. T. A. Hoffmann in Aufzeichnungen seiner Freunde und Bekannten: Eine Sammlung* (Munich: Winkler, 1974), 747.

38.   Wolfgang Menzel, *Die deutsche Literatur,* vol. 2 (Stuttgart: Franck, 1828), 106.

39.   Georg Wilhelm Friedrich Hegel, *Aesthetik,* vol. 1, ed. Heinrich Gustav Hotho (1836), vol. 12 of *Werke,* 3d ed. (Stuttgart: Fromann, 1953), 302.

40.   For a detailed survey of Russian interest in Hoffmann from the 1820s to the 1840s see Norman W. Ingham, *E. T. A. Hoffmann's Reception in Russia* (Würzburg: jal-verlag, 1974).

41. Heinrich Heine, *Die romantische Schule,* in *Sämtliche Werke,* ed. Ernst Elster (Leipzig: Bibliographisches Institut, n.d.), vol. 5, 302.

42. Joseph von Eichendorff, "Hoffmann," in *Geschichte der poetischen Literatur in Deutschland* (1847), vol. 9 of *Sämtliche Werke,* ed. Wilhelm Kosch et al. (Regensburg: Habbel, 1970), 447–55, 471; here 455.

43. Champfleury [pseud. Jules Fleury-Husson], "De l'introduction des Contes d'Hoffmann en France," in *Contes posthumes d'Hoffmann,* ed. and trans. Champfleury (Paris: Levy, 1856), ii–iii.

44. Charles Baudelaire, "Curiosités esthétiques" (1868), in *Œuvres complètes,* vol. 2 (Paris: Conrad, 1923), on Hoffmann 97–98, 151–52, 386–88, 393–95, 441; here 394–95.

45. Cesare Lombroso, *Der geniale Mensch* (1864), trans. M. O. Fraenkel (Hamburg: Actien-Gesellschaft, 1890), 107.

46. James G. Kiernan, "An Ataxic Paranoiac of Genius: A Study of E. T. A. Hoffmann," *The Alienist and Neurologist* 17 (1896): 295–310; here 305.

47. Marcel Demerliac, *Étude médico-psychologique sur Hoffmann* (Lyon: Rey, 1908), 89.

48. Ricarda Huch, *Ausbreitung und Verfall der Romantik* (Leipzig: Haessel, 1902), on Hoffmann 201–38; here 202.

49. Georg Ellinger, Introduction, *E. T. A. Hoffmann. Werke in 15 Teilen,* ed. Georg Ellinger, vol. 3, 2d enlarged ed. (Berlin: Bong, [1927]), 8.

50. Hermann Hesse, "E. T. A. Hoffmanns Werke," *Die Neue Rundschau* 35 (1924): 1199–1200; here 1200.

51. Edwin Keppel Bennett, *The History of the German Novelle,* ed. H. M. Waidson (Cambridge: Cambridge University Press, 1961), on Hoffmann 58–67; here 63.

52. Albert Béguin, "Le Lis et le Serpent (E. T. A. Hoffmann)," in *L'âme romantique et le rêve,* vol. 2 (Marseille: Cahiers du Sud, 1937), 266–91; here 281.

53. Jean-F.-A. Ricci, "Le Problème de la vraisemblance dans les 'Elixirs du Diable' de E. T. A. Hoffmann," *Les Langues modernes* 46 (1952): A29–A34; here A34.

54. Walter Muschg, *Tragische Literaturgeschichte,* 3d ed. (Berne: Francke, 1957), 81.

55. Hermann Schneider, *Geschichte der deutschen Literatur nach ihren Epochen dargestellt* (Bochum: Deutscher Buchklub, n.d. [1950s]), on Hoffmann 548–55; here 551.

56. René Wellek, Foreword, *E. T. A. Hoffmann: Selected Writings,* ed. and trans. Leonard J. Kent and Elizabeth C. Knight (Chicago: University of Chicago Press, 1969), vol. 1, 1–4; here 2.

57. Pauline Watts, *Music: The Medium of the Metaphysical in E. T. A. Hoffmann* (Amsterdam: Rodopi, 1972), [91].

58. Maria M. Tatar, "Mesmerism, Madness, and Death in E. T. A. Hoffmann's 'Der goldne Topf,' " *Studies in Romanticism* 14 (1975): 365–89; here 387.

59. Wolfgang Nehring, "E. T. A. Hoffmanns Erzählwerk: Ein Modell und seine Variationen," *Zeitschrift für Deutsche Philologie* 95, Sonderheft "E. T. A. Hoffmann" (1976): 3–24; here 24.

60. Inge Stegmann, "Die Wirklichkeit des Traumes bei E. T. A. Hoffmann," *Zeitschrift für Deutsche Philologie* 95, Sonderheft "E. T. A. Hoffmann" (1976): 64–93; here 93.

61. Ernst von Schenck, *E. T. A. Hoffmann: Ein Kampf um das Bild des Menschen* (Berlin: Verlag die Runde, 1939).

62. Friedrich Giselher Tretter, "Die Frage nach der Wirklichkeit bei E. T. A. Hoffmann," Ph.D. dissertation, University of Munich, 1961, 111.

63. Horst S. Daemmrich, *The Shattered Self: E. T. A. Hoffmann's Tragic Vision* (Detroit: Wayne State University Press, 1973), 9–10.

64. A. Leslie Willson, "Hoffmann's Horrors," in *Literature and the Occult: Essays in Comparative Literature,* ed. Luanne Frank (Arlington: The University of Texas at Arlington, 1977), 264–71; here 271.

65. Wilhelm Kosch, "E. T. A. Hoffmann," in *Die deutsche Literatur im Spiegel der nationalen Entwicklung von 1813 bis 1918: {Erster Teil} 1813–1848,* vol. 1 (Munich: Parcus, 1925), 113–52; here 114.

66. Werner Berthold, "Das Phänomen der Entfremdung bei E. T. A. Hoffmann," Ph.D. dissertation, University of Leipzig, 1953, 110.

67. Paul Reimann, *Hauptströmungen der deutschen Literatur 1750–1848: Beiträge zu ihrer Geschichte und Kritik* (Berlin: Dietz, 1956), on Hoffmann 540–54; here 542–43.

68. Georg Lukács, *Fortschritt und Reaktion in der deutschen Literatur* (Berlin: Aufbau, 1950), 69–70.

69. Hans Mayer, "Die Wirklichkeit E. T. A. Hoffmanns: Ein Versuch," in *E. T. A. Hoffmann. Poetische Werke,* ed. Gerhard Seidel (Berlin: Aufbau, 1958), vol. 1, v–lv; here xviii.

70. Hans-Georg Werner, *E. T. A. Hoffmann: Darstellung und Deutung der Wirklichkeit im dichterischen Werk* (Weimar: Arion, 1962), 46.

71. Sigmund Freud, "Das Unheimliche," in *Gesammelte Werke,* ed. Anna Freud et al., 2d ed., vol. 12: *Werke aus den Jahren 1917–1920* (London: Imago, 1955), 228–68, on Hoffmann 238–49; here 242 (first published 1919).

72. Emil Franz Lorenz, "Die Geschichte des Bergmanns von Falun bei Hoffmann, Wagner und Hofmannsthal," *Imago* 3 (1914): 250–301; here 264.

73. James M. McGlathery, *E. T. A. Hoffmann. Part One: Hoffmann and His Sources; Part Two: Interpretations of the Tales.* 2 vols. (Berne: Peter Lang, 1981–1985).

74. Martin Roehl, *Die Doppelgängerpersönlichkeit bei E. T. A. Hoffmann,* Ph.D. dissertation, University of Rostock, 1918 (Salzwedel: Menzel, [1918?]), 46.

75. Aniela Jaffé, "Bilder und Symbole aus E. T. A. Hoffmanns Märchen 'Der goldne Topf,' " in *Gestaltungen des Unbewußten,* ed. Carl Gustav Jung (Zurich: Rascher, 1950), 237–616. Republished in revised form as a volume under the same title (Hildesheim: Gerstenberg, 1978).

76.   William H. McClain, "E. T. A. Hoffmann as a Psychological Realist: A Study of 'Meister Floh,' " *Monatshefte für den deutschen Unterricht* 47 (1955): 65–80; here 77.

77.   Siegbert S. Prawer, "Hoffmann's Uncanny Guest: A Reading of 'Der Sandmann,' " *German Life & Letters* 18 (1965): 297–308; here 302.

78.   Diana Stone Peters, "The Dream as Bridge in the Works of E. T. A. Hoffmann," *Oxford German Studies* 8 (1973–1974): 60–85; here 85.

79.   Peter von Matt, *Die Augen der Automaten: E. T. A. Hoffmanns Imaginationslehre als Prinzip seiner Erzählkunst* (Tübingen: Niemeyer, 1971), 18.

80.   See the selected bibliography that follows.

81.   Maria M. Tatar. "Blindness and Insight: Visionary Experience in the Tales of E. T. A. Hoffmann," in *Spellbound: Studies on Mesmerism and Literature* (Princeton: Princeton University Press, 1978), 121–51.

82.   Friedhelm Auhuber, *In einem fernen dunklen Spiegel: E. T. A. Hoffmanns Poetisierung der Medizin* (Opladen: Westdeutscher Verlag, 1986).

83.   Susanne Asche, *Die Liebe, der Tod und das Ich im Spiegel der Kunst: Die Funktion des Weiblichen in Schriften der Frühromantik und im erzählerischen Werk E. T. A. Hoffmanns* (Königstein im Taunus: Anton Hain, 1985).

84.   Gerhard R. Kaiser. *E. T. A. Hoffmann,* (Stuttgart: Metzler, 1988).

85.   Barbara Elling, *Leserintegration im Werk E. T. A. Hoffmanns* (Bern: Haupt, 1973).

86.   Elizabeth Wright, *E. T. A. Hoffmann and the Rhetoric of Terror: Aspects of Language Used for the Evocation of Fear* ([London]: Institute of Germanic Studies, University of London, 1978), 1.

87.   Rudolf Drux, *Marionette Mensch: Ein Metaphernkomplex und sein Kontext von E. T. A. Hoffmann bis Georg Büchner* (Munich: Wilhelm Fink, 1986).

88.   David E. Wellbery, "E. T. A. Hoffmann and Romantic Hermeneutics: An Interpretation of Hoffmann's 'Don Juan,' " *Studies in Romanticism* 19 (1980): 455–73.

89.   Ursula Orlowsky, *Literarische Subversion bei E. T. A. Hoffmann: Nouvelles vom "Sandmann"* (Heidelberg: Winter, 1988).

90.   Detlef Kremer, *Romantische Metamorphosen: E. T. A. Hoffmanns Erzählungen* (Stuttgart and Weimar: Metzler, 1993).

91.   Elena Nährlich-Slatewa, *Das Leben gerät aus dem Gleis: E. T. A. Hoffmann im Kontext karnevalesker Überlieferungen* (Frankfurt am Main: Peter Lang, 1995).

Chapter Three

1.   Hoffmann's music criticism is discussed in the cultural context of its time by Robert Mühlher, "Das Bild der Wiener Klassik in den Werken E. T. A. Hoffmanns," in *Die österreichische Literatur: Ihr Profil an der Wende vom 18. zum 19. Jahrhundert (1750–1830); Teil I,* ed. Herbert Zeman (Graz: Akademische Druck-und Verlagsanstalt, 1979), 427–43.

2. *E. T. A. Hoffmann. Schriften zur Musik. Neubearbeitete Ausgabe,* ed. Friedrich Schnapp (Munich: Winkler, 1977), 23–24; hereafter cited in text as *SzM.*

3. For a survey of Hoffmann's reviews of Beethoven's compositions, see Fritz Felzmann, "E. T. A. Hoffmann als Rezensent Beethovens," *Mitteilungen der E. T. A. Hoffmann-Gesellschaft* 20 (1974): 48–64.

4. For an excellent discussion of Hoffmann's essay on church music in connection with his views on poetic literature see Jean Giraud, "Hoffmann's Vergangenheitswendung in der Kirchenmusik," *E. T. A. Hoffmann Jahrbuch* 3 (1995): 31–47.

5. *E. T. A. Hoffmann. Die Serapions-Brüder,* ed. Walter Müller-Seidel and Wulf Segebrecht (Munich: Winkler, 1966), 76–77; hereafter cited in text as *SB.*

6. The question of what constituted Hoffmann's ultimate ideal of romantic opera was addressed by Norbert Miller, "Hoffmann und Spontini: Vorüberlegungen zu einer Ästhetik der romantischen opera seria," in *Wissen aus Erfahrungen: Werkbegriff und Interpretation heute: Festschrift für Herman Meyer zum 65. Geburtstag,* ed. Alexander von Bormann (Tübingen: Niemeyer, 1976), 402–26.

7. The relationship between the peculiar ("das Wunderliche") and the miraculous ("das Wunderbare") in Hoffmann's writings is discussed by Lothar Pikulik, "Das Wunderbare bei E. T. A. Hoffmann: Zum romantischen Ungenügen an der Normalität," *Euphorion: Zeitschrift für Literaturgeschichte* 69 (1975): 294–319.

8. For a useful discussion of Hoffmann's theoretical views on opera, see Aubrey S. Garlington Jr., "E. T. A. Hoffmann's 'Der Dichter und der Komponist' and the Creation of the German Romantic Opera," *The Musical Quarterly* 65 (1979): 22–47.

9. *E. T. A. Hoffmann. Briefwechsel: Erläutert von Hans von Müller und Friedrich Schnapp,* ed. Friedrich Schnapp, 3 vols. (Munich: Winkler, 1967–1969), 408 (letter of 19 August 1813).

10. *E. T. A. Hoffmann. Schriften zur Musik/Nachlese,* ed. Friedrich Schnapp (Munich: Winkler, 1963), 598; hereafter cited in text as *Nachlese.*

11. *Fantasie- und Nachtstücke: Fantasiestücke in Callots Manier. Nachtstücke. Seltsame Leiden eines Theater-Direktors,* ed. Walter Müller-Seidel and Wolfgang Kron (Munich: Winkler, 1960), 638; hereafter cited in text as *FuN.*

12. The relationship between Hoffmann's enthusiasm for the theater and his storytelling was investigated in considerable detail by Heide Eilert, *Theater in der Erzählkunst: Eine Studie zum Werk E. T. A. Hoffmanns* (Tübingen: Niemeyer, 1977).

13. For a discussion of Hoffmann's essay comparing his use of fantasy in depicting figures from everyday life with Callot's graphic art, see Siegbert Prawer, "Die Farben des Jacques Callot: E. T. A. Hoffmanns 'Entschuldigung' seiner Kunst," in *Wissen aus Erfahrungen: Werkbegriff und Interpretation heute:*

Festschrift für Herman Meyer zum 65. Geburtstag, ed. Alexander von Bormann (Tübingen: Niemeyer, 1976), 393–401.

14. For an argument that the structure of Hoffmann's "Kreisleriana" is similar to that of certain musical compositions, especially Bach's "Goldberg" variations, see Jocelyne Kolb, "E. T. A. Hoffmann's 'Kreisleriana': A la Recherche d'une Forme Perdue?" *Monatshefte für deutschen Unterricht* 69 (1977): 34–44.

15. Siegbert S. Prawer discusses Hoffmann's "Berganza" in relation to Cervantes' tale and other earlier literary works in " 'Ein poetischer Hund': E. T. A. Hoffmann's 'Nachrichten von den neuesten Schicksalen des Hundes Berganza' and Its Antecedents in European Literature," in *Aspekte der Goethezeit,* ed. Stanley A. Corngold, Michael Curschmann, and Theodore J. Ziolkowski (Göttingen: Vandenhoeck & Ruprecht, 1977), 273–92.

16. For an exhaustive catalog of occurrences of animals in Hoffmann's works see Christa-Maria Beardsley, *E. T. A. Hoffmanns Tierfiguren im Kontext der Romantik: Die poetisch-ästhetische und gesellschaftliche Funktion der Tiere bei Hoffmann und in der Romantik* (Bonn: Bouvier, 1985).

17. A study of the statements about the theory of poetic art made by Hoffmann's Serapion brethren, comparing them to his artistic practice in stories contained in *Die Serapionsbrüder,* as well as to his earlier theoretical statements in the Callot essay of the *Fantasiestücke,* was made by Ilse Winter, *Untersuchungen zum Serapiontischen Prinzip E. T. A. Hoffmanns* (Mouton: The Hague, 1976).

18. For the influence of mesmerism on Hoffmann's tales, see Maria M. Tatar, "Blindness and Insight: Visionary Experience in the Tales of E. T. A. Hoffmann," in *Spellbound: Studies on Mesmerism and Literature* (Princeton: Princeton University Press, 1978), 121–51.

19. For a Jungian interpretation of the metaphor of the ladder as used here see Diana Stone Peters, "E. T. A. Hoffmann: The Conciliatory Satirist," *Monatshefte für deutschen Unterricht* 66 (1974): 55–73.

Chapter Four

1. An attempt to read this story and two other Hoffmann tales about musicians in terms of musical structures was made by Wolfgang Wittkowski, "E. T. A. Hoffmanns musikalische Musikerdichtungen 'Ritter Gluck', 'Don Juan' und 'Rat Krespel,' " *Aurora: Jahrbuch der Eichendorff-Gesellschaft* 38 (1978): 54–74. The relationship between Hoffmann's music criticism and his narrative depictions of musicians was investigated in detail by Thomas Wörtche, "E. T. A. Hoffmanns Erzählungen von der Musik," *Mitteilungen der E. T. A. Hoffmann-Gesellschaft* 33 (1987): 13–33.

2. Contemporary critics emphasized the element of fantasy in the tale: "The author has a departed spirit—who at the same time is more the spirit of his *own fantasy*—appear in the bustle of Berlin. Vision and reality here are

blended very boldly into one," Anon., *Allgemeine Literatur-Zeitung* [Halle] (1815), no. 134, col. 294; "The ghost's vision—a fantasy in the fantasy— . . . may not be viewed as a *characterization of the real Gluck,* because its 'new poetic' tone is after all very alien to the truly *great* presence of mind of the master," Anon., *Leipziger Literatur-Zeitung,* 2 June 1815, col. 1062. Another critic, though, took the piece to be a serious effort to portray the historical personage: "Who is there who has heard Gluck's music or about his manner who would not find this representation of the great master most ridiculous? . . . the description of his conduct, his bombastic, fantastic speeches, his *Euphon* that sounds and does not sound . . . form a yet more ludicrous contrast with Gluck himself"; Anon. [Karl Ludwig Woltmann], *Jenaische Allgemeine Literatur-Zeitung* 12, 4 (1815), no. 232, col. 419.

    3. For a Jungian interpretation of Ritter Gluck's visionary experience with the calyx, see Ronald J. Elardo, "The Maw as Infernal Medium in 'Ritter Gluck' and 'Die Bergwerke zu Falun,' " *New German Studies* 9 (1981): 29–49.

    4. A discussion of the story in relation to its historical context especially as regards music criticism and the "Euphon" is given by Günter Oesterle, "Dissonanz und Effekt in der romantischen Kunst: E. T. A. Hoffmanns 'Ritter Gluck,' " *E. T. A. Hoffmann-Jahrbuch: Mitteilungen der E. T. A. Hoffmann-Gesellschaft* 1 (1992–1993): 58–79.

    5. For a discussion of Hoffmann's tale in relation to Mozart's opera, see Hartmut Kaiser, "Mozart's 'Don Giovanni' and E. T. A. Hoffmanns 'Don Juan': Ein Beitrag zum Verständnis des 'Fantasiestücks,' " *Mitteilungen der E. T. A. Hoffmann-Gesellschaft* 21 (1975): 6–26.

    6. Two contemporary reviewers were quite taken with the figure of Donna Anna as interpreted by Hoffmann's enthusiast: "While the author with amazing acuteness has led us down into the depths of that 'opera of all operas,' he has revealed to us at the same time one of the most delicate secrets of sympathetic spirits; this Anna, she is indeed a 'winged, sacred being,' as the divine Plato calls the poet! . . . the divine woman elevates herself in song to the ultimate transfiguration, as the nightingale bursts its breast in hitting the highest note and the swan's tongue is unfettered to produce the sweetest song before it perishes," Anon. [F. G. Wetzel], *Heidelbergische Jahrbücher* 8, 2 (1815), no. 66: 1044; "Many who have long been acquainted with this *'opera of all operas'* can here *learn to understand it.* The hypothesis about Donna Anna is entirely original," Anon., *Leipziger Literatur-Zeitung,* 2 June 1815, col. 1064.

    7. Contemporary reviewers understandably saw Maria as the heroine and Alban as the villain: " 'Maria' is the gentlest female being, preserving in her breast with sweet, timid virginity the holy vestal flame: entirely the opposite of Alban—she the purest innocence and devotion—he the fiercest despotism, which digs with satanic ecstasy in the entrails of the butchered sacrifice at its feet," Anon. [F. G. Wetzel], *Heidelbergische Jahrbücher* 8, 2 (1815), no. 66: 1049; "Alban, the physician, sacrilegiously applies the forces of magnetism in order thereby to gain power over the soul of a charming girl, and, through the

power of magnetism, instead of love, to become her master unto death," Anon.,
Jenaische Allgemeine Literatur-Zeitung 12, 4 (1815), no. 232, col. 422.

8. A detailed analysis of this tale, especially as regards the sexual
aspects, was done by Hans-Walter Schmidt, "Der Kinderfresser: Ein Motiv in
E. T. A. Hoffmanns 'Ignaz Denner' und sein Kontext," *Mitteilungen der E. T. A.
Hoffmann-Gesellschaft* 29 (1983): 17–30.

9. For a discussion of the story with regard to recent theories of discourse and of reading, see Todd Kontje, "Biography in Triplicate: E. T. A.
Hoffmann's 'Die Abenteuer der Silvester-Nacht,' " *German Quarterly* 58 (1985):
348–60.

10. A contemporary critic justifiably complained: "The hurried conclusion of the fable does not resolve everything satisfactorily"; Anon., *Allgemeine
Literatur-Zeitung* [Halle] (1817), vol. 2, supps. 64, col. 506. For a recent representation of the generally held view that the story is about the conflict between
life as an artist and that of the bourgeois see Gunther Pix, "Der Variationskünst-
ler E. T. A. Hoffmann und seine Erzählung 'Der Artushof,' " *Mitteilungen der E.
T. A. Hoffmann-Gesellschaft* 35 (1989): 4–20.

11. A contemporary critic reasonably judged that the story was about
mental illness: "And why does this fellow [Coppelius] hound the sensitive
Nathanael? Out of mere idiosyncracy? . . . In short, a few caricatures flit past
our eyes without producing anything of significance that would have to appear
thoroughly rooted deep in Nathanael's soul, instead of mere sickliness that
awakens only the pity of the physician"; Anon. [Konrad Schwenk], "Über E. T.
W. Hoffmann's Schriften," 109. Jean Delabroy used Hoffmann's "Sandmann"
as a case in point to discuss the fictional representation of insanity in "L'Ombre
de la théorie: À propos de L'Homme au sable de Hoffmann," *Romantisme: Revue
du Dix-Neuvième Siècle* 24 (1979): 29–41.

12. Particular attention is drawn to the narrator's role by Christiane
Staninger, "E. T. A. Hoffmann's 'The Sand Man' and the Night Side of the
Enlightenment," in *Subversive Sublimities: Undercurrents of the German Enlightenment,* ed. Eitel Timm (Columbia, S.C.: Camden House, 1992), 98–104. As
Staninger asks in her conclusion, "[w]ho is this narrator and why does he know
what he knows?" (104). The narrator's admission of the fictive character of his
account about Nathanael is emphasized by Maria M. Tatar, "E. T. A. Hoff-
mann's 'Der Sandmann': Reflection and Romantic Irony," *Modern Language
Notes* 95 (1980): 585–608. For another essay focusing on the story's narrator,
see Claus Sommerhage, "Hoffmanns Erzähler: Über Poetik und Psychologie in
E. T. A. Hoffmanns Nachtstück 'Der Sandmann,' " *Zeitschrift für Deutsche
Philologie* 106 (1987): 513–34. An argument that Nathanael is the author of
his own story was made by Tobin Siebers, " 'Whose Hideous Voice Is This?':
The Reading Unconscious in Freud and Hoffmann," *New Orleans Review* 15, 3
(1988): 80–87. For a discussion of Helène Cixous's claim that Hoffmann's
sandman tale may be seen as an example of a literary precursor of feminine
writing, see Ricarda Schmidt, "E. T. A. Hoffmann's 'Der Sandmann': An Early

Example of Écriture féminine? A Critique of Trends in Feminist Literary Criticism," *Women in German Yearbook: Feminist Studies and German Culture* 4 (1988): 21–45.

13. For the view that Hoffmann meant this tale as a championing of "heated poetic temperaments" for engendering in his readers "the warmth of spontaneous, unreflective emotion," see Susan Brantly, "A Thermographic Reading of E. T. A. Hoffmann's 'Der Sandmann,' " *German Quarterly* 55 (1982): 324–35.

14. Helmut Merkel suggested that the mechanical doll represents for Nathanael a platonic eros that points beyond to suprasensual transcendence; "Der Paralysierte Engel: Zur Erkundung der Automatenliebe in E. T. A. Hoffmanns Erzählung 'Der Sandmann,' " *Wirkendes Wort: Deutsche Sprache und Literatur in Forschung und Lehre* 38 (1988): 187–99; see 190. For discussion of Nathanael's problem as solipsism, see Jochen Schmidt, "Die Krise der romantischen Subjektivität: E. T. A. Hoffmanns Künstlernovelle 'Der Sandmann' in historischer Perspektive," in *Literaturwissenschaft und Geistesgeschichte: Festschrift für Richard Brinkmann,* ed. Jürgen Brummack et al. (Tübingen: Niemeyer, 1981); also especially Thomas A. Kamla, "E. T. A. Hoffmann's 'Der Sandmann': The Narcissistic Poet as Romantic Solipsist," *Germanic Review* 63 (1988: 94–102. Jean Charue found the moral to be that to fall in love with a machine is to love death: "Peut-on s'éprendre d'une femme machine?: Remarques à propos de L'homme au sable d'E. T. A. Hoffmann," *Les Études philosophiques* 1 (1985): 57–75.

15. Particular attention to the motif of eyes is paid by Günter Hartung, "Anatomie des Sandmanns," *Weimarer Beiträge: Zeitschrift für Literaturwissenschaft, Ästhetik und Kulturtheorie* 23, 9 (1977): 45–65. For a critique of Freud's interpretation of the story as a depiction of castration fear arising from the Oedipus complex, see Ingrid Aichinger, "E. T. A. Hoffmanns Novelle 'Der Sandmann' und die Interpretation Sigmund Freuds," *Zeitschrift für Deutsche Philologie* 95, Sonderheft "E. T. A. Hoffmann" (1976): 113–32.

16. For an argument claiming that Clara, not only Coppelius and Spalanzani, is out to make Nathanael a puppet, see John M. Ellis, "Clara, Nathanael and the Narrator: Interpreting Hoffmann's 'Der Sandmann,' " *German Quarterly* 54 (1981): 1–18.

17. Regarding "Die Jesuiterkirche in G." a contemporary critic justifiably complained: "This story would be even more satisfying if it developed more profoundly how Angiolina [sic!], earlier worshipped, becomes ever more hated by this *Bertolt*," Anon., *Allgemeine Literatur-Zeitung* [Halle] (1817), no. 179, col. 598.

18. One contemporary critic found the point to be neoplatonically serious: "May, therefore, a voice from within always call out to the gifted artist: *the highest power,* which a god has bestowed on you, will be lost if the artist himself gets lost in the whirlpool of earthly sensuality"; A. Wendt, *Allgemeine Musikalische Zeitung,* 2 July 1817, col. 460. Another critic, though, complained

of a lack of seriousness: "Bettina can no longer sing because she once tried to perform sacred music with worldly thoughts in her heart. . . . This [Hoffmann's 'Sanctus'] is a playing with sacred things that is insincere"; Anon. [Konrad Schwenk], "Über E. T. W. Hoffmann's Schriften," 111–12.

19.   For an argument that "In Krespel the Romantic quest for knowledge and control of the spiritual universe reaches a final impasse; the end is resignation and silence"; see Gordon Birrell, "Instruments and Infidels: The Metaphysics of Music in E. T. A. Hoffmann's 'Rat Krespel,' " in *Literature and the Occult: Essays in Comparative Literature,* ed. Luanne Frank (Arlington: University of Texas at Arlington, 1977), 65–71; here 71.

20.   The narrator's reaction to Krespel's account of his relationship to the daughter is discussed by William Crisman, "E. T. A. Hoffmann's 'Einsiedler Serapion' and 'Rat Krespel' as Models of Reading," *Journal of English and Germanic Philology* 85 (1986): 50–69.

21.   For the positive view of Krespel that "he is a father who attempts to save his daughter from certain and imminent death. He is guilty of loving her not too little but too well," see Paul M. Haberland, *The University of South Florida Language Quarterly* 13, 3–4 (1975): 39–42; here 41.

22.   A contemporary reviewer objected to Hoffmann's depiction of seeming insanity in the figure of Krespel, seeing it as belonging rather in a medical journal; Anon., *Morgenblatt für gebildete Stände* 12, 2 (1818), Literaturblatt 19: 74.

23.   For discussion of the ghost in "Ein Fragment aus dem Leben dreier Freunde" from a parapsychological viewpoint, see Lee B. Jennings, "The Anatomy of 'Spuk' in Two Tales of E. T. A. Hoffmann," *Colloquia Germanica: Internationale Zeitschrift für Germanische Sprach- und Literaturwissenschaft* 17, 1–2 (1984): 60–78.

24.   Klaus Kanzog maintained that Hoffmann's choice of setting here does not amount to creation of a genre of Berlin stories but is rather owing to his general use of such settings to depict the opposition between customary life and poetic life; "Berlin-Code, Kommunikation und Erzählstruktur: Zu E. T. A. Hoffmanns 'Das öde Haus' und zum Typus 'Berlinische Geschichte,' " *Zeitschrift für Deutsche Philologie* 95, Sonderheft "E. T. A. Hoffmann" (1976): 42–63.

25.   Regarding the contradictory references to the beautiful young woman as "Edmonde" but also as "Edwine" in "Das öde Haus," see John M. Ellis, "Über einige scheinbare Widersprüche in Hoffmann's Erzählungen," *Mitteilungen der E. T. A. Hoffmann-Gesellschaft* 29 (1983): 30–35.

26.   The lack of rational explanation of the characters' motivations in this tale and in Hoffmann's storytelling generally is discussed by Marek Jaroszewski and Marek Wydmuch, "Das Phantastische in E. T. A. Hoffmanns Novelle 'Das öde Haus,' " *Germanica Wratislaviensia* 27 (1976): 127–35.

27.   For a discussion of the story as a criticism of feudal law and rule by the nobility see Stefan Diebitz, " 'Überhaupt eine gehässige Sache': E. T. A.

Hoffmanns Erzählung 'Das Majorat' als Dichtung der Hybris und der Niedertracht," *Mitteilungen der E. T. A. Hoffmann-Gesellschaft* 32 (1986): 35–49.

28. A contemporary critic understandably saw in the tale nothing but a ghost story: "The castle on the Baltic Sea is haunted because someone has been murdered there. For those who cannot believe this, the story is of no interest, since everything really only revolves around this ghost"; Anon. [Konrad Schwenk], "Über E. T. W. Hoffmann's Schriften," 86–143; here 112. For analysis of "Das Majorat" from a parapsychological viewpoint, see Jennings, "The Anatomy of 'Spuk.' "

29. Louis Gerrekens argued that the factual inconsistencies, including chronological impossibilities, are owing to faulty memory on the part of the nephew Theodor as narrator; "Von erzählerischer Erinnerung und literarischer Anamnese: Eine Untersuchung zu E. T. A. Hoffmanns 'Das Majorat,' " *Études germaniques* 45 (1990): 152–83. A detailed discussion of chronological inconsistencies in the story was offered by Gero von Wilpert, "Ausgerechnet: 'Das Majorat,' " *Mitteilungen der E. T. A. Hoffmann-Gesellschaft* 37 (1991): 53–59.

30. A contemporary reviewer found Xaver's "seduction" of Hermenegilde to be "absolutely base, punishable as a serious crime; [it] belongs before the courts, not in art, and cannot serve in this fashion as material for a poetic tale"; Anon. [Konrad Schwenk], "Über E. T. W. Hoffmann's Schriften," 113.

31. One contemporary reviewer found the message of "Der Kampf der Sänger" to be "[t]he so very true idea that poetry springs only from the soul"; Anon., *Zeitung für die elegante Welt* (1818), no. 212, col. 1711. Another, however, criticized the characterization of Wolframb von Eschinbach for its "mawkish affected piety"; Anon. [Konrad Schwenk], "Über E. T. W. Hoffmann's Schriften," 119.

32. A contemporary critic of "Doge und Dogaresse" asked, regarding Marguerita, "why the figure of the old woman must remind us so completely of a grotesque witch," but added, "we cannot avoid confessing that she contributes to the vividness of the whole"; Anon. [Theresa Huber], *Morgenblatt für gebildete Stände* 13, 1 (1819), Literaturblatt 7: 27.

Chapter Five

1. A contemporary critic found that "*Meister Martin* . . . gives a most congenial and appealing family portrait from those genuine, warm, and powerful times, to which our generation, not entirely without justification, looks back longingly"; Anon., *Zeitung für die elegante Welt* (1818), no. 216, cols. 1741–42. That positive acceptance of the story as historical depiction was seconded by another critic: "The costume of this story, both the *mores* and the way of thinking, seem to us to be most authentic! Nowhere [here] is there retouching, whether of feeling or of piety, and yet [it is] so sensitive and pious"; Anon. [Theresa Huber], *Morgenblatt für gebildete Stände* 13, 1 (1819), Literaturblatt 7: 25.

2. Angelika's susceptibility to seduction by the "uncanny guest" bothered a contemporary reviewer: "[E]ven the purity of the soul is not able to pro-

tect itself against the influence of this power"; Anon., *Heidelberger Jahrbücher* 14 (1821), no. 6: 99–100.

3. Elis failed to impress a contemporary critic: "[T]he youth was a superstitious fool given to fantasy, in whom the old loyal bride has lost much less than she believes"; Anon., *Morgenblatt für gebildete Stände* 14, 2 (1820), Literaturblatt 43: 171. Another critic considered the story's point to be "that no one is allowed to devote himself to anything except for its own sake, otherwise he shall perish"; Anon. [Konrad Schwenk], "Über E. T. W. Hoffmann's Schriften," 117–18.

4. For a parapsychological reading of the story see Lee B. Jennings, "The Downward Transcendence: Hoffmann's 'Bergwerke zu Falun,' " *Deutsche Vierteljahrsschrift für Literaturwissenschaft und Geistesgeschichte* 59 (1985): 278–89.

5. For an argument that "Elis' need for punishment is warning him that he is overreaching himself when he dreams of life with Ulla," see Doris T. Wight, "Masochism, Mourning, Melancholia: A Freudian Interpretation of E. T. A. Hoffmann's Tale 'The Mines of Falun,' " *Germanic Notes* 21 (1990): 49–55; here 53.

6. A Jungian interpretation of Elis's visionary relationship to the mine was made by Ronald J. Elardo, "The Maw as Infernal Medium in 'Ritter Gluck' and 'Die Bergwerke zu Falun,' " *New German Studies* 9 (1981): 29–49.

7. A contemporary critic judged the point of "Spielerglück" to be "[t]he abyss into which the gambling compulsion can plunge even a rather noble person"; Anon., *Zeitung für die elegante Welt* (1819), no. 216, col. 1723. Another critic found "the horrifying uncertainty of how Angela actually died magnificent in a way that is seldom encountered"; Anon. [Konrad Schwenk], *Hermes oder kritisches Jahrbuch der Literatur* 2 (1820): 217. Yet another critic wrote that "this story . . . leaves a wounding thorn in the reader's soul, since the only noble creature to appear here dies finally in a way that remains unclear"; Anon., *Heidelberger Jahrbücher* 14 (1821), no. 6: 101.

8. About the story's ending a contemporary reviewer wrote that it was "not so much aesthetically shocking as that, through the simulation of the corpse, it borders on the permissible, even if the merciless tormenting of poor Capuzzi might otherwise be defended artistically"; Anon. [Konrad Schwenk], *Hermes oder kritisches Jahrbuch der Literatur* 2 (1820): 202–3.

9. The tale has been discussed in considerable detail by Gerd Hemmerich, "Verteidigung des 'Signor Formica': Zu E. T. A. Hoffmanns Novelle," *Jahrbuch der Jean-Paul-Gesellschaft* 17 (1982): 113–27. Hemmerich points out (118) that the young artist's family name, Scacciati, means those who are chased, or chased away. He notes that the love story between Antonio and Marianne is not the main point (123) and that the prospect of the young protegé's marriage to her is an object of some trepidation for his mentor, Salvator Rosa (125). As Hemmerich importantly observes, while the historical Salvator Rosa married, "Signor Formica, the actual hero of Hoffmann's tale and its central figure, does *not*" (126; Hemmerich's emphasis).

10. A contemporary critic observed: "One . . . recognizes immediately that Euchar departs only in order to return again as Edgar and to bring along the beautiful Mignon-like creature with him"; Anon., *Heidelberger Jahrbücher* 14 (1821), no. 75: 1186. For a discussion of this tale see Stefan Diebitz, "Übersehen und verkannt: Hoffmanns serapiontische Erzählung 'Der Zusammenhang der Dinge,' " *Mitteilungen der E. T. A. Hoffmann-Gesellschaft* 33 (1987): 50–65.

11. For a discussion of this issue from a Marxist and Hegelian point of view, see Johannes Werner, "Was treibt Cardillac?: Ein Goldschmied auf Abwegen," *Wirkendes Wort: Deutsche Sprache und Literatur in Forschung und Lehre* 40 (1990): 32–38.

12. A contemporary critic commented on Hoffmann's creation of a type of suspense we have come to associate with detective stories: " 'Fräulein von Scudéry' . . . is suspenseful and well costumed; . . . it deceives the reader for the whole length, which results from the frequent introduction of the characters through their own speech"; Anon. [Theresa Huber], *Morgenblatt für gebildete Stände* 13, 4 (1819), Literaturblatt 48: 192. Another critic praised the depiction of "the pious and gentle Scudéry" but complained about Hoffmann's letting Cardillac "each time enjoy peace and spiritual contentment, as a constant condition, only after having committed a murder, a condition to which the fantasy about the evil star and the ghost does not suffice to lend permanence and truth, only the most direct influence of Satan"; Anon. [Konrad Schwenk], *Hermes oder kritisches Jahrbuch der Literatur* 2 (1820): 211. Schwenk subsequently wrote that Cardillac's "love of jewels is on the one hand neither so ghostly, nor on the other so obvious, that it might supplant the more general [motivation] of greed, which appears here as the most natural thing [i.e., as the actual motivation]"; Anon. [Konrad Schwenk], "Über E. T. W. Hoffmann's Schriften," 124. A third critic complained that assuming Cardillac was a fictional character, not a real person, "the author of the tale cannot possibly avoid the reproach of having misused his talent through the invention of a despicable moral monster"; Anon., *Allgemeine Literatur-Zeitung* [Halle] (1822), supp. 57, cols. 454–55. Hoffmann's Berlin contemporary Rahel Varnhagen von Ense complained, "[t]he silversmith is the greatest of artists because he was compelled, while still in his mother's womb, to become a devourer of jewels. How hideous, sick, useless, and actually without any moral basis or struggle! Like a hydrophobic whose biting one is required to excuse"; *Rahel: Ein Buch des Andenkens an ihre Freunde*, ed. Karl August Varnhagen von Ense, vol. 3, 14–15, entry dated February 1820.

13. For a discussion of the subjectivity of "the characters' interpretations and reconstructions" see Sheila Dickson, "Devil's Advocate?: The Artistic Detective in E. T. A. Hoffmann's 'Das Fräulein von Scuderi,' " *Forum for Modern Language Studies* 29 (1993): 246–56.

14. Sexuality in the story was investigated from a Freudian perspective by Peter Schneider, "Verbrechen, Künstlertum und Wahnsinn: Untersuchungen zur Figur des Cardillac in E. T. A. Hoffmanns 'Das Fräulein von Scuderi,' " *Mitteilungen der E. T. A. Hoffmann-Gesellschaft* 26 (1980): 34–50.

15. The tale was discussed as a detective story by Gisela Gorski, " 'Das Fräulein von Scuderi' als Detektivgeschichte," *Mitteilungen der E. T. A. Hoffmann-Gesellschaft* 27 (1981): 1–15.

16. For a discussion of the story in relation to the political situation in post-Napoleonic Europe, see Yvonne Holbeche, "The Relationship of the Artist to Power: E. T. A. Hoffmann's 'Das Fräulein von Scuderi,' " *Seminar: A Journal of German Studies* 16 (1980): 1–11.

17. A platonically idealistic interpretation of the figure of Mlle de Scudéry as portrayed by Hoffmann was offered by Klaus D. Post, "Kriminalgeschichte als Heilsgeschichte: E. T. A. Hoffmanns Erzählung 'Das Fräulein von Scuderi,' " *Zeitschrift für Deutsche Philologie* 95, Sonderheft "E. T. A. Hoffmann" (1976): 132–56. For an existentialist interpretation see Hermann F. Weiss, " 'The Labyrinth of Crime': A Reinterpretation of E. T. A. Hoffmann's 'Das Fräulein von Scuderi,' " *Germanic Review* 51 (1976): 181–89.

18. A philologically oriented discussion of this almost wholly neglected tale was offered by Anneliese W. Moore, "E. T. A. Hoffmann's 'Haimatochare': Translation and Commentary," *The Hawaiian Journal of History* 12 (1978): 1–27.

19. A contemporary critic applauded Hoffmann's exclusion of the supernatural in "Die Räuber": "If the gifted author would only give us more such poetic works full of nature and truth, instead of his numerous grotesqueries"; Anon., *Heidelberger Jahrbücher* 14 (1821), no. 78: 1231–32. That opinion was echoed by a second critic: "[T]he Robbers, by Hoffmann, grips the reader all the more certainly since the author's vivid imagination has known here how to keep itself within the bounds of physical possibility and psychological probability"; Anon., *Morgenblatt für gebildete Stände* 15, 4 (1821), Literaturblatt 100: 397. A third critic, however, complained that the tale was too realistic: "The translation into the realm of the natural could only deprive it [Schiller's play] of its grandeur"; Anon., *Literarisches Conversations-Blatt* (1825), no. 211: 842.

20. A comparison of the characters between the Schiller play and Hoffmann's story was made by Lowell A. Bangerter, " 'Die Räuber': Friedrich Schiller and E. T. A. Hoffmann," *Germanic Review* 52 (1977): 99–108. For a study of Hoffmann's tale "Die Räuber" and others of his late stories, connecting them particularly with the figure of the mad hermit "Serapion" in *Die Serapions-Brüder,* see Hans Toggenburger, *Die späten Almanach-Erzählungen E. T. A. Hoffmanns* (Bern, Frankfurt am Main, New York: Lang, 1983). For a discussion of the story as an attack on idealism of the sort exemplified by Schiller's play, see Reinhard Heinritz, "E. T. A. Hoffmanns 'Räuber': Schreibweisen und ihre parodistische Komposition," *Mitteilungen der E. T. A. Hoffmann-Gesellschaft* 34 (1988): 35–42. For a discussion of Hoffmann's tale in the context of the reception of Schiller's drama in Hoffmann's day, see Gerhard Kluge, "Franz Moor und Amalia in den böhmischen Wäldern: 'Die Räuber' von E. T. A. Hoffmann," in *Grenzgänge: Literatur und Kultur im Kontext,* ed. Guillaume van Gemert and Hans Ester (Amsterdam: Rodopi, 1990), 185–200.

21.   A discussion of this story was offered by Inge Kolke, " 'aus den Gräbern zerrst du deine Atzung, teuflisches Weib': Verwesung als struktur-bildendes Element in E. T. A. Hoffmanns 'Vampirismus'-Geschichte," *Mit-teilungen der E. T. A. Hoffmann-Gesellschaft* 33 (1987): 34–49.

22.   A contemporary critic objected "although we are not at all averse to [portrayals of] the horrifying, still we believe that this must find its limit when a higher moral power in man is no longer able to control it, and therefore we have to call this whole story a repulsive, diabolical invention"; Anon., *Heidel-berger Jahrbücher* 14 (1821), no. 75: 1187.

23.   For a Freudian interpretation, see Thomas A. Kamla, "E. T. A. Hoffmann's Vampirism Tale: Instinctual Perversion," *American Imago: A Psycho-analytic Journal for Culture, Science, and the Arts* 42 (1985): 235–53.

24.   For a discussion of "Der Elementargeist" in relation to Cazotte's pioneering fantastic tale, see Markus Winkler, "Cazotte lu par E. T. A. Hoff-mann: Du 'Diable amoureux' à 'Der Elementargeist,' " *Arcadia: Zeitschrift für vergleichende Literaturwissenschaft* 23 (1988): 113–32. Winkler interprets the story as being about poetic creativity.

25.   A contemporary critic complained "will this man of many talents never tire of entertaining the public with confused, feverish dreams?" Anon. [Wilhelm Müller], *Literarisches Conversations-Blatt* (1821), no. 275: 1099. Another critic, though, commented approvingly: "The leave which the colonel finally takes from his salamandress is touching"; Anon., *Heidelberger Jahrbücher* 14 (1821), no. 78: 1235.

26.   In the opinion of a contemporary critic, "how is it possible that this noble, worthy old woman . . . can be brought to decide to offer the young stu-dent her hand in marriage?"; Anon., *Literarisches Conversations-Blatt* (1825), no. 211: 842.

27.   A contemporary critic found the story to be "about a young botanist who . . . in the end . . . is made happy—happier indeed than he deserved—through the possession of a lovely, innocent girl, who grew up among the flowers of *his* garden, and whose until then unperceived worth revealed itself to him completely only at *that* point at which she had made up her mind to separate herself from him"; Anon., *Heidelberger Jahrbücher* 16 (1823), no. 28: 447.

28.   A contemporary reviewer was happy that Hoffmann did not intro-duce the devil himself into the story: "[T]he satanic principle here only dwells as a Jesuit proselytizer, but without a horse's hoof and rooster-feather, *and that is where it belongs*"; Anon., *Literarisches Conversations-Blatt* (1822), no. 232: 925.

29.   For an argument that Hoffmann's original concept for the story, evident in the first three chapters, was to depict Eugenius's straying into a humdrum philistine life, see Stefan Diebitz, "Der Spießer im Treibhaus: Ver-such einer Deutung und Wertung von E. T. A. Hoffmanns später Erzählung 'Datura fastuosa,' " *Mitteilungen der E. T. A. Hoffmann-Gesellschaft* 34 (1988): 52–66.

30. A contemporary reviewer rightly complained regarding the ending of "Meister Johannes Wacht": "[A]s a reward Jonathan receives the hand of the beloved and remains a lawyer. But the father, after all, had never doubted his good-heartedness"; Anon., *Literarisches Conversations-Blatt* (1824), no. 80: 317.

Chapter Six

1. Interpretations of Hoffmann's seven fairy tales from various perspectives are offered by Gisela Vitt-Maucher, *E. T. A. Hoffmanns Märchenschaffen: Kaleidoskop der Verfremdung in seinen sieben Märchen* (Chapel Hill and London: University of North Carolina Press, 1989).

2. A contemporary reviewer judged that *Der goldne Topf* was about the questions: *"What is the ultimate purpose of human existence? How is it achievable?"*; Anon., *Morgenblatt für gebildete Stände* 9, 2 (1815), Literaturblatt 4: 14–15. Another found it to be about "the mystery of all mysteries, the great mystical secret of all temporal creation, of the falling away and the return of the Transitory into Original Being"; Anon. [F. G. Wetzel], *Heidelbergische Jahrbücher* 8, 2 (1815), no. 66: 1051. That "the basic duality of Hoffmann's cosmos" can be demonstrated by stylistic analysis of this tale was proposed by Nils Ekfelt, "Style and Level of Reality in E. T. A. Hoffmann's 'Der goldne Topf,' " *Style* 22 (1988): 61–92; here 86. For an argument that the story was one of the artistic fairy tales that as this critic claims expressed a hope of achieving utopia in the wake of the French Revolution and Napoleonic period, see Knud Willenberg, "Die Kollision verschiedener Realitätsebenen als Gattungsproblem in E. T. A. Hoffmanns 'Der goldne Topf,' " *Zeitschrift für Deutsche Philologie* 95, Sonderheft "E. T. A. Hoffmann" (1976): 93–113.

3. The poetic use Hoffmann made of occult traditions in the tale was investigated by Detlef Kremer, "Alchemie und Kabbala: Hermetische Referenzen im 'Goldenen Topf,' " *E. T. A. Hoffmann-Jahrbuch: Mitteilungen der E. T. A. Hoffmann-Gesellschaft* 2 (1994): 36–56.

4. For a discussion of the tale in relation to mesmerism see Maria M. Tatar, "Mesmerism, Madness, and Death in E. T. A. Hoffmann's 'Der goldne Topf,' " *Studies in Romanticism* 14 (1975): 365–89.

5. Concerning the implication that Anselmus plunges into the river see Anthony Harper and Norman Oliver, "What Really Happens to Anselmus?: 'Impermissible' and 'Irrelevant' Questions about E. T. A. Hoffmann's 'Der goldne Topf,' " *New German Studies* 11 (1982): 113–22.

6. A contemporary critic judged: "Here the 'life in poetry' to which 'the most secret harmony of all beings reveals itself as the profoundest secret of nature' is depicted with jesting irony"; Anon., *Leipziger Literatur-Zeitung,* 2 June 1815, col. 1064. Another did not think much of Anselmus's sublimity: "Nothing about the student Anselmus, except at most his awkwardness, testifies to his poetic sensitivity, which indeed he does not possess"; Anon. [Karl Ludwig Woltmann], *Jenaische Allgemeine Literatur-Zeitung* 12, 4 (1815), no. 232: col.

422. For a recent judgment that "Hoffmann's mythical Atlantis in the last analysis is a world which can only be found between the covers of a book, such as the one which the narrator himself is composing," see L. C. Nygaard, "Anselmus as Amanuensis: The Motif of Copying in Hoffmann's 'Der goldne Topf,' " *Seminar: A Journal of German Studies* 19 (1983): 79–104; here 102–3. Another scholarly critic found the point to be that "the only meaningful position for man to be in is to be spread-eagled between empirical existence and the nether realm of ideal being"; John Reddick, "E. T. A. Hoffmann's 'Der goldne Topf' and Its 'durchgehaltene Ironie,' " *The Modern Language Review* 71 (1976): 577–94; here 593. An argument that the tale is about the development of poetic language as exemplified by the case of Anselmus was made by Hartmut Marhold, "Die Problematik dichterischen Schaffens in E. T. A. Hoffmanns 'Der goldne Topf,' " *Mitteilungen der E. T. A. Hoffmann-Gesellschaft* 32 (1986): 50–73.

7. A focus on Drosselmeier's storytelling for the goddaughter and on her developing it further in her imagination is found in Johannes Barth, " 'So etwas kann denn doch wohl der Onkel niemals zu Stande bringen': Ästhetische Selbstreflexion in E. T. A. Hoffmanns Kindermärchen 'Nußknacker und Mausekönig,' " *E. T. A. Hoffmann-Jahrbuch: Mitteilungen der E. T. A. Hoffmann-Gesellschaft* 3 (1995): 7–14.

8. A contemporary critic did not think much of the goddaughter and godfather: "Maria Stahlbaum, to whom the Nutcracker has been given as a Christmas present, is on closer observation herself, too, nothing but a wooden marionette; one therefore finds it quite all right for her to be in love with the nutcracker. . . . And Godfather Drosselmeier . . . is so much a puppet, like all of his listeners, who eagerly hear him tell about things which likewise were turned on the lathe of a Nuremberg woodworker"; Anon. [Heinrich Voß Jr.], *Morgenblatt für gebildete Stände* 11, 1 (1817), Literaturblatt 11: 44.

9. A contemporary critic saw Marie's adventures as taking place in her imagination: "[A] whole world appears with all of its fantastic images, as these have formed in the intuitive, innocent, and yet desirous soul in a child's ecstatic dreams"; Anon., *Heidelberger Jahrbücher* 12 (1819), no. 76: 1205. The important role of childlike imagination in the tale was investigated from a pedagogical point of view by Günter Heintz, "Mechanik und Phantasie: Zu E. T. A. Hoffmanns Märchen 'Nußknacker und Mausekönig,' " *Literatur in Wissenschaft und Unterricht* 7 (1974): 1–15.

10. A Jungian psychoanalytical interpretation of this tale was offered by Ronald J. Elardo, "E. T. A. Hoffmann's 'Nußknacker und Mausekönig': The Mouse-Queen in the Tragedy of the Hero," *Germanic Review* 55 (1980): 1–8.

11. Zaches is seen at base as a character from folktale, the "Thumbling," and a victim of his social origin, and therefore as the tale's central figure by Furio Jesi, "L'identità del 'Wechselbalg' in 'Klein Zaches genannt Zinnober' di E. T. A. Hoffmann," *Studi germanici* 11 (1973): 25–50.

12. With reference to the figure of Little Zachary, a contemporary critic commented: "If we understand the author correctly, this witches' doll is the soul's offspring—Sin"; Anon., *Allgemeines Repertorium* 1, 2 (1819): 78.

13. A contemporary critic wrote "after reading through this Märchen one gains an insight into what it means to elevate oneself humoristically above life, and how refreshing such a successful attempt can be for the mind and soul"; Anon., *Zeitung für die elegante Welt* (1819), no. 54, col. 427. For a discussion of the tale in connection with Hoffmann's biography and times, from a Marxist perspective, see Franz Fühmann, "E. T. A. Hoffmanns 'Klein Zaches,' " *Weimarer Beiträge: Zeitschrift für Literaturwissenschaft, Ästhetik und Kulturtheorie* 24, 4 (1978): 74–86. An analysis from the standpoint of social and political history as interpreted by Marxist theory was made by Jürgen Walter, "E. T. A. Hoffmanns Märchen 'Klein Zaches genannt Zinnober': Versuch einer sozialgeschichtlichen Interpretation," *Mitteilungen der E. T. A. Hoffmann-Gesellschaft* 19 (1973): 27–45. Walter argued that the tale was "a reflection of the political powerlessness . . . experienced by a large part of the middle-class intelligentsia in Germany around 1815" (44). For an interpretation of the tale as a depiction of negative effects of the Enlightenment on man and society, see Heidemarie Kesselmann, "E. T. A. Hoffmanns 'Klein Zaches': Das phantastische Märchen als Möglichkeit der Wiedergewinnung einer geschichtlichen Erkenntnisdimension," *Literatur für Leser* 2 (1978): 114–29.

14. For a Jungian interpretation see Ronald J. Elardo, "E. T. A. Hoffmann's Klein Zaches, the Trickster," *Seminar: A Journal of German Studies* 16 (1980): 151–69.

15. A contemporary critic wrote, regarding depiction of the supernatural in the story: "Ever since *Tieck* and *Hardenberg* [Novalis] opened up, like a hidden door in one's everyday living room, the new miraculous fairy tale realm, in which everything can be explained, dissolved, and formed anew, and yet still remain mysterious and independent, a number of authors have followed this path; none yet seems to have found his way so happily through this romantic wilderness as Hoffmann"; Anon., *Literarisches Conversations-Blatt* (1821), no. 68: 270–71. An interpretation of the tale as being about poetic creativity was made by Walther Hahn, "E. T. A. Hoffmanns 'Prinzessin Brambilla': Künstlerisches Selbstbewußtsein und schöpferischer Prozeß," *Michigan Germanic Studies* 12 (1986): 133–50.

16. A contemporary critic commented "[t]hat Giglio finally finds his princess, and Giacinta her prince, and that their realms on the Urdarsee flow into one another like quicksilver, goes without saying"; Anon. [Heinrich Voß Jr.], *Heidelberger Jahrbücher* 14 (1821), no. 47: 748. Another applauded "the charming idea" that Giglio and Giacinta discover in one another their dream beloved "so that in the end it turns out that they themselves were the prince and princess"; Anon., *Literarisches Conversations-Blatt* (1821), no. 68: 270–71.

17.   For a discussion of the tale with regard to the critic and theorist Mikhail Bakhtin's concept of "literary carnivals" see Detlef Kremer, "Literarischer Karneval: Groteske Motive in E. T. A. Hoffmanns 'Prinzessin Brambilla,' " *E. T. A. Hoffmann-Jahrbuch: Mitteilungen der E. T. A. Hoffmann-Gesellschaft* 3 (1995): 15–30.

18.   The tale is about self-knowledge and questions of self-identity according to Josef Quack, *Künstlerische Selbsterkenntnis: Versuch über E. T. A. Hoffmanns 'Prinzessin Brambilla'* (Würzburg: Königshausen & Neumann, 1993).

19.   For an argument that the tale is about overcoming inhibitions to sensuality and boundaries of the self, see Stephan Fischer, "E. T. A. Hoffmanns 'Prinzessin Brambilla': Auf der Suche nach der verlorenen Lust," *Mitteilungen der E. T. A. Hoffmann-Gesellschaft* 34 (1988): 11–34.

20.   A contemporary critic complained there was no point or guiding idea to the whole: "[T]he author's forcing [us] to follow him through a labyrinth of dream and insanity without a saving thread is as inartistic as it is unnatural"; Anon., *Leipziger Literatur-Zeitung* (1821), no. 267, col. 2136.

21.   A contemporary critic commented on the dreamlike quality of Anna's adventures but saw no point to it: "It is entertaining, to be sure, to see how in the midst of her prosaic life the good rural mistress sees a carrot field in her beloved vegetable garden arise and enter her life in a strangely teasing manner, as though she were suffering feverish delusions and fantasizing about her garden plots that have come alive in a dream. An anecdote of this sort, however, cannot lay claim to being anything more than teasingly entertaining"; Anon. [Konrad Schwenk], "Über E. T. W. Hoffmann's Schriften," 126.

22.   A discussion of the tale's poetic structure, including its ties to traditions of comedy and fairy tale, was offered by Alfred Behrmann, "Die Poetik des Kunstmärchens: Eine Strukturanalyse der 'Königsbraut' von E. T. A. Hoffmann," in *Erzählforschung 3: Theorien, Modelle und Methoden der Narrativik,* ed. Wolfgang Haubrichs, Zeitschrift für Literatur und Linguistik, supps. 8 (Göttingen: Vandenhoeck & Ruprecht, 1978), 107–34.

23.   The tale is about Peregrinus's path to inward perfection according to Min Suk Chon-Choe, *E. T. A. Hoffmanns Märchen 'Meister Floh'* (Frankfurt am Main, Bern, New York: Lang, 1986).

24.   Hoffmann's younger literary contemporary, Heinrich Heine, complained: "The psychic realm which Hoffmann knows how to depict so magnificently, is treated most prosaically in this novel [sic]. . . . The grand allegory into which everything dissolves at the end did not satisfy me. . . . I believe that a novel should not be an allegory"; Heine, "Briefe aus Berlin," 51–52 (in the third letter, 7 June 1822). For discussion of the role of Master Flea and other magical figures in the tale as allegorical representations of erotic sensuality, see Hans Sachse, "Gespräch über E. T. A. Hoffmanns Märchen vom 'Meister Floh' und Goethes Gedicht 'Das Tagebuch,' " *Goethe-Jahrbuch* 101 (1984): 310–20.

Chapter Seven

1. For a discussion of Hoffmann as novelist in the broader context of that genre see Hartmut Steinecke, "Hoffmanns Romanwerk in europäischer Perspektive," *E. T. A. Hoffmann-Jahrbuch: Mitteilungen der E. T. A. Hoffmann-Gesellschaft* 1 (1992–1993): 21–35.

2. The relationship between the supernatural and the psychological in the novel was discussed by Susanne Olson, "Das Wunderbare und seine psychologische Funktion in E. T. A. Hoffmanns 'Elixiere des Teufels,' " *Mitteilungen der E. T. A. Hoffmann-Gesellschaft* 24 (1978): 26–35. Hoffmann's deepening of the depiction of the subconscious in comparison with earlier examples of the gothic novel, such as Lewis's *Monk,* is emphasized by Wolfgang Nehring, "Gothic Novel and Schauerroman: Tradition und Innovation in Hoffmanns 'Die Elixiere des Teufels,' " *E. T. A. Hoffmann-Jahrbuch: Mitteilungen der E. T. A. Hoffmann-Gesellschaft* 1 (1992–1993): 36–47.

3. Medardus's adventures concern the task of giving himself an identity, especially in relation to the sins of his father and his own attraction to Aurelia, according to Johannes Harnischfeger, "Das Geheimnis der Identität: Zu E. T. A. Hoffmanns 'Die Elixiere des Teufels,' " *Mitteilungen der E. T. A. Hoffmann-Gesellschaft* 36 (1990): 1–14.

4. For an argument that "Medardus is an individual in search of his identity and his truth" and that "Aurelia raises him to her level and purifies him," see Alain Faure, "Du simple au double: Du 'Moine' de M. G. Lewis aux 'Élixirs du diable' de E. T. A. Hoffmann," *Europe: Revue Litéraire Mensuelle* 62, 659 (March 1984): 54–62; here 60–61. For a survey of critical reaction to the novel in the context of criticism on Hoffmann generally, as well as the interpretive view that the work is ultimately about "the challenge to sublimation and to transcendence of what is immediately present," see Wolfgang Nehring, "E. T. A. Hoffmann: 'Die Elixiere des Teufels' (1815/16)," in *Romane und Erzählungen der deutschen Romantik: Neue Interpretationen,* ed. Paul Michael Lützeler (Stuttgart: Reclam, 1981), 325–50; here 347.

5. *E. T. A. Hoffmann. Die Elixiere des Teufels/Lebens-Ansichten des Katers Murr,* ed. Walter Müller Seidel and Wolfgang Kron (Munich: Winkler, 1961), 291; hereafter cited in text as *ET/KM.*

6. For the view, from a perspective that echoes themes of Marxist criticism on German romanticism, that the novel is satirical, see Michael T. Jones, "Hoffmann and the Problem of Social Reality," *Monatshefte für deutschen Unterricht, deutsche Sprache und Literatur* 69 (1977): 45–57. Jones claims to demonstrate "Hoffmann's deadly serious intention of portraying the incongruity between the compensatory, overblown sentiments of German philosophy and poetry and the prevailing conditions of social misery in post-Napoleonic Germany" (56).

7. For a survey of critical reception of the novel up to about 1980 and a discussion of several major themes and aspects of the work, see Horst S.

Daemmrich, "E. T. A. Hoffmann: Kater Murr (1820/22)," in *Romane und Erzählungen zwischen Romantik und Realismus: Neue Interpretationen,* ed. Paul Michael Lützeler (Stuttgart: Reclam, 1983), 73–93.

8. In this connection see Charles Findlay, "The Opera and Operatic Elements in the Fragmentary Biography of Johannes Kreisler," *German Life & Letters* 27 (1973–1974): 22–34. Regarding Hoffmann's brand of humor in the novel, a contemporary critic complained: "Roaming from one extreme to the other . . . , he too often omits the *mediating* point of view and robs himself and his readers of the most sublime enjoyment of *that* irony which throws the rainbow bridge of *bold* courage across the terrifying chasm of Existence and Being, and mocks even mockery itself"; Anon. [Friedrich von Gruenthal], *Morgenblatt für gebildete Stände* 14, 1 (1820), Literaturblatt 12: 45. Another was of the same opinion: "Humor, in the higher sense of the term, we define as the universal view of the world which, by encompassing the limits of human knowledge and by relating the most sublime in spiritual contemplation to the lowest of ordinary phenomena, dissolves the conflicting opposites into the essential unity and puts the observer at a vantage point from which, beyond the dissension and conflict of earthly relationships, the view of a higher, conciliatory world of ideas is opened to him. . . . [H]is [Hoffmann's] portrayals are by no means imbued with genuine humor in the above sense"; Anon., *Allgemeine Literatur-Zeitung* [Halle] (1822), no. 123, col. 105.

9. On the presence of Shakespearean elements, especially with regard to the characterizations of Kreisler and Hedwiga, see Ritchie Robertson, "Shakespearean Comedy and Romantic Psychology in Hoffmann's 'Kater Murr,' " *Studies in Romanticism* 24 (1985): 201–22.

10. The juxtaposition of the tomcat story and the composer's biography was seen as a case of Hoffmann playing—in a mockingly ironic way—with the expectations of his broad readership by Stefan Diebitz, "Versuch über die integrale Einheit der 'Lebens-Ansichten des Katers Murr,' " *Mitteilungen der E. T. A. Hoffmann-Gesellschaft* 31 (1985): 30–39.

11. Social context and social criticism in the novel are emphasized by Martin Swales, " 'Die Reproduktionskraft der Eidexen': Überlegungen zum selbstreflexiven Charakter der 'Lebens-Ansichten des Katers Murr,' " *E. T. A. Hoffmann-Jahrbuch: Mitteilungen der E. T. A. Hoffmann-Gesellschaft* 1 (1992–1993): 48–57.

12. For an argument that the unity in the seeming disparateness and disjointedness of *Kater Murr* is of a sort that anticipates a "modern" concept associated with the crisis in literature at the turn to the twentieth century, see Anneli Hartmann, "Geschlossenheit der Kunstwelt und fragmentarische Form: E. T. A. Hoffmanns 'Kater Murr,' " *Jahrbuch der Deutschen Schiller-Gesellschaft* 32 (1988): 148–90. The question of the novel's continuation is discussed by Uwe Schadwill, "Der dritte Teil des 'Kater Murr': Überlegungen zu seiner Rekonstruierbarkeit," *Mitteilungen der E. T. A. Hoffmann-Gesellschaft* 34 (1988): 43–51.

Conclusion

1. For an essay on "Des Vetters Eckfensters" with special regard to its sources, see Werner Kraft, "Des Vetters Eckfenster: E. T. A. Hoffmanns letzte Geschichte," *Neue deutsche Hefte* 149 (1976): 26–37. For a comparison of Hoffmann's sketch with his chief source, Karl Friedrich Kretschmann, "Scarron am Fenster," in *Taschenbuch zum geselligen Vergnügen* 8 (1798), see Ulrich Stadler, "Die Aussicht als Einblick: Zu E. T. A. Hoffmanns später Erzählung 'Des Vetters Eckfenster,' " *Zeitschrift für Deutsche Philologie* 105 (1986): 498–515. The relationship of the piece to the history of theories of aesthetic perception was discussed by Günter Oesterle, "E. T. A. Hoffmann: 'Des Vetters Eckfenster': Zur Historisierung ästhetischer Wahrnehmung oder der kalkulierte romantische Rückgriff auf Sehmuster der Aufklärung," *Der Deutschunterricht* 39, 1 (1987): 84–110. The work is seen as an anticipation of trends in twentieth-century fiction toward "permanent self-reflection" by Rolf Selbmann, "Die Poetik von E. T. A. Hoffmanns Erzählung 'Des Vetters Eckfenster,' " *E. T. A. Hoffmann-Jahrbuch* 2 (1994): 69–77. A discussion with regard to notions of poetic genius from the earlier "Storm and Stress" period of German literature is found in Lutz Hagestedt, *Das Genieproblem bei E. T. A. Hoffmann. Am Beispiel illustriert: Eine Interpretation seiner späten Erzählung 'Des Vetters Eckfenster'* (Munich: Brehm, 1991).

Selected Bibliography

PRIMARY SOURCES

Works by Hoffmann

Sämtliche Werke. Historisch-kritische Ausgabe. Ed. Carl Georg von Maassen. Vols. 1–4, 6–8, 9/10. Munich: Müller, 1908–1928. Never completed.

Werke in fünfzehn Teilen: Auf Grund der Hempelschen Ausgabe. Ed. Georg Ellinger. 1912. 2d enlarged ed. 8 vols. Berlin: Bong, 1927.

Sämtliche Werke in fünf Einzelbänden. Ed. Walter Müller-Seidel, Friedrich Schnapp, Wolfgang Kron, and Wulf Segebrecht. 5 vols. Munich: Winkler, 1960–1965. The best of the completed editions for scholarly use:

Fantasie-und Nachtstücke: Fantasiestücke in Callots Manier (1814–1815). *Nachtstücke* (1816, 1817). *Seltsame Leiden eines Theater-Direktors* (1819). Ed. Walter Müller-Seidel and Wolfgang Kron, 1960.

Die Elixiere des Teufels (1815, 1816)/*Lebens-Ansichten des Katers Murr* (1819, 1821). Ed. Walter Müller-Seidel and Wolfgang Kron, 1961.

Die Serapions-Brüder (1819, 1820, 1821). Ed. Walter Müller-Seidel and Wulf Segebrecht, 1963.

Schriften zur Musik (1813–1821)/*Nachlese.* Ed. Friedrich Schnapp, 1963.

Späte Werke (1819–1822). Ed. Walter Müller-Seidel and Wulf Segebrecht, 1965.

Schriften zur Musik. Neubearbeitete Ausgabe. Ed. Friedrich Schnapp. Munich: Winkler, 1977. A reprint of the texts of the 1963 edition, with the same page numbers, but with additions to the notes, and without the *Nachlese.*

Nachlese: Dichtungen, Schriften, Aufzeichnungen und Fragmente. Ed. Friedrich Schnapp. Munich: Winkler, 1981.

Gesammelte Werke in Einzelausgaben. Ed. Hans-Joachim Kruse. 8 vols. Berlin: Aufbau, 1994.

Sämtliche Werke in sechs Bänden. Ed. Wulf Segebrecht and Hartmut Steinecke, with Gerhard Allroggen and Ursula Segebrecht. Frankfurt am Main: Deutscher Taschenbuch Verlag: Vol. 2, Pt. 1, 1993; Vol. 2, Pt. 2, 1988; Vol. 3, 1985; Vol. 5, 1992. When completed, this will likely be the standard edition for scholarly use.

Kinder-Märchen. Von C. W. Contessa, Friedrich Baron de la Motte-Fouqué und E. T. A. Hoffmann (1816, 1817). Ed. Hans-Heino Ewers. Stuttgart: Reclam, 1987.

E. T. A. Hoffmann im persönlichen und brieflichen Verkehr. Ed. Hans von Müller. 2 vols. in 4. Berlin: Paetel, 1912.

Briefwechsel: Erläutert von Hans von Müller und Friedrich Schnapp. Ed. Friedrich Schnapp. 3 vols. Munich: Winkler, 1967–1969.

Tagebücher und literarische Entwürfe. Ed. Hans von Müller. Berlin: Paetel, 1915.

Tagebücher: Nach der Ausgabe Hans von Müllers. Ed. Friedrich Schnapp. Munich: Winkler, 1971.

Juristische Arbeiten. Ed. Friedrich Schnapp. Munich: Winkler, 1973.

English Translations of Hoffmann's Works (in chronological order)

Hoffmann's Strange Stories. Trans. Lafayette Burnham. Boston: Burnham, 1855.

Hoffmann's Fairy Tales. Trans. Lafayette Burnham. Boston: Burnham, 1857.

The Serapion Brethren (1819, 1820, 1821). Trans. Major Alexander Ewing. 2 vols. London: Bell, 1886–1892. Still the only complete translation of these collected tales.

Weird Tales. Trans. J. T. Bealby. 1923. Reprint. Freeport: Books for Libraries Press, 1970.

Tales of Hoffmann. Trans. F. M. Atkinson. London: Harrap, [1932].

The Tales of Hoffmann: Stories by E. T. A. Hoffmann. Ed. Hugo Steiner-Prag. New York: Limited Editions Club, The Heritage Press, 1943.

Tales of Hoffmann. Ed. Christopher Lazare. 1946. Reprint. New York: Grove, 1960.

Tales from Hoffmann. Ed. J. M. Cohen. New York: Coward-McCann, [1951].

Eight Tales of Hoffmann. Trans. J. M. Cohen. London: Pan Books, [1952].

The King's Bride (1821). Trans. P. Turner. London: Calder, [1959].

The Devil's Elixirs (1815, 1816). Trans. Ronald Taylor. London: Calder, [1963].

The Tales of Hoffmann. Trans. Michael Bullock. New York: Ungar, 1963.

The Best Tales of Hoffmann. Ed. E. F. Bleiler. New York: Dover, [1967].

Selected Writings of E. T. A. Hoffmann. Trans. Leonard J. Kent and Elizabeth C. Knight. *Vol 1: The Tales; Vol 2: The Novels* [*Kater Murr* (1819, 1821)]. Chicago: University of Chicago Press, 1969.

Three Märchen of E. T. A. Hoffmann. Trans. Charles E. Passage. Columbia: University of South Carolina Press, 1971.

Selected Letters of E. T. A. Hoffmann. Ed. and trans. Johanna Sahlin. Chicago: University of Chicago Press, 1977.

E. T. A. Hoffmann. Tales. Ed. Victor Lange. New York: Continuum, 1982.

Tales of Hoffmann, 2d ed. Ed. and trans. J. R. Hollingdale, with Stella Humphries, Vernon Humphries, and Sally Hayward. Harmondsworth: Penguin Books, 1984.

E. T. A. Hoffmann's Musical Writings: Kreisleriana, The Poet and the Composer, Musical Criticism. Ed. David Charlton. Trans. Martyn Clarke. Cambridge: Cambridge University Press, 1989.

The Golden Pot and Other Tales. Ed. and trans. Ritchie Robertson. Oxford and New York: Oxford University Press, 1992.

SECONDARY SOURCES

English

Blackall, Eric A. "The Divided Self: Hoffmann." In *The Novels of the German Romantics*, 221–41. Ithaca and London: Cornell University Press, 1983. Focuses on literary form and philosophical aspects in Hoffmann's two ventures into the genre.

Daemmrich, Horst S. *The Shattered Self: E. T. A. Hoffmann's Tragic Vision*. Detroit: Wayne State University Press, 1973. An interesting, often stimulating attempt to understand Hoffmann from an existentialist viewpoint.

Hewett-Thayer, Harvey W. *Hoffmann: Author of the Tales*. Princeton: Princeton University Press, 1948. Reprint. New York: Octagon, 1971. Still the best general study of the life and works in English, though lacking the benefit of more recent research and critical studies.

Journal of English and Germanic Philology [Special E. T. A. Hoffmann Issue] 75 4 (1976). A volume of critical essays by scholars in America and England occasioned by the 200th anniversary of Hoffmann's birth.

McGlathery, James M. *Mysticism and Sexuality: E. T. A. Hoffmann. Part One: Hoffmann and His Sources; Part Two: Interpretations of the Tales*. Berne: Peter Lang, 1981–1985. Argues that Hoffmann wrote in a broad literary tradition of sexual jest and ironic portrayal of the psychology of desire.

McGlathery, James M. "E. T. A. Hoffmann and the Bildungsroman." In *Reflection and Action: Essays on the Bildungsroman*. Ed. James N. Hardin, 314–28. Columbia: University of South Carolina Press, 1991. Addresses the question of Hoffmann's relationship to this much discussed and debated novelistic form.

Negus, Kenneth. *E. T. A. Hoffmann's Other World: The Romantic Author and His 'New Mythology.'* Philadelphia: University of Pennsylvania Press, 1965. Discusses Hoffmann in relation to the call by German romantics such as Novalis and Friedrich Schlegel for a revival of myth for their time.

Taylor, Ronald. *Hoffmann*. London: Bowes & Bowes, 1963. Remains the best brief introduction in English to the life and works.

German and French

Allroggen, Gerhard. *E. T. A. Hoffmanns Kompositionen: Ein chronologisch-thematisches Verzeichnis seiner musikalischen Werke mit einer Einführung*. Regensburg: Bosse, 1970. Good introduction to and survey of Hoffmann as a musician.

Auhuber, Friedhelm. *In einem fernen dunklen Spiegel: E. T. A. Hoffmanns Poetisierung der Medizin*. Opladen: Westdeutscher Verlag, 1986. Shows the closeness of Hoffmann's depictions to medical literature of his time but goes too far in claiming that like those sources his aim as an author was therapeutic.

Dobat, Klaus-Dieter. *Musik als romantische Illusion: Eine Untersuchung zur Bedeutung der Musikvorstellung E. T. A. Hoffmanns für sein musikalisches Werk*. Tübingen: Niemeyer, 1984. Squarely addresses the crucial question of whether Hoffmann believed in the possibility of achieving transcendence through music.

Egli, Gustav. *E. T. A. Hoffmann: Ewigkeit und Endlichkeit in seinem Werk*. Zürich: Füssli, 1927. An early interpretive study concerned with platonic and metaphysical themes.

Ellinger, Georg. *E. T. A. Hoffmann: Sein Leben und seine Werke*. Hamburg and Leipzig: Voß, 1894. A pioneering scholarly presentation of the life and works that emphasized platonic and musical aspects.

Harich, Walther. *E. T. A. Hoffmann: Das Leben eines Künstlers*. 2 vols. Berlin: Reiß, [1920]. 3d ed. n.d. A dramatic presentation influenced by the experience of World War I and by the accompanying expressionism in German art and literature.

Hitzig, Julis Eduard. *Hoffmann's Leben und Nachlaß*. 1823. 3d revised and enlarged ed. 3 vols. Stuttgart: Brodhag, 1839. Reprint of the 1823 edition. Ed. Wolfgang Held. Frankfurt am Main: Insel, 1986. A memoir by Hoffmann's literary friend and judicial colleague that together with the documentary material included has been an important source of information for Hoffmann's biographers.

Kaiser, Gerhard. *E. T. A. Hoffmann*. Stuttgart: Metzler, 1988. A comprehensive introductory presentation of the author and his work with a good selected bibliography of scholarship on the respective aspects of the life and works.

Kleßmann, Eckart. *E. T. A. Hoffmann oder die Tiefe zwischen Stern und Erde: Eine Biographie*. Stuttgart: Deutsche Verlags-Anstalt, 1988. An extensive, well informed but subjectively presented accounting of the life and works colored by the author's conviction that Hoffmann was deeply religious and believed in God.

Köhn, Lothar. *Vieldeutige Welt: Studien zur Struktur der Erzählungen E. T. A. Hoffmanns und zur Entwicklung seines Werkes*. Tübingen: Niemeyer, 1966. Incisive analysis of narrative perspective, subjectivity, and psychology.

Korff, Hermann August. "E. T. A. Hoffmann." In *Geist der Goethe-Zeit: Versuch einer ideellen Entwicklung der klassisch-romantischen Literaturgeschichte*, IV: 543–639. 5th ed. Leipzig: Koehler und Amelung, 1962. A major attempt to understand Hoffmann and his works in the context of the peculiarly German, metaphysically oriented variety of intellectual history known as "Geistesgeschichte."

Funck, Z. [pseud. for Carl Friedrich Kunz]. *Erinnerungen aus meinem Leben in biographischen Denksteinen und andern Mitteilungen. Bd. 1: Aus dem Leben zweier Dichter: Ernst Theodor Wilhelm Hoffmann's und Friedrich Gottlob Wetzel's,* [Hoffmann] 1–172. Leipzig: Brockhaus, 1836. This memoir by Hoffmann's first publisher, the Bamberg wine merchant and lending librarian Kunz, remains an important though not wholly reliable source about these years in the author's life.

Matt, Peter von. *Die Augen der Automaten: E. T. A. Hoffmanns Imaginationslehre als Prinzip seiner Erzählkunst.* Tübingen: Niemeyer, 1971. An influential, often cited study centering on the creative powers of imagination exhibited by various figures in the tales.

Prang, Helmut, ed. *E. T. A. Hoffmann.* Darmstadt: Wissenschaftliche Buchgesellschaft, 1976. A quite arbitrary selection of reprinted items of secondary literature on Hoffmann covering the period 1906 to 1973.

Ricci, Jean F.-A. *E. T. A. Hoffmann: L'homme et l'œuvre.* Paris: Corti, 1947. A well-written comprehensive study still interesting for its attempt to interpret each of Hoffmann's narrative works in relation to his life.

Safranski, Rüdiger. *E. T. A. Hoffmann: Das Leben eines skeptischen Phantasten.* Munich: Hanser, 1984. Paperback edition, Frankfurt a. M.: Fischer, 1987. The best written, most readable, and most fascinating biography of Hoffmann to date, though one given rather overly to explanation of the works through psychobiography.

Schaukal, Richard von. *E. T. A. Hoffmann: Sein Werk aus seinem Leben dargestellt.* Zürich: Amalthea, 1923. An early attempt to relate depictions in the narrative works to what was known about Hoffmann's life.

Schenck, Ernst von. *E. T. A. Hoffmann: Ein Kampf um das Bild des Menschen.* Berlin: Verlag die Runde, 1939. Interestingly reflects a shift from the earlier expressionism of the World War I period to the existentialism of the pre– and post–World War II years.

Schnapp, Friedrich, comp. *E. T. A. Hoffmann in Aufzeichnungen seiner Freunde und Bekannten: Eine Sammlung.* Munich: Winkler, 1974. An important collection of documentary material containing contemporary reactions to Hoffmann as a person and as an author.

[Schwenck, Konrad.] "Über E. T. A. Hoffmanns Schriften." *Hermes oder kritisches Jahrbuch der Literatur* 3 (1823): 80–143. By far the fullest contemporary critical assessment of Hoffmann's works.

Segebrecht, Wulf. *Autobiographie und Dichtung: Eine Studie zum Werk E. T. A. Hoffmanns.* Stuttgart: Metzler, 1967. A pioneering argument for distinguishing between Hoffmann's life and his storytelling, in which his experiences underwent a marked poeticization.

Sucher, Paul. *Les sources du merveilleux chez E. T. A. Hoffmann.* Paris: Alcan, 1912. A partly superseded but still useful comparison of passages in Hoffmann's works with his literary sources, especially with regard to his depictions of miraculous happenings and occult beliefs.

Werner, Hans-Georg. *E. T. A. Hoffmann: Darstellung und Deutung der Wirk-lichkeit im dichterischen Werk.* 2d ed. Berlin: Aufbau, 1971. A major study that became the model for Marxist interpretation among critics in the German Democratic Republic.

Willimczik, Kurt. *E. T. A. Hoffmann: Die drei Reiche seiner Gestaltungswelt.* Berlin: Junker und Dünnhaupt, 1939. An interesting attempt to under-stand the life and works in accord with the cultural and literary climate of the Hitler period.

Zeitschrift für Deutsche Philologie. Band 95: Sonderheft E. T. A. Hoffmann. Berlin: Erich Schmidt, 1976. A volume of generally excellent critical essays in German occasioned by the 200th anniversary of Hoffmann's birth.

Index

The Author

James M. McGlathery is a professor of German and comparative literature at the University of Illinois at Urbana-Champaign. He is the author of *Mysticism and Sexuality: E. T. A. Hoffmann. Part One: Hoffmann and His Sources; Part Two: Interpretations of the Tales* (1981–1985); *Desire's Sway: The Plays and Stories of Heinrich von Kleist* (1983); *Fairy Tale Romance: The Grimms, Basile, and Perrault* (1991); *Grimms' Fairy Tales: A History of Criticism on a Popular Classic* (1993); and *Wagner's Operas and Desire* (in press). In addition, he has published essays in scholarly books and journals on those subjects, as well as on Annette von Droste-Hülshoff, Franz Kafka, eighteenth-century licentious tales, Bildungsroman, and madness as a theme in German romanticism. His next major project is a book on Heinrich Heine as a love poet. He edited volumes of scholarly essays including *The Brothers Grimm and Folktale* (1988) and *Music and German Literature* (1992), a special issue devoted to E. T. A. Hoffmann for the *Journal of English and Germanic Philology* (October 1976), and the anthology *German Source Readings in the Arts and Sciences* (1974), and has been a managing editor of the *Journal of English and Germanic Philology* since 1972. In addition to invited lectures, he has been a frequent presenter of papers at scholarly meetings and has published more than eighty book reviews in various scholarly journals. His undergraduate degree is from Princeton University (B.A. 1958) and his graduate degrees from Yale (M.A. 1959, Ph.D. 1964). He taught at Phillips Andover Academy (1959–1960) and Harvard University (1963–1965) before coming to the University of Illinois as assistant professor in 1965. He was a visiting professor at Harvard (summers 1966, 1970) and at the University of Göttingen, Germany (1993–1994). He served for ten years as head of his academic department (Germanic Languages and Literatures, 1985–1995).

The Editor

David O'Connell is professor of French at Georgia State University. He received his Ph.D. in 1966 from Princeton University, where he was a National Woodrow Wilson Fellow, the Bergen Fellow in Romance Languages, and a National Woodrow Wilson Dissertation Fellow. He is the author of *The Teachings of Saint Louis: A Critical Text* (1972), *Les Propos de Saint Louis* (1974), *Louis-Ferdinand Céline* (1976), *The Instructions of Saint Louis: A Critical Text* (1979), and *Michel de Saint Pierre: A Catholic Novelist at the Crossroads* (1990). He has edited more than sixty books in the Twayne World Authors Series.

.